THE POWER OF INTEREST FOR MOTIVATION AND ENGAGEMENT

D1592608

The Power of Interest for Motivation and Engagement combines research from educational psychology and neuroscience to explain the important role of interest in academics and life success. Drawing on cases both in and out of the classroom, the authors examine how interest is developed and sustained as well as how it can be assessed and interpreted. This volume is written for people who would like to know more about the power of their interests and how they could develop them: students who want to be meaningfully engaged, educators and parents wondering about how to facilitate motivation, business people focusing on ways in which they could engage meaningfully their employees and associates, policy-makers whose recognition of the power of interest may lead to changes resulting in a new focus supporting interest development for schools, out-of-school activity, industry, and business, and researchers studying learning and motivation. It draws on research in cognitive, developmental, and social psychology, as well as in the learning sciences, to demonstrate that there is power for everyone in leveraging interest for motivation and engagement.

K. Ann Renninger is the Eugene M. Lang Research Professor at Swarthmore College. She is the Chair of the Department of Educational Studies.

Suzanne E. Hidi is a Founding Fellow of the Senior College of the University of Toronto, and an Associate Professor of Educational Psychology.

THE POWER OF INTEREST FOR MOTIVATION AND ENGAGEMENT

K. Ann Renninger and Suzanne E. Hidi

Routledge
Taylor & Francis Group

NEW YORK AND LONDON

First published 2016
by Routledge
711 Third Avenue, New York, NY 10017

and by Routledge
2 Park Square, Milton Park, Abingdon, Oxon, OX14 4RN

Routledge is an imprint of the Taylor and Francis Group, an informa business

© 2016 Taylor and Francis

The right of K. Ann Renninger and Suzanne E. Hidi to be identified as authors of this work has been asserted by them in accordance with sections 77 and 78 of the Copyright, Designs and Patents Act 1988.

Library of Congress Cataloging in Publication Data
Names: Renninger, K. Ann, author. | Hidi, Suzanne, author.
Title: The power of interest for motivation and engagement / K. Ann Renninger and Suzanne Hidi. Description: New York, NY : Routledge, 2016. |
Includes bibliographical references and index.
Identifiers: LCCN 2015023516 | ISBN 9781138779785 (hardback) |
ISBN 9781315771045 (e-book) | ISBN 9781138779792 (pbk.)
Subjects: LCSH: Motivation in education. | Interest (Psychology) | Engagement (Philosophy) | Learning, Psychology of.
Classification: LCC LB1065 .R44 2016 | DDC 370.15/4–dc23
LC record available at http://lccn.loc.gov/2015023516

ISBN: 978-1-138-77978-5 (hbk)
ISBN: 978-1-138-77979-2 (pbk)
ISBN: 978-1-315-77104-5 (ebk)

Typeset in Bembo
by Out of House Publishing

We dedicate this book to our families. Their many interests and questions have contributed significantly to our understanding of interest. Their humor, patient explanations, and generous support of our interest in understanding interest have been essential.

CONTENTS

LIST OF ILLUSTRATIONS

Figures

Tables

ACKNOWLEDGMENTS

We want to acknowledge the contributions that our many colleagues and students have made to the field of interest research, our thinking, and this volume. We also appreciate the thoughtful comments of Jessica E. Bachrach, Jocelyn G. Hidi, Rose K. Pozos-Brewer, and J. Melissa Running on the chapters of this volume. We gratefully acknowledge support for work on the volume from the Senior College of the University of Toronto, the Swarthmore College Faculty Research and Travel Funds, and the Constance C. Hungerford Faculty Support Fund. Finally, we thank Rebecca Novack and the editorial support team at Routledge for their work with us.

INTRODUCTION

Interest is powerful. The triggering of interest initiates productive engagement and the potential for optimal motivation. A person is said to be interested in some activity, such as writing, playing bridge, or fantasy football, if they voluntarily engage in thinking about it, happily prioritize the problems that arise (e.g., a paragraph that does not work, a bridge hand that did not make, or having your first round draft pick be out for the season), and are willing to persevere to address them.[1] Until recently, it has not been clear that regardless of a person's age or prior experience, interests like these can be triggered and can be supported to develop. A person's interest makes persistence feel effortless and increases the possibility of achievement and creative contribution.

Being interested in something—a school assignment, a work-related responsibility, or a museum exhibit—has been repeatedly shown to benefit the interested person. People who are interested in what they are doing are recognizable because they tend to have positive feelings, be invigorated, and choose to reengage with a particular object/activity/idea, or content, repeatedly. Their engagement with the content is distinctive and appears to be self-sustaining; their interest positively affects their attention, goal setting, comprehension, motivation, and learning, and it can influence their ability to achieve and succeed in their careers.[2] Although having a more developed interest is optimal, any development of interest is beneficial. Many people do well with having focused interests in only a few content areas and less well-developed (but some) interest in others. The complications set in if there is no interest for content to be learned and no supports to trigger interest for the content to develop. As we will explain, evidence now exists that demonstrates that those who lack interest can have their interest triggered and can be supported to seriously engage content that previously was not of interest to them.

In his 1949 review of the history of interest, Berlyne pointed out that increasing understanding of interest has been a serious pursuit of psychologists and educators for centuries. Berlyne wrote that conceptualizations of interest were inadequate in early studies as they neglected important meanings of the word. He argued that many aspects of interest need clarification and that various aspects of motivation such as curiosity were particularly in need of clarification. He suggested that when such advances have been made:

> we shall be in a better position to give a clear, precise, operational definition of "interest" in one or several senses. And it will be easier to discuss such matters as: (a) the relation between different uses of the word; (b) the development of adult interests out of the behavior of animals and children; (c) the origins and progress of specific interests; (d) the measurement and classification of interests.
>
> (Berlyne 1949: 194)

Berlyne believed that eventually developments in research would make it possible to provide clarity about the relations among different approaches to interest, the development of interest in general and with regard to specific content, as well as the measurement of interest.

Armed with a developmental model of interest that distinguishes between earlier and later phases of development—the four-phase model of interest development—we can now provide the conceptual framework that Berlyne called for.[3] The four-phase model describes phases in the development of a person's interest that apply both in and out of school. It provides a framework for explaining how studies focusing on varying aspects of interest contribute to understanding of interest as a developmental process. It also allows us to identify indicators of different phases of interest that can be used by researchers and educators and positions them to address the power of the development of interest for motivation and engagement. For example, individuals with little interest in history might be encouraged to examine artifacts or documents and talk about what they notice. An educator (parent, after-school staff person, or museum docent) should respond to the connections that the individuals can make to the materials and/or provide additional relevant content. On the other hand, those who already have a more developed interest in history can draw on previously acquired knowledge and are likely to prefer engaging in discussions or debates about the evidence or perspectives provided by the artifacts. Having already made some connection to history, they are ready to continue to stretch what they know, and this, in turn, leads to the continuing development and deepening of their interests.

Only relatively recently have research findings demonstrated that interest develops. Because interest is a common phenomenon, there is folk wisdom that explains its origins and how it works. Although folk wisdom about interest has some aspects of truth, it also contains a number of misunderstandings about interest that need to be recognized and addressed. Addressing these misconceptions should allow the field of interest research to move forward and provide practitioners with information about how interest can be supported to develop. We briefly review some of these misconceptions here and address them in more detail in the chapters of this volume.

A critical misunderstanding about interest is that it is static. It has been studied and conceptualized as if it were either present or absent. When people think of interest, they often are not thinking about its potential to develop. They may be thinking of the psychological state of interest (the way that they or another person engages with interest) or of interest as a motivational predisposition (the motivating qualities of interest). In this volume, we explain that interest always includes both of these aspects, and, most importantly, that interest is dynamic. It always has the possibility to develop. The development of interest occurs through interactions with others (e.g., peers, educators, employers, and parents) and the environment.

A related misunderstanding is the erroneous description of interest as a personal characteristic, trait, or propensity, something that a person is born with.[4] This view of interest suggests that a person either has an interest in a particular discipline, such as mathematics, or does not, and that if a person does not have an interest in a particular school subject, business, or leisure time activity, etc., nothing can be done about it. Some people still mistakenly operate with this view; however, research findings suggest that this is not the case. Interest may be supported to develop, and, in fact, the support provided by the home environment has been widely acknowledged to be critical in providing a foundation as well as a language for engaging particular disciplines (e.g., music, science). Given its benefit for learning, and differences of early experience, it seems to be incumbent on educators, in particular, to take responsibility for supporting the development of their students' interest.

Yet another misconception is that interest is always easily measured by simply asking the person if they are interested or like the content. "Liking" does not provide enough information to distinguish among those with less and more developed interest. It is also essential to consider an individual's value for and knowledge of content, and/or the behaviors to enable assessment of this information.

Another misconception is that a person who has more developed interest does not need support; research shows that this assumption is not valid. Even when a person's interest is already developing, it is most likely to thrive when there is support for its continued development. Without opportunities to continue to deepen and develop, even a well-developed interest may go dormant or drop off. Parents, educators, and employers play an important role in how interest develops and whether it is sustained.

Finally, another misunderstanding about interest is the assumption that supporting the development of a person's interest is too complex and messy of a task to deal with. The complexity is related to the fact that people tend not to have a clear definition of interest (for example, they do not know if and how interest differs from curiosity), and they often do not recognize the characteristics of interest or its developmental trajectory. Interest that is in the process of being triggered and has not yet developed differs in predictable ways from more developed interest. Understanding the differences between earlier and later phases in the development of interest can be a reliable and useful tool for supporting learning and productivity. A person's phase of interest provides information about how a task or activity is likely to be experienced and can suggest ways that others could enable the person to make connections to it and persevere.

Findings from research on interest confirm that the development of interest contributes to a person's readiness to identify with a discipline, to think and work with content, and interest is used as an indicator in assessments of flow and grit.[5] There is mounting evidence that interest is instrumental in its relation to learning, and for motivation and engagement. For example, interest:

- predicts long-term growth in achievement;[6]
- is critical for learners' expectations and motivation to succeed; their awareness of the value of interest seems to precede their awareness of utility and attainment value (importance);[7]
- leads to meaningful engagement, and appears to precede changes in students' behavior and academic engagement.[8]

Moreover, evidence from neuroscience now confirms that people are hardwired to be interested and to engage in seeking behavior that activates the brain's reward circuitry.[9] This means that all persons can develop interest and also that, as interest develops, a person is likely to voluntarily seek the information and resources needed for continued learning. When interest is supported to deepen and develop, motivation and engagement are most likely to be effectively cultivated.

In 1946, the psychologist Allport wrote that, "One of our greatest defects is our lack of a consistent or adequate theory of interest" (1946: 341).[10] He acknowledged the power of interest and described the complications of not having enough information to be able to explain and/or harness its possibilities. In the last thirty years, research developments have begun to provide a basis for formulation and development of such a theory. In this book, we describe the theory and findings that now constitute the four-phase model of interest development.[11] In this model, interest is conceptualized as including affective and cognitive components that are biologically grounded; that is, they have roots in a person's physiological make-up. Furthermore, interest is dynamic and has the potential to develop. It develops in the interaction(s) of a person and the environment, or learning context.[12]

We open the volume by describing interest development as a trajectory that unfolds in relation to a person's interactions with the environment, whether these interactions take place in or out of school. In each of the book's six chapters, we focus on issues that are important to educators, business people, parents, and various research communities. Policy-makers could also benefit from reading the book.

In Chapter 1, we define interest. We acknowledge references to interest in everyday conversation, and explain how interest is studied by academics concerned with education and learning. We provide an overview and a case illustration of the four-phase model of interest development. We also explain the historical context of educational and psychological studies of interest and the roots of different approaches to the conceptualization of interest.

In Chapter 2, we review research on interest and its relation to learning, attention, and curiosity. We point to findings confirming the important role of interest in learning, and we revisit differences in researchers' interpretations of the relation between attention and interest. We use evidence from neuroscience to further clarify how learning, attention, and curiosity are related to interest, and to explain why interest is rewarding and powerful. We also argue that interest and curiosity should be conceptualized as related but distinct concepts.

In Chapter 3, we describe the process of triggering interest and how new interests can be supported to develop. We address what counts as interest and how interest can be identified and measured. We point to behaviors associated with the development of interest, and explain how and also why these behaviors provide reliable indicators for its measurement.

In Chapter 4, we define the terms "motivation" and "engagement" and discuss their relation to interest. Following this, we explain the links between interest and different types of motivational variables such as goals, self-efficacy, and self-regulation. We also explain that the ways in which they are related may change as interest develops; for example, in earlier phases of interest, the variables are distinct, and in later phases of interest they are more likely to be coordinated and mutually supportive.

In Chapter 5, we consider the paradox of declines in interest as learners advance in schooling. We discuss how interest is related to content knowledge, the relation between interest and identity, and the meaning of interest-driven learning. We also report on research conducted both in and out of school to provide an overview of interest research by domain.

In Chapter 6, we conclude by reviewing three major premises:

1. Interest is a variable that can be supported to develop and deepen, regardless of a person's age or prior experience.
2. In order for interest to develop, a person needs to make connections to the content of interest.
3. Neuroscience provides evidence that people are hardwired to find the pursuit of their interest rewarding.

We review resources for supporting the development of interest, and we address the implications of interest for subsequent research and for practice.

We draw on research findings to inform the discussion in each chapter and to identify what is not yet well understood. Because the principles of interest are generally applicable across disciplines, we have included case materials that refer to a wide variety of situations in order to provide context for readers. We have designed the volume to include text written for a wide range of readers, not all of whom specialize in motivation and learning; annotated notes are provided for researchers. This organization is intended to increase ease of reading for those new to the topic; it enables the chapters to be read without interruption by multiple citations and additional details. The sequencing of the chapters and the use of examples is intended to allow readers new to research on interest to develop their understanding; key ideas are also reiterated in each chapter in case readers choose to read chapters out of order.

Our goal is to provide readers with a research-informed follow-up to Dewey's now-classic essay that was published in 1913, *Interest and Effort in Education*.[13] We note that, like Dewey's, our focus is on typical development and the role of interest in learning. This volume does not address particular conditions, although we recognize that both researchers and practitioners may benefit by attending to the development of interests of those with attention-deficit hyperactivity disorder, Asperger's syndrome, or high-functioning autism.

Although not all of Dewey's ideas were supported by subsequent research, many of them were. Neuroscientific information was unavailable to Dewey. Now, this research suggests that there are biological correlates of interest indicating that interest is inherently rewarding. Recent findings suggest that interest is its own reward and that the development of interest is even more powerful than Dewey suggested.

Notes

1 Our focus throughout this volume is on individuals' participation with interest. Interest is both a psychological state and/or a motivational variable. We speak of a person having an interest in some content (e.g., domain of knowledge [such as mathematics, or playing tennis], object [such as trains or microscopes], or idea [such as leftist politics or cooperation in peace-making]). However, we do not focus on the specifics of the object of interest; rather, we describe the power of interest generally and its application across different contents of interest.
2 See Barron et al. 2014; Edelson and Josephs 2004; Illeris 2007; Renninger 2000; Renninger and Hidi 2002.
3 Hidi and Renninger 2006; Renninger and Hidi 2011; see also discussion in Renninger and Su 2012.
4 This is not to deny that some individuals are born with major predispositions to develop their individual interests such as in music, mathematics, or chess. However, the point we are making is that even when no such strong predisposition is present, interest may be developed, if triggered and supported.
5 Flow refers to the psychological state of engagement during which a person is so focused on activity that they may lose track of time (e.g., Csikszentmihalyi

1990; Jackson 2012). Grit refers to the determination to master content, especially when interest and its facilitating effect on effort is not present (e.g., Duckworth et al. 2007).

6 Murayama et al. 2013.
7 This is our interpretation of Wigfield et al.'s (2006) explanation that is described in terms of prediction.
8 Reschly and Christenson 2012; see discussion in Renninger and Bachrach 2015.
9 Hidi 2006, 2015; see also Berridge 2012; Panksepp 1998.
10 cf. Berlyne 1949; Renninger and Hidi 2011.
11 The four-phase model describes phases in the development of a person's interest, a process that is initiated by triggering. Interest may then be sustained as a relatively enduring predisposition to return over time to particular classes of content such as writing, playing bridge, or cooking (Hidi and Renninger 2006; see also Renninger and Hidi 2011; Renninger and Su 2012).
12 Schiefele (1978) was among the first to emphasize that it was essential to study interest as a significant component of motivation and to explain how and why students become interested in particular content and how interest can be sustained.
13 The present volume also follows Silvia's *Exploring the Psychology of Interest*, published in 2006. As we discuss in more detail later, Silvia's research questions focus on cognitive appraisals that result in the emotion of interest. Notably, Silvia is not focusing on interest as a cognitive and affective variable that can be supported to develop. Rather he focuses on the emotional component of interest as an aspect of personality. Whereas we acknowledge that interest has an emotional component, we also maintain that interest is the product of an interaction between a person and their environment and that it is through this interaction that interest is supported to develop. Because Silvia focuses on the pattern of cognitions, or appraisal structures, that lead to feelings of interest, he suggests that evaluations (appraisals) of events, not the events themselves, result in emotional experiences. Instead, we draw on research from neuroscience that describes seeking behaviors as a biological root of interest (Panksepp 1998) and the interactions of the person with the environment as the basis of interest development. As such, although we do not deny that individual differences exist in the depth and breadth of interests of individuals (see Ainley 1987), we do not presume that conscious cognitive evaluations precede the psychological state of interest or that interests are necessarily stable aspects of personality.

1

DEFINING INTEREST

What is interest and how has it been conceptualized and studied?

What is the definition of interest? A momentary fixation, attraction, fascination, or curiosity? A preference or an attitude? Love of learning or even a passion? A motivational belief or a trait-like characteristic? Is it an emotion?[1] Until recently, academics have not been able to reach a consensus about how to define interest, because so many of these ways of describing interest seem to be intuitively correct. In order to avoid confusion about our definition, we specifically focus on interest and its development beginning with the initial triggering of attention and extending through to the formation of a well-developed individual interest. In the course of its development, interest is very likely to include or reflect all of the above definitions.[2]

In our definition, interest has a dual meaning: it refers to the psychological state of a person while engaging with some type of content (e.g., mathematics, bass fishing, music) and also to the cognitive and affective motivational predisposition to reengage with that content over time. That is, interest is a psychological state and a motivational disposition that exists in, or is the product of, the interaction of people's characteristics and their environment (see Figure 1.1).[3] Much of the research on interest focuses on one or the other of these two aspects of interest, although they have been, and perhaps should be, considered together.

A Psychological State and a Motivational Variable

Interest as a psychological state is grounded in a person's physiological/neurological reactions to a wide range of things, including other people, objects, and tasks. Interest also describes a unique, content-specific, motivational variable that is responsible for the processes underlying how people act, feel, engage, and learn.[4]

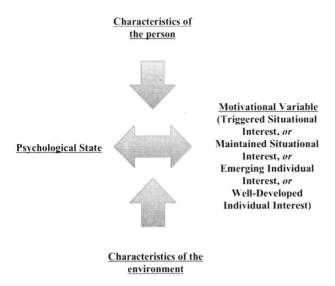

Characteristics of the person

Psychological State

Motivational Variable
(Triggered Situational
Interest, *or*
Maintained Situational
Interest, *or*
Emerging Individual
Interest, *or*
Well-Developed
Individual Interest)

Characteristics of the environment

FIGURE 1.1   The Dual Meaning of Interest: A Psychological State and a Motivational Variable.

As a psychological state, interest is characterized by increased attention, effort, concentration, and affect during engagement. As a motivational variable, the term makes a distinction between shorter-term or situational interest and longer-term or individual interest, which is characterized by reengagement over time.

Two children who are playing chess and are in different phases of interest may be in the same psychological state but may differ in their predisposition to return to playing chess another time. The child with less developed interest (triggered or maintained situational interest), may or may not continue to seek opportunities to play, depending on available and competing opportunities; on the other hand, the child with more developed interest in chess (emerging individual or well-developed individual interest) will be motivated to return to play: he will not want to be called away from the game, and, if he is, he is likely to seek opportunities to play chess again just as soon as he can.[5]

The two meanings of interest—as both a psychological state and as a motivational disposition—are interrelated. On one hand, if the psychological state of interest is generated, or triggered repeatedly, it may support the development of interest as a motivational variable. On the other hand, the level or phase of interest as a motivational variable determines the types of environmental supports (e.g., from other people and/or the design of tasks or opportunities) that are needed to enable the continued triggering and maintaining of the psychological state of interest.

Integral to the development of interest as a motivational variable are two types of interest: situational and individual.[6] Linked, they describe the potential

TABLE 1.1 A Case Example of a Triggered Situational Interest That Is Maintained.

Julia is in her last term of college. While nervously waiting for a medical appointment, she picks up and flips through a magazine. Her attention is drawn to an article about a man who is an engineer and who recently gave up his partnership in a successful consulting practice to become a facilitator. A facilitator is a person who tries to help people or groups resolve conflicts before they go to litigation. Julia likes the idea of working with people and wants to read more even though she has never heard of the occupation of facilitator before now. Meanwhile, she is called to meet the doctor. She carefully marks the page she is reading and leaves the magazine on the table. Following her appointment, she goes back to the table, finds the magazine, and sits down to finish reading the article.

Source: Hidi and Renninger 2006: 116.

trajectory of interest development in which situational interest may trigger and support the development of individual interest (see Table 1.1).

They have also been studied separately. We consider each briefly and explain the links between them. We then provide detail about the four-phase model of interest development, which describes phases in interest development as including triggered situational, maintained situational, emerging individual, and well-developed individual interest. Following this, we review conceptualizations of interest in their historical contexts and discuss their implications for better understanding interest as a variable that develops.

Situational, Individual, and Topic Interest

Situational interest—also referred to as an early phase of interest development, or less developed interest—is a reaction to particular content or activity. It has an affective component that frequently is positive but can also involve negative feelings such as fear or disgust.[7] Situational interest is characterized by focused attention to particular content and may be shorter-term (triggered situational interest) or may be maintained over a somewhat longer period of time (maintained situational interest).[8] Two types of factors have been identified as characterizing situational interest:

1. structural characteristics such as novelty, surprise, complexity, and ambiguity;[9]
2. content features such as human activity, life themes, intensity, and personalization.[10]

These factors may naturally occur in the environment, can result from educators' organization of school activities (e.g., hands-on activities)[11] or, in the case of older individuals, may be self-generated (e.g., with the intention of staying on task).[12] Linnenbrink-Garcia et al. (2010) have shown different aspects of the mathematics classroom can provide triggers: the presentation of course materials (triggered situational interest), students' feelings about the materials as enjoyable or engaging (maintained situational interest feeling), and students' perceptions of the materials' importance (maintained situational interest value).[13] Moreover, they reported that situational interest promoted change in the students' individual interest over the school year.

Individual interest—also called a later phase of interest development, more developed interest, and/or personal interest—is a relatively enduring pre-disposition to reengage particular content over time. The repeated experience of the psychological state of interest predicts the likelihood of continued self-sustained engagement[14] when opportunity is available,[15] as well as the experience of flow.[16] Typically, learners who have an emerging individual interest are invested and excited by their developing knowledge. When learners have a well-developed individual interest they are also likely to be concerned with the relation between their understanding and what others have said or may have figured out.[17] Individual interest tends to develop slowly through repeated triggers from the environment that can be provided by other people[18] or may be self-generated.[19] Individual interest is associated with positive feelings as well as a recursive relation of knowledge and value for the content of interest. The development of knowledge contributes to the deepening of value, and, as value develops, it leads to continued engagement and yet more deepening of knowledge.[20]

In addition to situational and individual interest, some researchers have studied topic interest (e.g., space travel).[21] Topic interest is triggered by the presentation of topics and themes.[22] This type of interest was considered to be a form of situational interest in some early studies,[23] while other investigators referred to topic interest as a form of individual interest.[24] Subsequently, Ainley et al. (2002) reported that topic interest can be influenced by both situational (e.g., a topic such as space travel is mentioned and people want to know about it) and individual factors (e.g., people have an already developed interest in space travel). Their research identified the contributions of both of these factors to the psychological state of interest that was triggered by four expository topics.

It is now clear that situational interest can be triggered in earlier as well as later phases of interest development. In fact, triggering occurs in each phase of interest, and when triggers "take," interest can develop.[25] In earlier phases of interest, the person needs triggering to support engagement with the content. In later ph~~
of interest, continued triggering of interest is necessary for ~~
interest to continue. For example, a person's interest can k
early phases of interest development and also by novelty ~~
development,[26] although what is novel or even compre~~
ent for persons with less and more developed interest in
(1999: 89) provided some good illustrations of how indivi~~
information they find novel and interesting:

> What is an exciting filmed chase scene for most people, may be boring to the jaded film critic who has seen too many chase scenes. A fascinating magazine account of a war escape may be old news, and inaccurate to boot, to the teen war aficionado who has already read several detailed book-length accounts of the escape.[28]

Initially, researchers studying interest did not see that situational and individual interest were linked. They did not recognize that the psychological state of interest could be the same for both situational and individual interest (as described in the example of the boy playing chess) and that the phase of a person's interest would influence the level of his or her motivation. Rather, they thought that situational and individual interest were two different forms of interest.[29] However, study findings emerged that led us to question the distinction between situational and individual interest.[30] Subsequently, based on a review of the empirical literature, we found that we could identify four phases of interest and proposed the four-phase model of interest development, a proposition that has now been validated empirically.

The Four-Phase Model of Interest Development

As its name implies, the four-phase model of interest development describes four phases (not stages) in the development of interest: triggered situational, maintained situational, emerging individual, and well-developed individual interest (see Table 1.2). These phases characterize interest development across age levels and contexts, both in and out of formal settings such as the workplace or school. The term "phase" is used rather than "stage" because the length and character of a given phase may vary between and within individuals based on experience and temperament, among other factors. Without self-generated or environmental support for continued engagement, it is also possible for a person's interest in something to decrease or drop off altogether.[31]

As depicted in Table 1.2, the first phase is a *triggered situational interest*. In this phase, people's feelings about their own interest may be positive or negative and may or may not result in sustained engagement. Triggers in this phase are most likely but not necessarily external to the individual. As Dewey (1902, 1913) predicted, whether a triggered interest is maintained depends on a person's prior experience, strengths, and needs, as well as the facilitation provided by others and the features of available interest-related tasks and activities. The form of facilitation, moreover, is likely to be informed by whether the person is aware that help could be beneficial, asks questions, and/or takes advantage of potential input.[32]

If triggered interest is sustained and people begin and/or are supported to begin making connections between the content of interest and their own skills, knowledge, and prior experience, this may lead to the second phase of interest

TABLE 1.2 The Four Phases of Interest Development.

Phases of interest development

	Less developed (earlier)		More developed (later)	
	Phase 1: Triggered situational interest	Phase 2: Maintained situational interest	Phase 3: Emerging individual interest	Phase 4: Well-developed individual interest
Definition	• Psychological state resulting from short-term changes in cognitive and affective processing associated with a particular class of content	• Psychological state that involves focused attention to a particular class of content that reoccurs and/or persists over time	• Psychological state *and* the beginning of relatively enduring predisposition to seek reengagement with a particular class of content over time	• Psychological state *and* a relatively enduring predisposition to reengage a particular class of content over time
Learner characteristics	• Attends to content, if only fleetingly • May or may not be reflectively aware of the experience • May need support to engage from others and through instructional design • May experience either positive or negative feelings • May not persevere when confronted with difficulty • May simply want to be told what to do	• Reengages content that previously triggered attention • Is developing knowledge of content • Is developing a sense of the content's value • Is likely to be able to be supported by others to find connections to content based on existing skills, knowledge, and/or prior experience • Is likely to have positive feelings • May not persevere when confronted with difficulty • May want to be told what to do	• Is likely to independently reengage content • Has stored knowledge and stored value • Is reflective about the content • Is focused on their own questions • Has positive feelings • May not persevere when confronted with difficulty • May not want feedback from others	• Independently reengages content • Has stored knowledge and value • Is reflective about the content • Is likely to recognize others' contributions to the discipline • Self-regulates easily to reframe questions and seek answers • Has positive feelings • Can persevere through frustration and challenge in order to meet goals • Appreciates and may actively seek feedback

Source: This is a revised version of a table originally presented in Renninger and Su 2012.

development: *a maintained situational interest*. When people have a maintained situational interest, they are likely to experience positive affect and to continue to develop their knowledge of and value for the content of interest. However, much of the support for the continued development and deepening of interest still comes from features of the environment, including other people, activities, and resources.

When people begin taking initiative by independently reflecting and reengaging, seeking answers and/or identifying resources that allow their knowledge to deepen, they can be said to have an *emerging individual interest*. In this phase, people begin to self-generate interest, to self-regulate, and to prioritize further understanding and involvement with the object of interest over other things.[33] However, they are also primarily concerned with their own questions and may or may not be responsive to feedback, even though they continue to need support to develop skills and understanding of the content.

When an interest has developed into a *well-developed individual interest*, people are able to focus on information about the content of interest beyond what is immediately connected to their own questions.[34] In this phase of interest, they have positive feelings and voluntarily and independently reengage. People with a well-developed individual interest have a long-range vision of their own participation and are able to overcome frustrations from needing to rework, or rethink, issues that arise. They are able to recognize others' contributions to the discipline, may actively seek to understand those contributions, and are likely to seek feedback.

For example, Harackiewicz et al. (2008: 118) provided empirical validation of the model in their study of the situational interest, individual interest, and academic performance of 858 undergraduate students over seven terms:

> Our results offer strong support for the four-phase model of interest development recently advanced by Hidi and Renninger (2006), which identifies four phases of interest development and outlines the progression from situational interest to individual interest. According to their model, the first phase of interest development is a *triggered situational interest*, in which attention, liking, or involvement is initiated by an external cue. Our lecture-specific measures of catch correspond to this early phase of interest development. If sustained over time or contexts, triggered situational interest evolves into the second phase a *maintained situational interest*, and this phase of interest may be reflected in our measures of hold, which assessed interest in the course material. A third phase, characterized as an *emerging individual interest*, may develop out of the second phase, if individuals begin to value the object or topic beyond the situation that first stimulated their interest. In this phase, individuals may be predisposed to seek out opportunities on their own to reengage with the topic of interest. This phase of

interest may be reflected in our behavioral measure of continued interest, which examined students' course choices after completion of the introductory course. The third phase of interest development can then lead to the fourth, a *well-developed individual interest*, which is associated with personal meaning, value, and knowledge (Renninger, 1990). Our psychology major variable, which represents a student's extensive experience with and investment in a domain of study, seems to correspond to a well-developed individual interest.

Many studies have now been published that provide support for the model.[35]

A logical question about interest development concerns its relation to boredom. Is boredom simply a lack of interest, or is it a more aversive state? In terms of the four-phase model, we would expect that the reasons for boredom depend on the phase of a person's interest development (or lack of it). More specifically, it would be expected that those with no interest might not yet have made connections to present content and therefore experience boredom.[36] For those with developing interest, on the other hand, boredom might be expected if their existing connections to content are mismatched with the available tasks, information, and/or opportunities for action. In each case, we would also expect that boredom could be offset by appropriate opportunities to seriously engage with content, whether these are provided through interactions with other people or are self-generated through activities and tasks.

A Case Illustration of Interest Development

Consider, for example, the case of an adolescent whom we call Emma who received a camera from her parents for her birthday. Within hours of receiving it, she began using the camera to photograph the flowers in her garden. Her case illustrates how interest can develop:

> Emma's situational interest in photography is triggered by the gift of the camera. She is not aware that she is developing an interest in photography; she thinks of herself as being interested in flowers. She takes pictures of all sorts of flowers and decides to put the pictures in an album, at which point, her interest in photography can be said to have shifted from being a triggered to a maintained situational interest.[37] As the season changes, her photos begin to include fading foliage. She begins to distinguish between the photos that she thinks work and throws away the others.
>
> One day as she is putting her camera away, she sees directions in the bottom of the case. She pulls them out and begins reading. She learns about distance, focus, sharpness, exposure, and light. As such, her interest

in photography begins to shift from being a maintained situational interest to an emerging individual interest because she begins applying her newly acquired knowledge, and, as she does, her understanding of the possibilities and the challenge of taking good pictures grows, as does her value for the camera. She feels positive about photography, and, whether or not she is aware that her value for the camera increases as she gains knowledge about it, she begins to see the importance and the benefit, or utility, of using the camera correctly.

She still describes herself to others as interested in flowers even though her interest in photography has developed into an emerging individual interest. In assembling an album of her photos, she sets goals to use light and shadow as the grouping strategy rather than organizing them by flower type. She feels proud of this decision and of her pictures and decides that she should find out whether she could submit her photos to the school talent fair, and when the school camera club meets. At the club meeting, she is very excited to find out that special workshops on how to develop photos will be held and that she is welcome to join. She does, and over the months, she learns that her original understanding of light and shadow was not accurate. She prioritizes her time so that she can attend the workshops and ask questions, follow recommendations for additional resources, and invest time in practicing what she has learned. She is receptive to the feedback she receives and is undaunted in her efforts to master photography. At this point, she has clear goals, feels self-efficacious, and is able to self-regulate. She also identifies as a photographer. She now has a well-developed interest in photography and is presently working to better understand light and shadow.

Characteristics of Interest

In addition to providing an example of how a new interest can develop, Emma's case illustrates key characteristics of interest. First, Emma's interest is content, or object-specific: She is interested in flowers, the camera, photography, light, and shadows. Interest is always related to particular objects, events, activities, or ideas. Second, Emma has numerous environmental supports for her initial, continuing, and deepening engagement with the camera; she receives the camera from her parents, reads directions that accompanied the camera, joins the camera club, and, as a camera-club member, begins to develop her own photos. Third, Emma enjoys both taking and looking at her pictures as well as figuring out how to improve their quality. Interest includes both affect and cognition. Emma is cognitively engaged in photographing the flowers and their parts in the different seasons, ordering the photos by light and shadow, and perfecting her ability to develop photos. She experiences positive affect, and she is able to overcome the occasional negative experience such as pictures not coming out as expected or finding out that she has a lot to learn in order to work effectively with light and shadow. Fourth, Emma is so absorbed in her work with the camera that she may not be aware that she is developing an interest in photography until it has developed. Often people are not aware that their interest is triggered, or developing, because they are fully engaged in "doing" the interest. A fifth characteristic of interest that is not explicitly illustrated by Emma's case is that the affective and cognitive components of interest have a physiological/neurological basis (biological roots). In other words, Emma's brain activation when she is engaging in photography is different from when she is engaged with other activities that she is not interested in.

In each phase of Emma's developing interest in photography, she experiences a psychological state of interest, although the triggers for her developing interest in the earlier phases are not the same as in the later phases. In each phase, we see some voluntary reengagement with the camera, although it is not until she begins to change the way in which she interacts with it (e.g., using the information in the directions to explore light and shadow) that she seems to be clear about what she wants to learn. As she begins identifying with photography, her interest seems to be self-sustaining, and she appears to be setting goals for herself. The shift in the development of her interest in photography is related to her developing knowledge and increased value for photography.

Emma's interest development could have been thwarted. For example, the instructions for using the camera might have been too hard for Emma to understand; she might have gone to an exhibit of a famous photographer and decided that she could never take pictures that would be as good as those in the exhibit; her camera could have been stolen; the album she assembled might have been dismissed by the members of the camera club; or the school might not have had a camera club. In earlier phases of her interest development, Emma might not have made needed connections to using the camera (e.g., her use of the camera to record types of flowers over time as they grew) and become bored; and, once her interest in photography had begun to develop, she might have exhausted her own abilities to do new and more challenging things with the camera. In this case, she also might have become bored. Even though the development of interest is sequential, interest can go dormant, meaning that it can fall off. The availability and the nature of environmental supports inform the trajectory of interest development during all phases.

Following publication of the four-phase model, studies of interest development have begun to focus on distinctions between earlier and later phases of interest.[38] Such studies provide research evidence of the positive role of interest on learners' attention, motivation, engagement, strategy use, and goal setting.[39] In them, the researchers assume that interest develops and that its support includes the interaction of the person, other persons, and the tasks of the environment. Their findings point to the roles of early experiences for developing and maintaining interest,[40] interest as a support for learning,[41] the organization and facilitation of the classroom environment as supporting the development of interest, or not,[42] and the importance of the teacher's own interest in content to be taught.[43]

Studies have also established that interest has a reciprocal relation to other variables such as goals, self-efficacy, and self-regulation.[44]

Historical Context and Conceptualizations of Interest

Early discussions of interest and education recognized the impact of interest on learning. For example, psychologists and educators such as Dewey (1913), Herbart (1965), James (1890), and Pestalozzi (2004) each pointed to the centrality of interest in supporting learning. They noted the importance of interest in supporting effort, focused attention, and persistence to understand and that the design and/or sequencing of tasks was likely to promote learners' interest in content to be learned. Dewey (1913) described the presence of interest as rendering effort effortless. He said that interest improved understanding and facilitated learning as well as personal involvement. He also pointed to the interaction of the person and the environment as basic to interest and acknowledged that learning could be influenced by personal interest as well as by the interestingness of tasks and objects. Similarly, Herbart (1965) described interest and meaningful learning as being closely related. He suggested that interest contributes to the accuracy of understanding, the development of knowledge, and the motivation to learn. James (1890) elaborated on these points, further noting the impact of interest on what learners pay attention to, as well as what they have learned. In the context of social reform, Pestalozzi (2004) argued that if the goal was to enable all students to learn, pedagogical practices needed to be revised to address learner interests.

Psychologists such as Arnold (1910) and Claparède (1905) further suggested that interest was a biological force that affected learning, although it is only recently that neuroscientists have been able to demonstrate the biological roots of interest.[45] Arnold and Claparède were limited in their abilities to fully explain the biological process and were instead challenged to make links to pedagogy that practitioners could use. Importantly, Arnold described interest as an attitude toward a situation that influenced feelings and future possibilities and attention as a possible support for interest, but his insight about the role of biology was considered shallow, and he was not able to provide information that practitioners desired.[46] Similarly, Claparède (1905) was well regarded for his recognition of the failings of educational systems that were not centered on children and their interests and wrote the introduction to Dewey's (1913) volume, but he was later described by Hameline (2000) as ill equipped to move beyond generalizations about interest to its needed application. Hameline also observed that because Claparède was not able to provide details about interest as a motivational variable, he was repeatedly misunderstood as if he had suggested that the use of interest in teaching was more about entertainment than rigor.

Even if particulars about the role of interest in learning were not well under-stood, its power was recognized. This gave momentum to efforts to improve under-standing of interest. There was a proliferation of inventories by educators wanting to assess the strengths, needs, and interests of learners, as suggested by Dewey (1913) and by psychologists to identify interests and their duration.[47] Inventories of topics that children found interesting were developed and used to identify texts for use in teaching.[48] In describing responses to inventories, Thorndike (1912) suggested that interests developed early in a person's life were related to later experience and that such interests might be expected to be fairly permanent by adulthood. However, Thorndike and other researchers also acknowledged that their studies of the relation between interest and learning indicated that interest was more complex than they had previously realized. They found that the strength of interest might predict its endurance and that the environment made more of an impact on interest when interest was not so strong; taken together, these findings suggested that interest worked differently depending on both the person and the environment.

According to Fryer (1931), surveys also began to be refined for use as a tool in career and vocational guidance following World War I, during which the need to classify enlisted persons suggested that surveys could be useful for matching people to jobs. Moore (1921) was one of the first to employ methods of interest assessment to distinguish the fit of potential engineers to different types of engi-neering. The success of this effort quickly spread to other technical fields. Under the leadership of Strong's[49] research group at Stanford University and Paterson's[50] at the University of Minnesota, vocational interest inventories expanded to include other career paths.[51] These researchers also pushed for methodologi-cal advancements such as longitudinal study and the reliability and validity of measures.

Concern about measurement increasingly characterized developments in many academic fields as researchers became aware that their methods affected their results. For interest researchers, as well as those in other fields, the objectiv-ity of experimentation became a central concern.[52] In order to ensure objectiv-ity, many researchers began using invented nonsense words and objects in their experiments on the assumption that if participants had prior experience with the content being studied, its already acquired meaning would influence study results.[53] The concern for objectivity led to discrete studies that were focused on the prediction and control of behavior, in terms of the relation between stimuli and the responses that they elicited, an approach to the study of learning that came to be associated with behaviorism and learning theory.[54] Under the aegis of behaviorism, study of internal mental states such as cognition, emotion, and mood were considered too subjective for effective experimentation in learning, even though researchers such as Bartlett (1932) stressed that interest played a major role in what individuals remember, and that study of nonsense words was too simple to make a significant contribution to understanding learning.

Adaptation of behavioral principles to teaching described (a) knowledge as a repertoire of observable behaviors that could be learned (and unlearned) if stimuli were targeted and appropriate reinforcement (or rewards) were provided, and (b) teaching as a technology that involved use of appropriate stimuli in the transmission of learning.[55] In response, progressive educational thinkers such as Dewey (1933) and his followers had begun to be placed on the defensive about their recommendations for practice (e.g., using the interests of learners to help them develop connections to the materials they needed to learn).[56]

There were behaviorists who recognized the limitations of focusing too narrowly on either stimuli or responses, however. For example, Tolman (1932) pointed to learning as occurring in the interaction with the environment and determined by an organism's motivational state (e.g., expectations, beliefs). McDougall (1932), another behaviorist, challenged prevailing discussions about reinforcement, suggesting that even in animal research, the importance of instinct and motivation should be recognized. By the 1940s and 1950s, distinctions were being made among various categories of research in psychology, e.g., abnormal, social, and so forth. Within different subfields, the push to better articulate the measurement of constructs, decisions to employ one or another type of measure or methodology, and ensuing scholarship along one rather than another line of methods appear to have led to increasingly distinct lines of inquiry and sometimes to parallel sets of constructs and analyses.[57]

The psychological studies of interest that followed tended to focus on one or another particular aspect of interest (although some addressed combinations of these aspects), including interest as emotion, interest as influenced by the experience of interest, interest as value, or interest as vocational interest. These studies typically assessed interest at one point in time and in a single context. Sometimes the studies assessed the interest of participants at different ages in order to consider issues of development, but they did not consider how the interest of a person, once triggered, might be supported to develop. Often the indicators employed focused solely on liking and knowledge was not considered to be coordinated with either feelings or value. These differing approaches to the study of interest are reviewed briefly as each represents a contemporary conceptualization of interest that also informs understanding of the four-phase model.

Interest as Emotion

Studies of interest as an emotion focus on the feelings experienced during interested engagement rather than on either value or knowledge. A concern in early studies was whether it was appropriate to consider interest as an affect and, if so, whether it was distinct from joy and how to target it in investigations. Tomkins (1962) was one of the first to use facial expressions, and distinguished between interest and enjoyment as two primary positive affects.[58] He proposed that interest–excitement motivates exploration of what is novel and intriguing, whereas enjoyment–joy is a sense of satisfaction and reward that is generated through the activity. Izard (1977) elaborated on this position suggesting that interest is a feeling of wanting to investigate, become involved, be engaged and absorbed in an activity, as well as of being curious or fascinated. Izard also considered enjoyment to be distinct from interest.[59] More recently, Izard (2007, 2009) pointed to the complementary and reciprocal functions of interest and joy in the expansion of ideas and knowledge in constructive and creative activities.

Ainley and Hidi (2014) have reviewed the literature on interest and enjoyment and suggested that the relation between these constructs may vary based on students' developmental levels and past experience. They noted that feelings of interest motivate exploration and information seeking, whereas feelings of enjoyment manifest pleasure. They also concluded that the development of relatively enduring individual interest that supports achievement is contingent on the individual experiencing both interest and enjoyment in their learning. Reeve and his colleagues (2015) have also noted the importance of understanding feelings generated during engagement more generally as these influence interest. Silvia (2006) too has argued that interest is an emotion; he attributed the triggering of interest to inherently interesting features of the environment. He suggested that the origins of interest lie in individuals' cognitive processing, that is, in their appraisals of events.[60]

Neural mechanisms have now been identified that indicate emotions can be activated without cognitive appraisals.[61] Hetland and Vittersø's (2012) study of BASE jumpers who parachute from fixed structures or cliffs provides evidence that this is the case and further suggests that one emotion may suppress another.[62] Specifically, the BASE jumpers report enthusiasm at the time of the jump and joy at the end of the jump; however, the camera captures the facial expression of fear during the jump, an emotion that the participants do not report or seem to be aware that they have had. The logical explanation of this is that the strength of their interest, enthusiasm, and subsequent joy suppresses or renders unconscious their fear. It also raises the likelihood that other emotions may be involved when experiencing interest. The possibilities that a person may not be aware of co-occurring emotions and also that other emotions may be related to the experiencing of interest are important for establishing the role of various emotions in the development of interest.

No suggestions have yet emerged to explain how interest develops when interest is conceptualized as an emotion. Neuroscientific findings showing the separation of the psychological aspects of liking and wanting complicate consideration of interest as only an emotion. For example, Berridge (2012) demonstrated that liking (referred to as hedonic impact) and wanting (referred to as incentive salience) are distinct psychological identities and have distinguishable neural processes. This has direct implications for measuring and understanding the developmental process of interest.[63]

Interest Based on Task Features or Interest Experience

Interest research addressing the influence of task features (e.g., characteristics such as novelty, surprisingness, and so forth; topics; and activity structure) tends to focus on situational interest.[64] Studies that specifically examine the contribution of the environment to task experience also address how the experience of interest can maintain interest. Examples of this type of study include:

- inventories used to identify topics for assigned work and/or remediation;[65]
- questions generated by students;[66]
- the design of courses around examples (e.g., use of medical examples in physics lectures for pre-medical students) in order to optimize student engagement and understanding.[67]

Investigations have also addressed the nature of seductive details that trigger interest (e.g., interesting but irrelevant text segments) and the placement of information on a page or in a presentation.[68]

Initially, these studies focused on how interest elicited when reading a text (text-based interest) affected processing. Two hypotheses emerged about interest in text-processing:

1. Increased interest resulted in better memory of text.[69]
2. Increased interest meant basic text-processing required fewer cognitive resources, which would, in turn, make resources for higher-order processing more available.[70, 71]

McDaniel et al. (2000) tested these hypotheses by conducting studies of undergraduates reading stories that they rated as being of higher or lower interest. McDaniel et al. found that fewer cognitive resources are required by more interesting than by less interesting text, and that text-based interest results in qualitative differences in the kind of information that is processed and encoded. In discussing their findings, they suggested that level of interest for the text should be taken into consideration in the assignment of study strategies. Task features that promoted feelings of competence (e.g., flexibility) and extended time to explore have also been found to provide support for interest and enhanced problem-solving.[72]

Studies that have referred to interest experience, the role of experiencing interest as a support for interest, describe the psychological state of interest associated with situational interest.[73] They have pointed to particular features of the environment that trigger and can serve to sustain activity, findings that are consistent with the four-phase model. They indicate that the level of a participant's initial interest for a task or activity affects their ability to work with additional information.[74] Sansone and her colleagues (e.g., Thoman et al. 2007) have also provided more specific information about the contribution of task features in the context of group activity. They found that opportunities to talk together following an activity promoted interest and influenced the quality of social interactions (e.g., eye contact, verbalization). They also reported that listener responsiveness influenced whether interest was maintained. Findings from other studies of participants with less and more developed interest have similarly suggested that not all learners respond to task characteristics or even to the same classroom context in the same way.[75]

Interest as Value

Studies of interest as value consider interest to be a belief on which a person can consciously report (e.g., "We are learning valuable things in math class this year." Linnenbrink-Garcia et al. 2010: 19). Although these studies may address a person's feelings in addition to their value, they typically do not address the developmental aspects or the knowledge component of interest. Such studies range from including conceptualizations of interest as a set of valence beliefs (positive or negative appraisal)[76] to interest as a source of value that together with importance, utility, and cost, may be used to describe a person's motivations, as described in expectancy-value theory.[77] Moreover, studies in which interest is conceptualized as value may, or may not, be studies of interest, per se. They can also be studies of other constructs (e.g., attitude, engagement, or grit) that build on or are informed by interest.

Interest is considered to be a relatively enduring characteristic of a person that is responsive to (a) the conditions of the environment (e.g., parental modeling) and (b) the decisions made in responding to these (e.g., engaging in one rather than another after-school activity).[78] People are assumed to be conscious of their decision-making, and their beliefs about interest are considered to inform their decisions.[79] Schiefele (1999, 2001, 2009), for example, has described interest as a set of valences, or beliefs, that when activated affect a person's motivation. Findings from his and his colleagues' work with the Study Interest Questionnaire suggested that value, feelings, and the choice to engage content are all associated and are not independent factors.[80]

In developing expectancy-value theory, Eccles et al. (1983) pointed to two sets of self- and task-related beliefs to explain school achievement. One set of beliefs was related to individuals' expectations of success, based on their self-concept of ability. The second set was linked to subjective task value and identified task interest by asking participants how much they liked particular content (e.g., "How much do you like mathematics?").[81] As Eccles et al. (2015) noted, their model focuses on behaviors that are the result of explicit (conscious) decisions associated with academic and career choices—behaviors that are motivated by interest "represent a subset of potential patterns of motivational beliefs" (2015: 219).[82]

Interest as Vocational Interest

Studies of vocational interest focus on the features of personality that align with task demands of different disciplines and careers. Such studies of vocational interest provide insight into how individuals may adjust their demands or expectations in order to effectively pursue academic and/or career pathways, and related studies of counseling psychology associate learners' beliefs to their perceptions of the workplace. However, studies of vocational interest do not address the origins of interest or how the continued support of interest might enable interest to develop. Instead, studies of vocational interest consider interests to be trait-like preferences that have implications for course and career selection.[83] Although it is acknowledged that vocational interests may change over one's life span, interests are considered to be relatively stable. It is on the basis of their stability that they are used to guide academic and career choices and can affect career development.[84]

Vocational interest is identified using surveys, and respondents are assumed to be aware of these interests and in a position to describe them. Items on vocational interest scales include both the potential content of interest and activities that are associated with it, such as mathematics and problem-solving. Holland's (1959, 1996) theory of vocational behavior, for example, identified types of people and their environments in terms of one of six categories (realistic, investigative, artistic, social, enterprising, and conventional). It suggested that the workplace can be associated with personality traits on the basis of these assignments.[85]

Rounds and Su (2014) have distinguished among interests that include identity and influences on the choices that are made in the school or workplace environment, and characteristics of the person (e.g., extroversion), or personality traits.[86] A person is considered to either be making choices to engage that are suited to their interest or identity or working to change the environment in ways that are consistent with this identity.[87] Rounds and Su (2014) provide evidence that interest influences behavior and as a result also affects achievement. They also report that interests can be even more powerful than either cognitive ability or personality as predictors of fit to the environment when controlling for contributions of cognitive ability and personality; equally able individuals are seen to do better or worse depending on their interests.

In their social cognitive career theory, Lent et al. (1994) provide a different explanation of how career choices are made. From a counseling perspective, they draw on Bandura's social learning theory (1977) that people learn from observing others, to link workplace and career interests to a person's beliefs. They suggest that context, including opportunities to observe others, influences perceptions of probable success and consequently affects a person's interest. They find that if learners view themselves as successful and value available compensation, they will continue to develop expertise and abilities; this, in turn, reinforces feelings of self-efficacy and interest.[88] In this model, interest is considered to be an outcome of cognitive evaluation and similar to the conceptualization and measurement of interest as value. Unexamined in approaches to vocational interest is the possibility that career interest can be supported to develop.

Concluding Thoughts

We began this chapter describing interest as having two meanings: It is both a psychological state and a motivational variable that can develop. It is noteworthy that throughout history interest has been recognized as a powerful influence on motivation and engagement. Focusing on one or the other conceptualization of interest did not diminish recognition of its impact. However, acknowledging that interest can develop and that it needs support to develop is critical. It seems likely that without support to develop interest some of the greatest achievements of humans might not have been realized, such as Mozart's interest in music, Einstein's interest in physics, Curie's interest in medicine, Mitchell's interest in writing and the South, Navratilova's interest in tennis.

With the emerging understanding of interest as something that can be supported to develop, a number of previously held assumptions are no longer appropriate. Specifically:

1. Interest is not static, nor is it a trait, although it can have trait-like properties when it is well developed. Because it emerges in relation to the support and challenges of the environment, it also can fall off when this support is not present. Therefore it is incorrect to assume that people with well-developed interest no longer need support. To the contrary, because interest exists in relation to the environment, continued support and challenges are needed, and the nature of these differs depending on the person's phase of interest.
2. Interest is not necessarily measured solely by asking people if they are interested, or if they like one or another content. Whereas such questions may work for indicating some level of interest, they do not distinguish among phases of interest.
3. Interest is not a genetic given. Although a person may have a biological, social, psychological, or physical predisposition to develop interest, interest can also be triggered and supported to develop.
4. Interest is not simply a cognitive appraisal or belief. For example, in early phases of interest development, people are not in a position to provide either a consistent cognitive appraisal or a belief, because they do not yet have a knowledge base on which it could be based. In later phases of interest, people may be more likely to be able to report on their interest, but they may also be too involved to reflect on their engagement.
5. Interest is not too complex or messy to be dealt with. In fact, we would argue that interest must be included in discussions of motivation, engagement, and learning. Interest has the potential to drive effective educational interventions.

Notes

1 Hidi and Ainley (2008) characterize these definitions of interest as ranging from a motivational belief that is fundamentally a cognitive conceptualization to a frequently experienced positive emotion (e.g., Panksepp 2000; Reeve et al. 2015; Silvia 2001; Tomkins 1962; Zimmerman 2002). These various ways of defining interest include differing amounts of cognition and affect.

2 We note that none of these definitions of interest describe interest as developing over time; rather, other definitions of interest provide insight into one or another aspect of interest development (see Renninger and Hidi 2011).

3 Figure 1.1 is a revision of Figure 1.1 in Krapp et al. (1992). We have intentionally omitted use of the term "actualized" and replaced it with the term "psychological state of interest" (e.g., Hidi 2000). At the time of the 1992 publication, it was not clear that both situational and individual interest shared the same psychological state; however, research has since indicated that this is the case.

4 It is instructive to note that items used to assess interest have been included in scales that assess grit, flow, engagement, and motivation, suggesting that the critical role of interest is recognized, even if it is not explicitly acknowledged by the researchers.

5 The more a child plays chess, the more likely that his interest in chess will continue to develop. Once his interest develops, different supports are needed for it to be sustained. For example, he will play given the opportunity but may need encouragement after losing repeatedly or if he improves to the point where he no longer feels challenged by weaker players. See Renninger 2000.

6 Silvia (2006) poses the only opposition that we know of to the use of our terms "situational interest" and "individual interest." Although he acknowledged the similarity between our terms and the terms he uses, he suggested that they be replaced with his terms "interest" and "interests" (Silvia 2006: 184–189). Silvia stated that the distinction between interest and interests is analogous to the classic distinction between states and traits. He defined *interest* "as a part of emotional experience, curiosity, and momentary motivation" (2006: 4), and *interests* "as a part of personality, individual differences and people's idiosyncratic hobbies, goals, and avocations" (2006: 4). Furthermore, his criticism of our definition of interest was based on early publications. In a chapter from the edited volume, *The Role of Interest in Learning and Development*, Krapp et al. (1992) used the terms "individual," "situational," "actualized individual interest," and "psychological state of interest." At that point, it was not clear that both situational and individual interest shared the same psychological state.

In the same book, Hidi and Anderson (1992) noted that this was an important question that had not been considered. Silvia's criticism of the confusion created by the use of four terms at that time was justified. However, a lot of research was undertaken between 1992 and the time of his publication (2006), that clarified the meaning and use of these terms. In addition, in the more than two decades that passed between 1992 and 2015, research on situational and individual interest burgeoned, resulting in a number of changes. First, the term "actualized interest" was dropped and replaced unequivocally by the term "psychological state of interest" (e.g., Hidi 2000; see also Renninger 2000). Second, it was argued that the psychological state of interest could be the outcome of either situational or individual interest (Renninger and Hidi 2002). Third, situational interest and individual interest were linked in a developmental continuum (Hidi and Renninger 2006; Renninger and Hidi 2011). As a result of empirical support for these changes, situational and individual interest are now among the most frequently used concepts in interest research.

7 Researchers have pointed out that whereas interest has been associated with positive feelings in most of the interest literature, something that elicits a negative reaction may also be a trigger for interest (Hidi and Harackiewicz 2000; Iran-Nejad 1987). To support

this, Hidi (2000) provided the example of a student who is not interested in science but happens to watch a television show that demonstrates how black holes can "suck up" things. Although somewhat frightened, the student's interest is triggered and her attention is focused. Her negative emotion may be driven by fear as to what might happen to the world in her lifetime. Should the interest described in this episode be maintained and the student become interested in astronomy, we would expect the negative emotions to disappear and positive feelings to become associated with the subject.

8 In an early investigation, Schank (1979) identified conditions that elicit readers' interest in story-processing and argued that they played an important role in what inferences readers drew. He also postulated that certain concepts such as death, danger, power, and sex are "absolute interests," and that certain characteristics such as unexpectedness and personal relatedness are "relative operators" when linked to these concepts. For example, as Hidi and Baird (1986) noted, the death of an eighty-two-year-old man from a heart attack would not be as interesting as if he died from a blow on the head. If the man were an uncle rather than a stranger, this relationship would even further amplify the level of interest. Around the same time that Schank published his paper on interestingness, Kintsch (1980) similarly addressed the issue of how interest is produced by various forms of discourse. He emphasized the cognitive aspects of interest and suggested that they were different from emotional interest.

Subsequently, studies that focused on isolated sentences indicated that text-based interest could be generated by segments such as "the huge gorilla smashed the bus with its fist" (Anderson 1982: 300), "when a fly moves its wings about 200 times in a second, you hear a buzzing sound" (Garner et al. 1989: 46), and "adult wolves carry food home in their stomachs and bring it up again or regurgitate it, for the young cubs to eat—the wolf version of canned baby food" (Hidi 1990: 555). Moreover, when children were given an expository text that included scientific information about the gorilla, the best-remembered idea was that the leader of the group was called the silverback because of grey hair that ran down his back. Researchers also found that more interesting sentences tended to be recalled more often and included four types of factors: character identification, novelty, life themes, and activity level.

In addition, they concluded that the term "situational interest" should be adopted to describe environmentally triggered interest of which text-based interest is one sub-type. Furthermore, they noted that situational interest, once triggered, may or may not have a long-term effect on the learner. As research on situational interest progressed, investigators demonstrated that in addition to text features, interest can be triggered by a visual stimulus such as viewing a picture or a play object, an auditory stimulus such as hearing a conversation, or a combination of visual and auditory stimuli as found in a film or television show.

9 See Berlyne 1960.

10 Anderson et al. 1987; Hidi and Baird 1988; Mayer et al. 2008; Renninger et al. 2002; Walkington 2013; Walkington and Bernacki 2014; Walkington et al. 2013.

11 See, for example, Renninger and Bachrach 2015.

12 See, for example, Azevedo 2011, 2015.

13 Linnenbrink-Garcia et al.'s (2010) Situational Interest Survey (SIS) reliably distinguished among factors of situational interest and has been frequently used in subsequent studies. For example, O'Keefe and Linnenbrink-Garcia (2014) reported that self-regulatory resources were optimized when both affect and value-related interest were high. They concluded that different levels of value and enjoyment interact, resulting in differing self-regulation and performance outcomes.

14 See extended discussion of self-sustained, interest-driven learning in Barron et al. 2014. We add to this consideration that although more developed interest can appear to be self-sustained, it is the product of the interaction between the person and the environment. As such, for interest to continue to be self-sustained, opportunities to continue engagement must be present (see discussion in Renninger 2000).

15 Silvia (2001) has described this phase as magnification. Although he did not develop the use of this term in his 2006 volume, we agree with his notion that reengaging with particular content has the potential to explain the consolidation of and development of interest.

16 As noted earlier, Csikszentmihalyi (1990) defines flow as a state of focused motivation. In our opinion, flow describes one aspect of the psychological state of developed interest.

17 Lipstein and Renninger 2007a; Renninger 2009.

18 For example, in the organization of tasks (Hidi and Baird 1986, 1988; Hidi and Berndorff 1998) or from activity (e.g., Renninger and Bachrach 2015; Swarat et al. 2012).

19 See Renninger 2000, 2010; Sansone et al. 1992.

20 Another conceptualization of value is provided by Eccles et al. (1983) and will be discussed later in the chapter.

21 Bathgate et al. (2013) report a strong correlation between interest assessment based on topic (e.g., cells) and domain (e.g., biology). They describe the utility to practitioners of working with specific topics such as animals and plants and the benefits to researchers of considering the more general domain of science.

22 Ainley et al. 2002; Hidi 2000, 2006.

23 Hidi and McLaren 1990, 1991.

24 Schiefele 1996; Schiefele and Krapp 1996.

25 It should be noted that triggers may not take (Renninger and Bachrach 2015; Renninger and Su 2012). This issue is addressed in Chapter 3.

26 See Renninger and Bachrach 2015.

27 In Chapter 2, we describe the importance of novelty as it relates to the physiological functioning of the reward circuitry.

28 See Hidi and Harackiewicz 2000: 155.

29 Hidi 1990; Hidi and Baird 1986; Renninger 1990.

30 These discussions were initially undertaken with Andreas Krapp. However, Krapp's (2002b) publication of the *Learning and Instruction* article, "Structural and Dynamic Aspects of Interest Development: Theoretical Considerations from an Ontogenetic Perspective," in which three phases of interest were mentioned, did not acknowledge our joint efforts to describe the developmental model of interest. Krapp had also begun to be increasingly focused on the development of identity and its relation to the psychological needs described in self-determination theory, whereas we undertook a review of existing empirical literature on which we based the four-phase model.

31 See related discussion in Hidi and Renninger 2006; Renninger and Riley 2013; Renninger and Su 2012.

32 See discussions in Lipstein and Renninger 2007b; Renninger 2010; Renninger and Su 2012.

33 This use of the term "initiative" is similar to that discussed by Larson 2000.

34 See discussion in Renninger 2000.

35 Nolen (2007b), for example, reported on a three-year longitudinal study of children's reading and writing in two classrooms from Grades 1 through 3. Content analysis of interviews with the children and their teachers was complemented by class observation. Findings indicated that situational interest developed into individual interest. While the importance of mastery goals peaked at Grade 2 when the children had acquired basic skills in reading and writing, interest was the salient motivator in both reading and writing over time.

Cabot (2012) has developed a survey that reliably allows her to distinguish among learners in the first three phases of interest for learning English as a second language. Maintaining situational interest was found to enable the development of emerging individual interest.

Lipstein and Renninger (2007b) used a combination of surveys and in-depth interviews to create portraits (composite cases based on survey and interview data) of middle-school-aged language-arts students in each of the four phases of interest. Findings allowed description of differences among the learners in each phase based on the goals that they set for themselves and their conceptual competence (disciplinary understanding), strategies, self-efficacy, effort, and feedback preferences.

36 There are many definitions of boredom in the literature, and these researchers do not typically cite each other. For example, Pekrun et al. (2010) defined boredom as a negative emotion that is associated with students' perceptions that they lack control over their activities and lack value for them. Goetz and Hall (2014: 312) further noted that: "whereas lack of interest can reasonably be assumed to be an important antecedent of boredom, it is clear that the two constructs are not identical in that lack of interest is affectively neutral, whereas boredom is prototypically negative in valence (e.g., 'the torments of boredom,' Berlyne, 1960, p. 192)."
    Gerritsen et al. (2014) suggested that three cognitive causes predict boredom propensity: inattention, hyperactivity, and executive dysfunction, and Eastwood et al.'s (2012) definition of boredom could be related to predictions of the four-phase model. Eastwood et al. argued that boredom is the aversive experience of wanting satisfying activity but being unable to engage in it. More specifically, they determined that boredom—an aversive state—occurs when an individual is not able to pay attention to internal (e.g., feelings or thoughts) or external (stimuli) information necessary to participate in a satisfying activity.

37 The fact that Emma continues to reengage with the camera and continues with related activities is an indication that her interest is maintained; it is not the cause of the shift. She may or may not be meta-aware of her actions.

38 Durik and Harackiewicz 2007; Linnenbrink-Garcia et al. 2010; Renninger, Kensey et al. 2015.

39 See Potvin and Hasni 2014; Renninger and Hidi 2011. These studies are being conducted by researchers from a wide number of fields, not just in the area of motivation.

40 Ainley and Ainley 2015; Alexander et al. 2015; Crowley et al. 2015.

41 Crouch et al. 2013; Reber et al. 2009; Renninger et al. 2014; Walkington and Bernacki 2014.

42 Pressick-Kilborn 2015; Turner et al. 2015; Renninger, Kensey et al. 2015.

43 Pressick-Kilborn 2015; Turner et al. 2015; Xu et al. 2012.

44 These variables and their relation to different phases of interest are addressed in more detail in Chapter 3.

45 Gruber et al. 2014; Hidi 2006, 2015; Kang et al. 2009.

46 In reviewing Arnold's (1910) volume, Baldwin (1910) suggested that more attention to developmental processes in the volume would have benefited practice. In particular, consideration was needed: the nature of children's interests at different stages, "how dormant interests might be awakened, and how sustained interest may be developed" (Baldwin 1910: 120). It is important that it was Baldwin, an educator, who pointed to these as essential questions to be addressed.

47 See discussion in Fryer 1931.

48 For example, Bell and Sweet 1916; Whitley 1929.

49 For example, Strong 1925.

50 Paterson et al. 1930.

51 Fryer (1931) noted that the scope and work to standardize Strong's Vocational Interest Blank and Patterson et al.'s (1930) Minnesota Interest Inventory were among the most successful. He also pointed to the proliferation of inventories being developed at this time.

52 Claparède (1905) and Thorndike (1912) were among those calling for objectivity.

53 Ebbinghaus 1885; see also Bartlett 1932.

54 For example, Skinner 1935, 1976; Thorndike 1905; Watson 1913.

55 See discussion in Skinner 1976.

56 Private schools that had been started on the basis of Dewey's writings and that followed his philosophy continued to thrive as sources of child-centered education; however,

public schools were caught between Dewey's and his followers' suggestions that children should be supported to develop their interests and principles from behavioral learning theory that became the basis of most teacher training and promoted the transmission of information to children without considering the role of the child in this process (see Zilversmit 1993).

57 Bruner (1966) extended Dewey's (e.g., 1913) discussion to identify four principles for learning: personalizing instruction through interest, attending to the structure of the content to be taught and learned, the need to appropriately sequence information for learning, and recognizing the role of rewards, the reward that real learning represents.

58 See Ainley and Hidi 2014.

59 Although Izard (1977) acknowledged that the two emotions may occur together, he also foreshadowed subsequent neuroscientific developments suggesting that increases in information corresponded to increases in interest.

60 This suggests that the experience of interest may change or end as appraisals of a situation are discontinued. However, this does not address how interest develops. Once the novelty that triggers engagement, or engagement of one or another type, ceases, the description of the coping potential does not distinguish between an interest that does and does not develop, nor explain the process of an individual continuing to search for new information.

61 Berridge 2012.

62 BASE is an acronym that refers to fixed sites from which a person can jump: Buildings, Antennas, Spans, and Earth.

63 Neuroscientific findings are further discussed in Chapter 2.

64 Berlyne (1960) identified five perceptual features (novelty, surprisingness, incongruity, uncertainty, and complexity) as collative variables of tasks. As Konečni (1978) explained, Berlyne called these variables collative to explain their effect was based on discrepancies between a person's experiences in the past and their present response, and also to distinguish this form of perceptual response from the ecological and psychophysical characteristics of tasks.

65 For example, Bathgate et al. 2013; Dawson 2000; Flippo 2014.

66 Hagay and Baram-Tsabari 2011.

67 Crouch et al. 2013; see related discussion in Walkington and Bernacki 2014.

68 Garner et al. 1989; Mayer et al. 2008.

69 For example, Anderson 1982.

70 For example, Hidi and Baird 1988; see Hidi 1990, 1995.

71 The role of interest in making resources available and their role in attention has been widely debated (e.g., Shirey and Reynolds 1988) and will be discussed further in Chapters 2 and 4.

72 Azevedo 2006.

73 Sansone and Thoman 2005; Sansone et al. 2011; Sansone et al. 2015; Tsai et al. 2008.

74 cf. Sansone et al. 2011.

75 See Durik et al. 2015; Lipstein and Renninger 2007b; Renninger 2010; Renninger et al. 2015.

76 Schiefele 2001, 2009.

77 Expectancy-value theory is a motivational theory developed by Eccles et al. (e.g., 1983; Wigfield and Eccles 2000; Wigfield et al. 2006) to explain the relation of behaviors and decision-making in relation to a person's value for and expectancies about goals. See Eccles et al. 1983; Eccles et al. 2015; see also discussion in Sansone 2009.

78 See Barron et al. 2014; Simpkins et al. 2015.

79 It should be noted that this line of study does not describe how interest can be supported to develop, but rather focuses on interest once it has developed.

80 Schiefele et al. 1993.

81 More specifically, the authors hypothesized that subjective task value has four components: task interest (enjoyment one gets or expects to get from engaging in an

activity), utility value (the instrumental value towards fulfilling one's goal), attainment value (linking the task to one's sense of self and identity), and cost associated with a particular choice.

Valuing more specifically refers to the components (task interest, task value or importance, task utility, and cost) of Eccles' (e.g., 1983) expectancy-value theory. However, expectancy-value theory assumes that a person is aware of the process or fact of changed valuing, a point on which interest theory and expectancy-value theory differ, in part because expectancy-value theory does not assess interest alone, nor its development from an earlier to a later phase (see discussion in Eccles et al. 2015). From the perspective of interest theory, the development of the knowledge and value components of interest contribute to the deepening or development of interest.

82 In an extension of the expectancy-value model, Harackiewicz and Hulleman and their colleagues (e.g., Harackiewicz et al. 2014; Hulleman and Harackiewicz 2009) have demonstrated that interest can be supported by helping the learner connect to the value, relevance, or utility of new information. This type of intervention has been found to support learners with low interest to better connect with the content to be learned, and to encourage learners with little interest to enroll in additional mathematics and/or science coursework.

83 For example, Fryer 1931; Lent et al. 1994; Nye et al. 2012; Strong 1943; Walsh and Osipow 1986.

84 Rounds and Su 2014.

85 See McCrae and Costa 1990; Schinka et al. 1997.

86 Rounds and Su 2014.

87 Low et al. 2005.

88 For example, Lent et al. 2013.

2

INTEREST, ATTENTION, AND CURIOSITY

What explains the power of interest?

Why are students who have an interest for the disciplinary content that they are to learn more likely to continue to reengage and develop more conceptual sophistication?

Over 100 years ago, Dewey (1913) published *Interest and Effort in Education*. He pointed out that the presence of interest makes learning feel effortless, but he was not in a position to explain why. Dewey did not distinguish between less and more developed phases of interest, nor did he understand how earlier phases of interest could be triggered even though he pointed to the importance of catching learners' attention. Years later, Hidi (1990) explained that interest not only has a profound facilitative effect on cognitive functioning but is central to how we select and persist in processing information. She also suggested that the psychological and physiological processes associated with learning interesting information have unique aspects and suggested the possibility that individual interest may develop from situational interest.[1]

Research has now demonstrated such development[2] and has shown that the process involves a sequence of increasingly complex phases.[3] Investigations have also provided evidence that there are physiological processes associated with the experience of interest, indicating that interest involves seeking or searching for information that is inherently rewarding.[4] In other words, interest is its own reward, and because of this the development of interest is even more powerful than Dewey suggested.[5] There is also solid evidence that interest develops in relation to a person's interactions with the environment; and that interest is a tool that educators, parents, employers, etc., can harness.[6] Of particular importance in this regard is the fact that interest has a facilitating effect on learning at any age, whether in or out of school.

In this chapter, we describe how interest affects learning, and interest's association with attention and the brain's reward circuitry. We explain that developing an interest may not require external incentives because it is inherently rewarding to seek or search for information relating to the content of interest. In order to further clarify the power of interest for practice, we also address the relation between interest and curiosity, since each involves seeking information.

Interest and Learning

The benefits of interest to learning are many. Interest has been found to positively affect learning outcomes as well as learning processes.[7] Support for people to develop interest enables them to make personal connections to their learning[8] and improves their performance.[9] It engages them in developing conceptual understanding,[10] leads to subsequent course enrollment,[11] and provides them with knowledge that they can do the work of the discipline.[12] When individuals have an interest in a task to be accomplished or subject matter to be learned, they have focused attention,[13] goals,[14] and learning strategies;[15] they are more likely to feel self-efficacious[16] and be able to self-regulate.[17] Depending on how developed their interests are, they persevere to understand more.[18] They can be expected to expend effort without it feeling effortful, seek feedback, make an effort to find additional resources, and create opportunities for themselves that allow them to more fully engage their interests.[19]

Interest must be triggered, however, in order for it to develop and continue to deepen.[20] "Triggering interest" refers to the capture of attention in response to the environment (which includes other people; e.g., Emma receiving the camera from her parents), which is likely to result in continued engagement. After a person's attention is triggered, the activities of others as well as the conditions of the environment may (or may not) support continued focus and development of interest. In later phases of interest, triggers can also be self-generated. Thus, for example, once Emma learns about light and shadow and begins to apply what she has learned, she begins to self-generate triggers: she wants to read more about light and shadow, find people to talk to about light and shadow, and use what she learns to produce better pictures.

Through the process of triggering, shifts between phases of interest may occur. For example, Andre and Windschitl (2003) reported on challenge as a trigger for students' developing interest when conflicting findings from experimentation with electrical circuits challenged what the students thought they already knew. When challenged, the students' interest developed and their understanding of circuits improved. Andre and Windschitl (2003) described student interest as enabling this conceptual change.[21] Out-of-school programming in music, science, or sports that provide opportunities for individuals to explore can serve a similar function.[22] It can call attention to various additional ways in which a content of interest might be engaged, prompting new forms of participation, as well as searching for new information.

However, when people are new to content and interest has yet to develop, the triggering process needs to focus their attention on the key elements of the content. Renninger et al. (2014), for example, found that when youth with little to no experience with formal science were supported to focus their attention by reflecting and then elaborating on project activity (a mink dissection), they developed their interest and their understanding of science. In this study, the youth were encouraged to focus their attention by reflecting and then elaborating on project activities (e.g., a mink dissection) as they completed ICAN probes in their laboratory notebooks, e.g., "I can use a microscope to understand a cell"; "I can create and fill in a chart to predict the possible genotypes for the offspring of a species"; "I can use a model to explain the cell cycle." The researchers found that even though the target and control groups both reported experiencing fun and excitement during the project-based work, only those who had been supported to reflect on their activity by writing responses to the ICAN probes developed their science interest and understanding. For these learners, the triggering of interest provided by project activity would have been a missed opportunity for science learning without support to reflect on it.[23]

In summary, learners with a less developed interest may or may not continue to engage with content, and are likely to need support from others and/or from the design of the environment (e.g., the use of probes in their lab notebook, activities, programming, etc.) to continue to engage. Without support for continued engagement with the content, such a learner may enjoy the experience of triggering but may not recognize opportunities or try to create opportunities that would sustain engagement.[24] Learners with a more developed interest, by contrast, are likely to continue to engage or to independently seek reengagement with content. Because their attention is focused, they can develop or continue to develop their ability to see and seize opportunities that are available and/or seek out opportunities to reengage that deepen their interest and also their understanding. We now turn to the fundamental question of why interest is such a powerful motivator and facilitator of learning.

Interest and Attention

The strong association that exists between interest and attention is one of the reasons that interest is considered to have such an important facilitating effect on learning. Historically, researchers maintained that attention and factors that contribute to attention (attentional factors) make a critical contribution to the effect that interest has on human performance and learning.[25] However, there was a debate among researchers about this link as some questioned its validity. Developments in neuroscience now provide confirmation of the association between attention and interest in learning. In the discussion that follows, we draw on relevant research findings from the fields of psychology and neuroscience to describe how attention is linked to interest.

Psychological Investigations of Links between Interest and Attentional Processes

James (1890) described interest as schooling, or focusing, attention and many current researchers continue to subscribe to this position. Renninger and Wozniak (1985) provided confirmation for this effect in their study of young children at ages three and four. Memory researchers had previously considered this age group to be too young to detect differences in recognition and recall.[26] Using a combination of naturalistic and experimental techniques, they found that the children they tested were more likely to shift their focal attention to the toys (e.g., trains, dolls) they were interested in than to those that were not of interest. The children also shifted their attention to the toys that were of interest to them first and did so more frequently.[27] Importantly, similar effects were found for both recognition (ability to identify items in an array) and recall (ability to remember) memory, demonstrating that interest influences even young children's attention, engagement, and memory.

However, some researchers questioned this association.[28] For example, Anderson and his colleagues wondered whether attention explained the facilitative role of interest in reading text segments.[29] They based their studies on the selective attention model, which was originally developed to explain why structurally important text segments resulted in superior recall. They adopted the model to explain the processing of interesting text segments. The original model assumed that when readers begin a passage they process text elements at some minimal level and rate them for importance. As they continue to read, they selectively allocate more attention to the processing of important information, resulting in longer reading times, slower reactions to other stimuli, and better recall.[30]

Assuming that interesting text segments are processed the same as important text segments, Anderson and his colleagues predicted that increased attention would result in slower reading and secondary reaction times and better recall. However, research demonstrated that interest actually reduced the reading and secondary reaction times of adults. On the basis of causal modeling, the researchers further concluded that attention did not mediate the effect of interest on recall and that attention and better recall were independent effects of interest.

Hidi and colleagues questioned the applicability of the selective attention model for the processing of interesting information.[31] They pointed to a critical distinction between importance and interest in text-processing and argued that the attentional processes involved in reading important text differ from those involved in reading interesting text. They maintained that in order to establish importance, readers have to evaluate text segments relative to previously processed, stored, and retrieved information or to self-generated standards. Once such rated importance is established, readers can selectively focus their attention on what has been judged to be important information. Both of these operations require allocation of attention that should add significantly to reading and secondary reaction times. Consequently, longer reading times and secondary reaction times can be assumed to indicate more attention allocation to the passages.

However, establishing interestingness of text does not require the same kind of evaluation and decision-making process as establishing importance. Readers tend to seek out and instantly recognize interesting information and are likely to spontaneously allocate attention as they process it. Therefore, the processing of interesting information should be more efficient and faster than less interesting information. In fact, Shirey and Reynolds' (1988) finding that adults read interesting sentences significantly faster than less interesting ones supports this hypothesis.[32]

In a related study, McDaniel et al. (2000) examined how interest influences processing of more and less interesting stories. They hypothesized that reaction times would not differ at the beginnings of the stories when all stories tended to be equally interesting to all readers. As the storylines developed, however, differences in secondary reaction times could be expected, based on a reader's level of interest. To test this hypothesis, the authors presented secondary task probes at various points in the stories, predicting differences in processing due to the level of interest that emerged as the stories unfolded. The results showed that readers' reaction times did indeed significantly vary only during the second half of the more and less interesting narratives. Compared to readers with more interesting stories, moreover, readers of less interesting stories had significantly longer reaction times to the secondary probes when reading the second half of the stories. In addition, readers' reaction times were significantly slower while reading later parts of less interesting narratives than during earlier parts. No such differences were found for the more interesting narratives. These findings indicated that readers consciously allocated more attention to the latter half of the low-interest stories. McDaniel et al. concluded that the data supported Hidi et al.'s hypothesis that interest can generate spontaneous (automatic) attention, resulting in more efficient and faster processing of information.[33]

Silvia (2006) also argued that attention does not mediate the effects of interest on learning. He reached his conclusion based on interpreting Anderson and colleagues' studies as proof that attention is not a critical factor in the facilitative effect of interest on learning. However, it should also be noted that Silvia (2006) misunderstood the evidence refuting this position. He stated that Hidi (1990, 1995) provided an alternative, counterintuitive view that suggests that interest reduces the amount of attention devoted to text. The point made by Hidi and colleagues was not that interest reduces the amount of attention devoted to reading but that the spontaneous attention allocated to text segments should result in shorter reaction times. He similarly misunderstood empirical evidence provided by McDaniel and his colleagues.

In another study that has implications for understanding attention, Schraw and Dennison (1994) reported three experiments in which assigned purposes for reading led to changes in both ratings of interestingness and recall of texts. In each of the experiments readers were asked to read a neutral story from three perspectives. The material consisted of a five-page story that centered on two boys who skip school and spend their afternoon at one boy's "opulent house." The story was embellished with a number of details that were of varying interest to readers, depending on their assigned perspectives, which were burglar, home-buyer, and neutral. Interesting information from the burglar perspective included the location of valuable objects, the presence of security alarms, and access to the house. Interesting information from the homebuyer perspective referred to the size of the house and its salient features. In the control condition, interesting information included skipping school, drinking beer, and playing loud music. The findings showed that interestingness of the text segments indeed varied as a func-tion of readers' perspectives and that the perspective-relevant segments not only were more interesting but were also recalled better. Notably, these finding were replicated when perspectives were provided after the initial reading of the text. The authors concluded that providing perspectives for readers (read this story "as if you were found to be thinking about robbing this house," or read this story "as if you were interested in buying this house") increased the interestingness of text information that Schraw and Dennison referred to as purpose-driven interest.

We would argue that the novelty of the perspectives triggered and maintained situational interest and led to focused attention and searches for relevant informa-tion that were rewarding as they activated the reward circuitry.[34] Developments in neuroscience to be discussed next, substantiate this discussion and clarify the importance of the relation between interest and attention in learning. In other words, neuroscience provides substantive triangulation for psychological research findings.

Neuroscientific Investigations: Attention, the Reward Circuitry, and Its Links to Interest

Developments in neuroscientific research point to connections between interest, attention, and the reward mechanism in the brain. Panksepp (1998) was the first neuroscientist to identify the physiological basis of the psychological state of inter-est. In his seminal *Affective Neuroscience*, he presented empirical research to propose that there are multiple emotional and motivational systems that all mammals share. More specifically, he argued that the brain contains a seeking system that is char-acterized by foraging, exploration, investigation, curiosity, interest, and expectancy. He called the brain a harmoniously operating neuroemotional system that drives and energizes "many mental complexities that humans experience as persistent feelings of interest, curiosity, sensation seeking, and, in the presence of a sufficiently complex cortex, the search for higher meaning" (Panksepp 1998: 145). He iden-tified dopamine, one of the important neurochemicals of the brain, as critical for feelings of engagement and excitement. Panksepp suggested that without dopamine, "human aspirations remain frozen, as it were, in an endless winter of discontent" (1998: 144) and the potential of the brain cannot be realized.

Since the publication of *Affective Neuroscience*, neuroimaging studies have provided evidence for the existence of a dopamine-fueled reward circuitry in the brain.[35] These studies show the association of interest and rewards.[36, 37, 38] Findings indicate that the reward circuitry is activated when individuals participate in certain activities such as anticipating, searching for information, and/or receiving rewards, and that these activities facilitate memory formation[39] and are critical to learning.[40] Importantly, all types of rewards activate the reward circuitry, including information seeking and continued experiences of developing understanding that characterize interested engagement.[41] Finally, rewards have been found to have three components that can be distinguished both psychologically and physiologically: liking, wanting, and learning.[42] These components may or may not co-occur, and have implications for how we measure interest.[43]

Studies have also shown that novelty acts as a bonus when a person is responding to reward anticipation or a reward itself. For example, Bunzeck et al. (2010) argued for the existence of a common mechanism for evaluating reward and novelty, and suggested that novelty is a fundamental signal that is associated with attracting attention, promoting memory encoding, and modifying goal-directed behavior. Neuroscientific studies such as Fenker et al. (2008) have also indicated that rewards have a strong influence on individuals' attention allocation. Hickey et al. (2011) demonstrated that objects associated with rewards become visually salient. In a related investigation, Anderson et al. (2011) found that inconspicuous, task-irrelevant items, previously associated with monetary rewards, slowed down visual search of these items. They called this type of reward-related significant distraction "value-driven attentional capture," suggesting that a person's previous associations with rewards are an involuntary influence on the attention required for a visual search.

Much of the early research in neuroscience focused on extrinsic rewards and showed many benefits of the activation of the reward circuitry to attention and memory.[44] More recently, neuroscientists have started to examine intrinsic rewards such as curiosity and interest.[45] The impetus for these investigations came from questions about the underlying mechanisms of exploring, seeking, and obtaining information without extrinsic rewards, as if learning was rewarding in and of itself.[46] This work provides evidence for the association between interest and rewards. Interestingly, neuroscientists have tended to conflate curiosity and interest or use the terms interchangeably, without recognizing their similarities and differences (a point that is further discussed in the next section of this chapter). Since both interest and curiosity involve information-seeking and do not require extrinsic rewards, their conflation can be easily understood. Whereas we argue that the two concepts should be considered distinct, it is also the case that the psychological state of each during the seeking of information is similar, and, thus, their relation to reward circuitry can be expected to be similar, as well. Therefore, neuroscientific findings related to curiosity can frequently be expected to apply to interest.

For example, in examining computational and neural mechanisms of information-seeking, curiosity, and attention, Gottlieb et al. (2013: 2–3) reported that "information seeking can also be intrinsically motivated, that is, a goal in and of itself. The fact that animals, and particularly humans, show intrinsic curiosity and seem to avidly seek out information without apparent ulterior motive suggests that the brain generates intrinsic rewards ... that assign value to information." Like Berlyne (1960), these researchers further concluded that intrinsic rewards may be based on uncertainty, surprise, and learning progress and that such rewards may be learned or innate. Gottlieb et al. explained the benefits of information-seeking as motivation for learning for its own sake. They also pointed out that information-seeking is evolutionarily adaptive as it maximizes long-term evolutionary fitness in rapidly changing environmental conditions.

In a relatively early study, Kang et al. (2009) examined the underlying neural mechanism of curiosity.[47] They used functional magnetic resonance imaging (fMRI) of changes in blood flow to assess the brain activity of individuals reading trivia questions that elicited varying levels of curiosity. Their data demonstrated that the level of individuals' curiosity while reading was correlated with the activation of the reward circuitry.[48] They also reported on imaging and behavioral data indicating that curiosity enhanced memory for novel information, pointing to its cognitive benefits. Kang et al. linked their findings to those of Adcock et al. (2006); together, the studies provide evidence that curiosity (internal reward) and anticipated monetary reward (external reward) activate similar neural circuits and have similar facilitative effects on memory.

Gruber et al.'s (2014) study of curiosity replicated and expanded on the findings of Kang et al., both with respect to the activation of the reward circuitry and its benefits on memory.[49] In the Gruber et al. study, curiosity, interest, and intrinsic motivation appear to be used interchangeably, and, therefore, we refer to their work as curiosity/interest. They reported that curiosity/interest activated the reward system and facilitated learning. They also found that (a) the benefit to memory was driven by the anticipation of activity (the seeking of information), not level of interest in the answers themselves; and (b) there were benefits to incidental learning. They further concluded that these findings may even underestimate the effects of curiosity/interest in everyday situations.

Curiosity and Interest

The relation between the constructs of curiosity and interest has not been addressed in the above-mentioned neuroscientific investigations. This state of affairs may be related to the fact that the terms "curiosity" and "interest" are often used interchangeably in everyday speech.[50] For example, one could say either "I am curious who is going to be the next mayor of our city" or "I am interested to find out who is going to be the next mayor of our city."

By contrast, two relatively distinct literatures have developed in psychological research on curiosity and interest, suggesting that they are conceptualized as two different constructs. However, researchers have not agreed on their similarities and differences. Without clearly defining their relation, confusions in research designs and interpretations of results may emerge. In the following section(s), we review various conceptualizations of curiosity and their relation to individual differences and consider how curiosity and interest are comparable.

Conceptualizations of Curiosity

This discussion of curiosity reflects a parsimonious selection of an extensive literature. Conceptualizations of curiosity are based on the premise that once curiosity is triggered, a form of information-seeking occurs. However, a range of definitions and categories of curiosity exist. For example, perceptual curiosity has been identified as the search for information elicited by novel, ambiguous stimuli related to sensory experience; whereas epistemic curiosity is considered to be a uniquely human search to gain knowledge that motivates inquisitiveness underlying intellectual development and achievements.[51] Another important conceptualization of curiosity has centered on how specific or general a person's search for information is. Berlyne (1949), whose work was seminal in the area of curiosity research, originally distinguished between specific exploration (when an animal is disturbed by lack of information) and diversive exploration (when an animal searches for optimal stimulation). As Markey and Lowenstein (2014) point out, however, Berlyne in his later papers (1966, 1978) only considered specific exploration as curiosity when it was based on having received partial information. Markey and Lowenstein further quote Berlyne (1966) who wrote that as diversive exploration is not due to having received partial information, it seems to be motivated by factors quite different from curiosity. In addition, Berlyne and associates viewed curiosity as a drive that motivates the search for information. This drive was assumed to initially be associated with negative feelings; positive affect would result once the desired information was acquired.

Some of the research that followed focused on incongruity theories, the types of stimuli that arouse drive. The underlying assumption of incongruity theories was that curiosity was triggered by violations of expectations such as collative variables: stimulus characteristics that produce incongruity (e.g., uncertainty, surprise, etc.).[52] These collative variables vary along lines such as familiar-novel, simple-complex, and clear-ambiguous and affect the psychological state of individuals by eliciting uncertainty and conflict.

Other related theories, also based on Berlyne's work, were curiosity-drive theories. These focused on affective states associated with curiosity. The most prominent curiosity-drive theory is Lowenstein et al.'s knowledge-gap theory.[53] According to this formulation, a curious person is motivated to search for a missing piece of information in order to reduce an aversive state of deprivation, and such reduction in the knowledge gap is enjoyable. These researchers further suggested that the magnitude of the gap determines the extent of individuals' sense of deprivation and the triggering of their curiosity.[54]

It is noteworthy that neuroscientists Jepma, Verdonshot, van Steenbergen, Rombouts, and Nieuwenhuis (2012) reported empirical findings that were consistent with Berlyne's and Lowenstein's conceptualizations that curiosity both triggers an aversive state whose termination is rewarding and facilitates memory. They investigated the neural correlates of human perceptual curiosity and found that:

- Induction of perceptual curiosity through the presentation of ambiguous visual input activated brain regions sensitive to conflict and arousal (anterior insula and anterior cingulate cortex).
- The termination of the aversive state by new information (visual disambiguation) activated a region of the brain (the striatum) that has been related to reward processing.
- The relief of perceptual curiosity with the activation of the reward circuitry was also associated with enhanced incidental memory.

To address the question of whether curiosity should be perceived as feelings of deprivation or as feelings of interest, Litman et al.[55] subsequently proposed the interest/deprivation model (the I/D model),[56] which suggests that feelings of deprivation and feelings of interest could reflect two different forms of curiosity. These researchers argued that interest-type curiosity involves anticipated pleasure from new discoveries, whereas the deprivation type of curiosity is concerned with reduction of uncertainty and the elimination of an undesirable state of ignorance. The researchers further maintained that more intense expressions of curiosity and exploration are associated with experiencing deprivation than with feelings of interest.[57]

More specifically, I-type epistemic curiosity is concerned with adding new ideas to one's knowledge base; it motivates diversive exploration and involves positive feelings related to improving intellectual understanding. On the other hand, deprivation-type epistemic curiosity reflects a need that energizes specific exploration aimed at problem-solving and is associated with setting performance-oriented learning goals. Similarly in his book, *Curious*, Leslie (2014) did not distinguish between curiosity and interest, nor did he consider that they might not be interchangeable terms. However like Litman, he recognized that there are different types of content that people are curious about or interested in. More specifically, he noted that the desire to know more about the religious rituals of the Mayan civilization is not the same as wanting to know how Ryan Gosling looks without his clothes. Leslie also had problems conceptualizing seeking, finding answers to only fill knowledge gaps as was suggested by Lowenstein (1994). Instead of distinguishing curiosity from interest as suggested by Markey and Lowenstein (2014), he talked about two types of curiosity, a position similar to Litman et al.'s description.

Given that Litman et al.'s description of epistemic curiosity of the I type corresponds to the way in which interest is described in the interest literature, we suggest that rather than identifying two types of curiosity, the D type should be considered curiosity, given its consistency with Berlyne (1966) and Markey and Lowenstein's (2014) work, and the I type should be considered interest. We discuss this suggestion further when we consider similarities and differences between curiosity and interest later in this chapter.

Curiosity and Individual Differences

A significant number of researchers have considered curiosity to be a personal characteristic or trait that is stable, varied across individuals, and related to differences in cognitive functioning and learning goals.[58] Although we do not review the earliest work on curiosity already reviewed by Silvia (2006), we acknowledge the work of Ainley (1987), who distinguished between depth and breadth of curiosity in the approach to novelty,[59] two factors for which a number of subsequent and independent studies provided verification.[60]

Litman et al. have conducted the most extensive and continuing investigations on the topic of individual differences in trait-curiosity since Silvia's (2006) review.[61] These researchers hypothesized that the I/D distinction not only describes two types of curiosities but that individual differences can be established on the basis of this distinction as well. More specifically, they reported that the degree to which the two types of curiosities are experienced and behaviorally expressed varies according to individual differences in relatively stable I- and D-type epistemic curiosity traits. Using assessment tools that have been shown to provide valid and reliable measures of individual differences, they found that people who prefer diverse exploration and learning completely new information can be distinguished from those who focus on specific exploration aimed at reducing uncertainty.[62] They have further linked the two categories to mastery-oriented learning and performance-oriented learning, respectively. Notably, the scales for adults (including college students and nonstudents) and versions appropriate for adolescents and young children have been validated by investigations that were conducted in the United States, Germany, and the Netherlands.

Despite this evidence for categorizing individuals based on the two types of curiosity, we argue for distinguishing between the two constructs of curiosity and interest. As interest researchers, we have noticed that some people are more likely to develop individual interest than others. Perhaps this is due to the same types of individual differences that explain why some people's curiosity focuses on filling knowledge gaps while others search and seek more diverse information.

Disambiguating Curiosity and Interest

Consider Ekeland and Dahl's (2015) description of tourists who arrive in Norway and want to see the Northern Lights.[63] They studied 400 people who waited for four days on a tourist boat to be able to see the Northern Lights; the weather was difficult, there was cloud cover. The tourists are eventually told that, given the weather, if they were going to see Northern Lights they would see them in the next three hours:

> They wait on the bow of the ship; there is silence, and finally when they do see the Northern Lights, there is exclamation and awe. An hour later, the tourists complete surveys indicating that sighting the Northern Lights was a peak experience. Twenty hours later, when interviewed about the trip, none of them mention the Northern Lights.

We would suggest that this is an example of having had a curiosity; the tourists wanted to see the Northern Lights, but once the experience of the psychological state of interest was fulfilled, the phenomenon was no longer of interest to them. In other words, consistent with the Jepma et al. (2012) findings, curiosity triggered an aversive state the termination of which was rewarding and facilitated incidental memory. Because the knowledge gap was closed at the sighting of the Northern Lights, for this group of people, the Northern Lights may have only been a curiosity and not a triggered interest that might develop. On the other hand, had there been a physicist on board who brought to the sighting some understanding of the role of the cloud cover in what could be seen, and who in seeing the Northern Lights had some residual questions that he resolved to take back to his laboratory to study, for that person the opportunity to see the Northern Lights might have been both a curiosity and a question related to their individual interest.[64]

Markey and Lowenstein (2014) are among the investigators who have pointed to curiosity and interest as different constructs.[65] Curiosity, in their view, only results from a desire to close an information gap. It is distinct from interest, defined as a psychological state that involves engagement in order to learn more about a subject generally. More specifically, they suggested that curiosity differs from interest in three ways:

> We define interest as a psychological state that involves a desire to become engaged in an activity or know more, in general, about a subject. If an

individual is interested in pottery, for example, that person may want to sit down and throw pots, or that person may want to know more about the technique, the materials, and the history. Curiosity, in contrast, according to our definition, only arises when a specific knowledge gap occurs, such as, "What is the difference between high and low fire pottery?" Thus, curiosity and interest differ by their objects of desire (specific knowledge vs. general knowledge/activity engagement). Furthermore, while interest is often subdivided based on its causal source—situational interest is generated by particular conditions in the environment, and individual interest is generated by relatively enduring predispositions—curiosity is agnostic about its origin. A final distinction is phenomenology, which refers to what each state feels like. Interest is often, though not always, associated with positive affect (Hidi, 2000: 312). In contrast, while the satisfaction of curiosity provides pleasure, curiosity itself is an aversive state associated with deprivation (e.g., Day, 1982; Litman and Jimerson, 2004; Lowenstein, 1994; Todt and Schreiber, 1998).

(Markey and Lowenstein 2014: 231)

Reeve (1996) similarly argued that curiosity and interest are distinct; curiosity is associated with an aversive state and interest with a positive state. In contrast, Silvia (2006), while acknowledging that the distinction between curiosity and interest is complex and tricky, stated that equating the two constructs is justified as no convincing evidence has been presented that would support the distinction between them.[66]

Many other researchers simply have used the terms "curiosity" and "interest" interchangeably, as if they were synonymous.[67] For example, Rotgans and Schmidt (2014) described three studies in which situational interest and epistemic curiosity were considered interchangeable terms. Lack of clarity about the definitions of these two terms led to conclusions about the role of knowledge in interest development that contradict published research and may be a source of confusion.[68] More specifically, in the case of curiosity, knowledge acquisition results in a resolution and reduced motivation; in the case of interest, increased knowledge is likely to lead to further seeking and increased motivation.

We maintain that although the psychological states and the physiological responses of curiosity and interest have common elements, they should be considered related but not interchangeable concepts. Whereas they both involve seeking or searching for information, they have different types of triggers, different affective markers, and different durations.[69] Curiosity involves specific kinds of searches that are triggered by knowledge gaps and tend to involve collative variables.[70] By contrast, interest researchers have identified many different triggers for interest.[71]

The affective markers of interest also differ from those of curiosity. Whereas curiosity is described as involving an aversive psychological state that is replaced by positive feelings as curiosity is satisfied, interest might be initiated by either positive or negative feelings.[72] Finally, inherent in the definition of curiosity is a relatively short-term psychological state, in as much as it lasts only until the information gap is closed or the conflict is resolved. The psychological state of interest, on the other hand, has no such limitations and often continues as interest develops. An early observation of Hidi and Anderson (1992) illustrates this point: readers of a mystery are curious to find out who committed the crime, but, once the identity of the killer is known, uncertainty is reduced, and they stop reading as the book loses most of its appeal. By contrast, readers of an essay might initially think that the essay is boring but then become interested because the ideas are original and well presented. These readers may eagerly continue reading the essay in order to acquire more information; their interest is situational, triggered by the text, and may develop into an enduring interest.

Let us return briefly to Emma's initial experience with the camera. At the moment that Emma first picks up the instructions to the camera, we would be hard-pressed to decide whether she is curious or interested to see the instructions. However, as Emma's interest develops, it informs her activity. It drives her to search for information about how she might organize her pictures and also how she could join the camera club at the school. But these searches are not limited to looking for specific information. Although the searches may seem like they stem from a desire to close knowledge gaps, they are driven by her developing knowledge and valuing of photography, and result in continued longer-term engagement. Therefore, they are not limited by the expectation of specific answers and are not type-D curiosity as defined in the literature. Rather, they are searches that support subsequent engagement and the development of her interest. That is, as Emma finds answers, she generates further questions and searches for information with no apparent external incentives.

Although research has demonstrated that the factors that trigger curiosity are not the same as those that trigger situational interest, and that the affective state in the triggering phase and the duration of the two motivational states are distinct,[73] neuroscience does suggest that the psychological states experienced by both curious and situationally interested individuals are likely to involve the activation of the reward circuitry.[74] However, it is important to note that once individuals have emerging or well-developed interest for the related content, their search for information may be different from both situational interest and curiosity in several ways.

First, even if a person with individual interest in a topic or subject area is looking for specific information, negative feelings do not necessarily accompany the search. That is, the underlying emotional tone of this type of information search is likely to be positive, unless serious problems are encountered. Second, once this individual finds the specific information, the reduction of uncertainty is unlikely to result in the termination of engagement with that content. It is more likely that they will continue to engage in a search for related information, leading to reflection that, in turn, may result in self-triggering.[75] For example, consider a student whose passion is mathematics and who is trying to find a solution for a mathematical problem. This search may not feel like deprivation or an aversive condition, and, once a solution is found, the student might continue the so-called exploration to find more related problems to solve, cherishing the challenge of the activity. This type of exploration cannot be classified simply as either diversive or specific as the individual has developed knowledge of and value for the content. In this case, we suggest that it is new, situationally interesting triggers for which the student is searching.[76]

Concluding Thoughts

Interest has repeatedly been shown to be beneficial to learning processes and outcomes. In this chapter, we have explained that the presence of interest enables learners to make connections to the learning that they are doing, which is rewarding and impacts conceptual understanding. The association of interest with attention contributes to the power of interest in learning. Triggers for interest serve to direct learners to particular content, and interventions that require reflection have been shown to positively influence learners' interest development and understanding. Although we have presented an argument for distinguishing curiosity from situational interest, we acknowledge that once an individual closes a knowledge gap (e.g., finds out who the candidates for the mayoral election are), it is possible that when curiosity is satisfied it will lead to a triggering of interest (e.g., one of the mayoral candidates is exciting and champions issues that feel personally relevant, leading to a decision to become involved in the following administration). There is also a question to be posed about how curiosity is related to existing individual interest: how is a knowledge gap closed when it is related to an existing individual interest?

Notes

1 See also discussion in Hidi 2006.
2 For example, Harackiewicz et al. 2008; Lipstein and Renninger 2007b; Nolen 2007a, 2007b; Pressick-Kilborn 2015.
3 See Lipstein and Renninger (2007b) for portraits of learners in each phase of interest development.
4 For example, Berridge et al. 2009; Gottlieb et al. 2013.
5 Dewey (1913) specifically suggested that teachers should not try to trigger interest, because he makes the assumption that such triggering would be superficial. This is a point that is also made by Reeve et al. (2015).
6 See Azevedo 2006, 2013a, 2013b, 2015; Harackiewicz et al. 2008; Lipstein and Renninger 2007b; Renninger, Kensey et al. 2015; Renninger and Hidi 2002; Sansone et al. 2011.
7 Dewey 1913; Renninger 2003; Lipstein and Renninger 2007b.
8 For example, Alexander et al. 2015; Azevedo 2015; Crowley et al. 2015; Nieswandt and Horowitz 2015; Pressick-Kilborn 2015; Pugh et al. 2015; Renninger, Kensey et al. 2015; Turner et al. 2015.

9 Hulleman and Harackiewicz 2009; Hulleman, Godes et al. 2010; Renninger et al. 2014.

10 Conceptual understanding, or sophistication, refers to both the organization and processing of information, its accuracy, and its productivity. See discussions, for example, in Andre and Windschitl 2003; Renninger et al. 2014; Renninger, Kensey et al. 2015; Schiefele 1999, 2001.

11 Harackiewicz et al. 2002.

12 Bong et al. 2015; Durik et al. 2015; Renninger et al. 2014.

13 Ainley et al. 2002; Hidi 1995, 2000; McDaniel et al. 2000; Renninger and Wozniak 1985.

14 Harackiewicz et al. 2000; Durik and Harackiewicz 2003; Pintrich and Zusho 2002; Sansone and Smith 2000; Senko and Harackiewicz 2002.

15 Alexander 1997; Alexander and Murphy 1998; Azevedo 2013a, 2013b; Hoffmann 2002; Köller et al. 2001; Krapp and Fink 1992; Renninger 1989, 1990; Renninger et al. 2002; Renninger, Kensey et al. 2015; Renninger and Hidi 2002; Sadoski 2001; Schiefele 1999; Schiefele and Krapp 1996; Schraw and Dennison 1994; Wade et al. 1999.

16 Bong et al. 2015; Durik et al. 2015; Hay et al. 2015; Jones et al. 2015; Kim et al. 2015; Renninger, Kensey et al. 2015; Sansone et al. 2015.

17 Renninger and Hidi 2002; Sansone et al. 1992; Sansone et al. 2012; Sansone et al. 2015.

18 Lipstein and Renninger 2007b; Renninger and Hidi 2002.

19 Lipstein and Renninger 2007b; Renninger, Kensey et al. 2015.

20 Although some people use "catch" to refer to a trigger, Hidi (2000) pointed out that "trigger" and "catch" do not necessarily describe the same thing. Triggering could be associated with differing sources including a state of boredom, whereas catching suggests that an already existing interest is being captured or diverted in the situation.

21 Conceptual change refers to change in existing conceptions (e.g., understanding, beliefs, ideas, and so forth) regarding, for example, nature, that are changed through learning (e.g., Duit and Treagust 2003; Sinatra and Pintrich 2003). Changes in a learner's understanding may be facilitated by conditions in the environment that can enable the learner to recognize the discrepancy between previous and new understanding.

22 Ainley and Ainley 2015; Alexander et al. 2015; Barron et al. 2014; Crowley et al. 2015; Renninger, Kensey et al. 2015.

23 Presumably because of the open-ended yet directed nature of the probes, this intervention worked for those with less and those with more developed interest. (See also Zhu et al. 2009.)

24 Renninger 2010; see also related discussions in Durik et al. 2015.

25 Berlyne 1960; Dewey 1913; James 1890; Simon 1967; Thorndike 1935.

26 For example, Myers and Perlmutter 1978; Perlmutter and Lange 1978; Perlmutter and Myers 1974, 1976.

27 Renninger and Wozniak 1985; see also related discussion in Renninger 1990.

28 For example, Silvia 2006.

29 Anderson 1982; Reynolds and Anderson 1992; Shirey and Reynolds 1988; see also related discussion in Hidi 1995.

30 The measurement of attention by secondary task reaction time is based on the assumption that cognitive capacity is limited. Because performance on primary and secondary tasks draws on the same limited resources, allocation to one task may reduce availability for the other task. Thus, if participants are reading and also have to respond to a tone that sounds intermittently, their response time to the tone reflects the intensity of attention paid to reading (Hidi 1995).

31 Hidi 1995, 2001; Hidi and Anderson 1992.

32 In the subsequent phase of text-processing when information has to be integrated with previously read text segments, reading speed may also depend on how the interesting text segments fit in with preceding materials. If text includes unimportant and possibly distracting information on new topics (seductive details: e.g., Garner et al. 1989; Wade and Adams 1990), reading requires particular focus of attention for the integration of

text elements, and slower reading times can be expected. Wade's (1992) finding, that readers spent 50 percent more time reading seductive details than other interesting text segments, provided confirmation of this assumption and suggested the need to acknowledge differences in the facilitating effects of attention on various types of text segments.

33 Another issue with reaction time as a reflection of attention has to do with the way in which attention influences new learning as opposed to skilled performance. Hidi and Berndorff (1998) note that both reading times and secondary task reaction times may be inadequate performance measures of attention. They pointed out that distinguishing between those who are simply performing an already-learned task from those whose task involves new learning may help distinguish the outcome of attentional factors in tasks. They provide an example to illustrate this point: "If one pays attention to sorting a deck of cards into four suits, the task is achieved faster than if one daydreams while sorting," in contrast, if the task of sorting cards into suits includes having to learn new information (e.g., remembering unfamiliar faces of the Kings), the relation between attention and speed of performance might be reversed; more attention in this case should result in slower performance. Correspondingly, although competent adult readers' reading speed should increase with attention, the reverse might be true when the task also includes learning important information" (Hidi and Berndorff 1998: 84–85).

34 In discussing attention, Csikszentmihalyi (2014) pointed to the primacy of two crucial psychological processes, consciousness and attention. More specifically, he described consciousness as information, and attention as the form of psychic energy that controls what information gets processed, and thus regulates consciousness. Csikszentmihalyi explained this difference by presenting an analogy to approaches used in the biological sciences to study animal behavior. One approach describes animals' anatomy, biochemistry, etc., of the species, whereas the other approach focuses on observing animals in their natural habitat. Csikszentmihalyi further noted that there are two ways to study attention, which he considers the central question of psychology. One way to establish how attention functions is to focus on the physiologically established attentional processes. The other way, which Csikszentmihalyi said he prefers, is to explore how attention, as a process, can be observed by studying individuals interacting in their usual environments. That is, Csikszentmihalyi chose to focus on behaviors associated with attention such as flow without addressing the underlying biological mechanisms.

35 These findings have been made possible by developments in neuroscientific techniques that continue to revolutionize the way in which human brain activation can be researched. One of the most frequently used of these relatively new methods is the noninvasive functional magnetic resonance imaging (fMRI), which records changes in blood oxygenation and reflects neural activities in various brain regions (Ernst and Spear 2009; Fareri et al. 2008; Gunnar and de Haan 2009; Hidi 2015; Knutson and Wimmer 2007).

36 Berridge 2012; Martin-Soelch et al. 2001; Schultz 1998.

37 A very interesting and important new study showed that expectations of reward, motivation, and response to novelty increased dopamine production in patients with Parkinson's Disease (PD), an illness that affects nerve cells in the brain involved in planning and controlling body movements. Dopamine is the chemical (neurotransmitter) that is required for normal functioning of this system. When a substantial percentage of dopamine-producing nerve cells in the brain (more specifically, in the substantia nigra) die off, PD symptoms (tremor, stiffness, slow movements, etc.) start to occur. Research on drugs designed to improve the symptoms has shown a strong placebo effect. That is, a pharmacologically inactive substance administered as a drug can result in improvements due to PD patients' raised expectations. Espay et al. (2015) showed that the placebo effect can be increased by patients' belief that they are being administered a more expensive ($1,500 a shot) versus a less expensive

($100 a shot) injection. Espay et al. concluded that people who receive the injections thinking they received the more effective drug appear to have even greater expectations of a reward response, which is normally associated with release of dopamine, similar to the response to an actual reward. Thus, this study demonstrates how increased belief, novelty, and the expectation of rewards can underlie the placebo effect.

38 Bunzeck et al. (2009) conducted an investigation relevant to this topic. They measured how long it took humans to distinguish novel from familiar items and compared the results to primates performing the same task. Findings indicated that neural novelty signals were detected by humans significantly more slowly than by primates. They hypothesized that the difference between species may have been due to the provision of reinforcement only in the animal studies. Subsequently, Bunzeck et al. found that under the contextual influence of reward motivation, humans detected behaviorally relevant novelty signals much faster than had been previously reported. The findings that rewards can accelerate novelty detection support the idea that rewards motivate attention and energize behavior leading to decreased response time and increased vigor (Hidi 2015).

39 For example, Adcock et al. (2006) showed that anticipated monetary rewards also modulate activation of the reward circuitry and promote memory formation prior to learning.

40 For example, Fareri et al. 2008.

41 Similar patterns of activation are found for primary rewards (which are necessary for the survival of the species, such as food or sexual contact) and secondary rewards (which derive their value from primary rewards, such as money) (see, e.g., Schultz 2007).

42 Berridge et al. 2009.

43 Further discussion of this point is undertaken in Chapter 3.

44 See Hidi 2015.

45 Other researchers who study intrinsic motivation mechanisms have focused on curiosity-driven seeking and learning within systemic and multidisciplinary approaches, and have developed models with algorithmic and robotic tools (e.g. the First Interdisciplinary Symposium on Information Seeking, Curiosity, and Attention [November 2014] organized by P.Y. Oudeyer, J. Gottlieb, and M. Lopes). Although artificial systems and robotics are not topics that we discuss in this book, the emphasis these researchers place on curiosity, information-seeking, and attention is supportive of our position on the importance of seeking behavior and its link to neural mechanisms, as well as on the physiological activities underlying the psychological state of interest.

46 Gottlieb et al. (2013) referenced Berlyne (1960) and noted that exploration-searching/seeking information alters the observers' epistemic state without external rewards, and concluded that this type of behavior and the high degree of motivation associated with it generates intrinsic rewards in the brain and assigns value to information or learning.

47 They referred to "curiosity" rather than "early phases of situational interest" even though, as Ainley and Hidi (2014) have pointed out, their findings are similarly applicable to interest and curiosity, as each can be described as an internally driven search for more information.

48 More specifically, the caudate in the striatum that has been previously associated with anticipated rewards.

49 Later in this chapter, we address these potential distinctions. Here we report their findings referring to "curiosity/interest." Gruber et al. (2014) asked participants to rate their level of curiosity about the answer to a trivia question (extremes of scale; 1 = "I am not interested at all in the answer," and 6 = "I am very much interested in the answer") (2014: 9).

50 For example, Leslie (2014: 46 and 47) referred to both interest and curiosity when he measured a baby's activities.

51 Berlyne 1960.
52 Berlyne 1960.
53 For example, Lowenstein 1994; Markey and Lowenstein 2014.
54 Silvia (2006) criticized the theory on a number of issues, most importantly on the premise that the subjective experience involves both negative and positive affective states. He concluded that this prediction requires empirical support, as it contradicts findings that people rate curiosity as a positive affective state.
55 For example, Litman 2005, 2008, 2010; Litman and Jimerson 2004; Litman and Mussel 2013; Litman et al. 2010; Piotrowski et al. 2014; Richards et al. 2013.
56 Litman (2005) has suggested that the I/D model maps onto the neuroscience of liking and wanting (Berridge and Robinson 1998), and that there are two neural systems that can be assumed to underlie motivation and affective experience. However, this interesting suggestion has not been further examined (personal communication, Litman, July 16, 2014).
57 Litman (2008) reported on four studies that examined interest and deprivation factors of epistemic curiosity and their relations to diversive and specific curiosity. He concluded that the "concepts of I- and D-type curiosity extend beyond those of diversive and specific exploration" (2008: 1594).
58 Self-reports, trait inventories, and teacher reports are some of the tools researchers have used to measure curiosity as a trait.
59 In earlier work, Ainley used the terms "depth" and "breadth of interest curiosities"; she has clarified that these were categories of curiosity rather than interest (personal communication, October 15, 2014).
60 For example, Byman 2005; Fulcher 2008; Reio et al. 2006.
61 For example, Litman 2005, 2008; Litman and Jimerson 2004; Litman and Mussel 2013; Piotrowski et al. 2014.
62 For example, Litman 2008; Litman and Mussel 2013; Piotrowski et al. 2014; Richards et al. 2013.
63 We use Ekeland and Dahl's (2015) example (with their permission) to provide an illustration of the distinction between curiosity and interest; however, it should be noted that their work addresses the emotions of the tourists in this context and emotions in the development of interest.
64 Personal communication with Christian Ekeland (May 11, 2015) further indicated that there was a tourist who reported having waited much of her life to see the Northern Lights. However, given that she did not continue to focus on them following the sighting, we suggest that she had only a long-standing curiosity to see them, not a developing interest.
65 Lowenstein 1994; Markey and Lowenstein 2014.
66 Based on his consideration of curiosity as being the equivalent of interest, Silvia (2006) criticized Lowenstein's conceptualization, not realizing that he was talking about curiosity and not interest (see Silvia 2006: 51). Whereas Silvia is correct in saying that interest theory should cover triggers other than uncertainty and knowledge gaps, this criticism of Lowenstein is in our opinion inappropriate since Lowenstein's is a clearly defined theory of curiosity.
67 For example, Izard 1977, 2007; Panksepp 1998.
68 Rotgans and Schmidt (2014: 37) investigated how situational interest is related to knowledge acquisition, and defined situational interest as a "motivational response to a perceived knowledge deficit." They suggest that interest is triggered in situations when a knowledge deficit becomes manifest, such as in confrontation with a problem (Rotgans and Schmidt 2014: 37). This definition is in essence identical to Lowenstein and his colleagues' definition of curiosity (e.g., Lowenstein 1994). Using this conceptualization, Rotgans and Schmidt reported that situational interest decreased with increasing knowledge of a given problem and concluded that their

findings supported a knowledge-deprivation account of situational interest. They further claimed that the results were at variance with the commonly held assumption that situational interest and knowledge are positively associated.

Rotgans and Schmidt (2014) interpret their findings as suggesting that once the knowledge gap is closed, curiosity is satisfied and interest falls off. The problem with their conclusion is that the authors are working with their own definition of situational interest, one that others have used to describe curiosity: "Situational interest is construed as a motivational response to a perceived knowledge deficit" (Rotgans and Schmidt 2014: 37). Second, though their findings are consistent with findings on curiosity, they not only are working with their own definitions of interest but argue that published research about the role of knowledge in interest development is incorrect: according to interest theory, knowledge is an increasingly significant component of interest as it develops.

69 More specifically, we accept both Lowenstein et al.'s definition of curiosity and Litman et al.'s definition of D-type curiosity, as both argue that curiosity is triggered by a desire to close a knowledge gap and reduce uncertainty.

70 Hidi and Berndorff 1998.

71 For example, some concepts like power, death, and sex have been shown to be universally interesting (Schank 1979). They also have pointed to factors that produce interesting text segments, such as traditional story elements, goal-directed activities, human factors, novelty, life themes, character identification, and intensity (Anderson et al. 1987; Hidi and Baird 1986, 1988). Furthermore, interest triggers that work for one person may not work for the next, depending on individual characteristics (see Renninger and Bachrach 2015). For example, group work is not a trigger for interest for an individual who is low on sociability, whereas a person who is high on sociability is likely to have their interest triggered by group work.

72 Leslie (2014: 80) also recognized that although closing a knowledge gap has an aversive aspect, this does not apply to all types of information search: "…when we come up on a field of knowledge that we feel sure will occupy us for a long time to come, whether it's neuroscience or languages, it's because we know we'll never get to the end of our ignorance. That feeling isn't uncomfortable or, as the psychologists say, 'aversive'."

73 It should be noted that situationally interested individuals may include those in earlier or later phases of interest development.

74 Ernst and Spear 2009; Hidi 2015; Knutsen and Wimmer 2007.

75 We point to reflection, rather than the terminology of "curiosity questions" which have previously been referenced (e.g., Renninger 2000, 2010) because reflection provides a more accurate description of the process (see Renninger et al. 2014).

76 Leslie (2014) explained the distinction between what he referred to as two types of curiosity by pointing to qualities of the content that elicited it: puzzles that have definite answers and mysteries that posed questions that cannot be answered definitely. Such answers according to Leslie may depend on a complex and interrelated set of factors, some known and others unknown. Whereas this conceptualization focuses on the object of interest, the four-phase model is focused on the interaction of the person and the environment.

3

MEASURING INTEREST

What is known about assessing existing interest?

How do new interests develop?

How can the phase of a person's interest be identified and measured?

People are hardwired to have interest(s) and to continue to develop new interest(s) throughout their lives. It is rewarding to have an interest triggered, to figure something out, to engage in seeking behavior, and to find relevant information. This involvement is something that characterizes all typically functioning individuals.[1] The triggering of interest initiates engagement and the possibility of interest development. Interest is sustained when a person begins to engage and has the ability as well as the opportunity to continue participation. In this chapter we consider how a person's existing interest(s) can be assessed, how new interests can be supported to develop, and how the phase of a person's interest can be identified and measured.

Existing Interest(s)

Some of the first assessments of existing, or already developed, interest(s) used inventories of topics.[2] For educators of school-age students, these provided insights about possible topics (e.g., dogs, sports, writing) that were the focus of their instruction. For counselors of young adults, similar assessments could be used to provide advice about course selection and career options. Findings from studies of such inventories reveal that people typically have four to five developed interests at one time,[3] and that the focus of interest for one person is likely to vary from that of the next person, even if they have an interest in the same domain (e.g., a child might be interested in training dogs for show, whereas another may be interested in breeding and raising puppies, and yet another may be interested in teaching their dog tricks).[4]

Findings from Bathgate et al.'s (2013) study of ten- to twelve-year-old children's science motivation are instructive. They reported on the roles of setting (e.g., in or out of school, formal or informal context), manner of interaction (e.g., working with new information, analysis, activity type such as hands-on activities), and topic (e.g., physics, biology, earth science) in science motivation. The researchers were particularly interested in exploring the role of the topic, in contrast to the role of the more general domain (e.g., science), as influencing children's perceptions. They found little variation when their analyses focused on the settings or the manner of interaction, and few differences based on topic. Bathgate et al. reported a high correlation (r =.84) between participants' responses to individual topics (e.g., cells, animals, plants) and responses to more basic domains (e.g., biology, science). They interpreted these findings to suggest that use of information should determine whether specific topics or domain information should be the basis of assessment. They explained that having specific topic information could be useful to the educator (the person developing museum exhibits and so forth); however, for those whose needs include only a more general reading on science, referencing the simpler category is appropriate and has fewer methodological constraints (e.g., requires use of fewer items, less time to administer the survey).

There are a range of approaches to identifying existing interest in topics, including:

• lists of topics that respondents are asked to rate;[5]
• surveys such as the O★Net Interest Profiler Short Form (Rounds et al. 2010), which include items that identify existing interests based on personality characteristics;[6]
• Häussler and Hoffmann's (2002) Interest Scale, which has items reflecting three dimensions of student interest in physics (individual interest for the domain, interest in particular topics, and interest in activity types);
• Ely et al.'s (2013) My Interests Now for Engagement online tool that allows exploration of the topics prior to selection.

These surveys all assume that the person is aware of their interest, a hypothesis that may or may not be accurate.[7] As Bathgate et al.'s findings indicated, even though the "what" of existing interests may vary, existing interests can be expected to (a) be present in both in- and out-of-school contexts and (b) continue to develop, provided that the kinds of interactions a person has are positive and enable continued engagement.

The Development of a New Interest

Research on intrinsic interest has centered primarily on how extrinsic incentives affect high interest when it is already present rather than on how to develop it when it is lacking. It is the latter problem that presents major challenges.[8]

(Bandura and Schunk 1981: 596)

As Bandura and Schunk (1981) pointed out, a critical question is how to support people to find potential contents of interest rewarding. As discussed, findings from neuroscience indicate that the process of seeking, or wanting to figure something out, is linked to the reward circuitry. This explains why those whose engagement is associated with interest do not need additional rewards as discussed by Deci and Ryan (e.g., Ryan and Deci 2000) and also suggests that persons who are new to content that could potentially be of interest, may need external support from others or from the design of the environment (e.g., activities, software) to begin experiencing the process of making connections to content rewarding.[9]

In other words, the situational interest of those with little to no present interest needs to be triggered, by using a number of options (e.g., through pointers to its relevance or utility, personalizing the content by including a topic of already existing interest, etc.). Once interest is triggered, attention is piqued, and support from the environment can enable individuals to continue to develop interest, because of connections that they can make to their prior experiences and the new content due to relevance, utility, personalization, etc. (See a case illustration of the development of an interest in mathematics provided in Table 3.1.)

Active participation is critical for interest to develop.[10] It is rewarding for mathematics students with developed interest to work on and then discuss problem-solving, because such forms of engagement extend their understanding; this type of activity characterizes the high interest to which Bandura and Schunk referred in the excerpt above. It is likely to involve wondering and thinking with other people, but might also characterize independent exploration of related ideas outside of the class context. Bandura and Schunk (1981) asked how a person with little, if any, present interest in particular content could be supported to seriously engage with that content. Research evidence has since indicated that the answer to their question has two parts:

1. A person needs to make a connection to the content and then be able to sustain this through active participation.
2. Enabling engagement by others involves understanding what the person in question already knows about the content.

When a person picks up a magazine and starts reading an article that leads him or her to seek additional information, or he or she finds out that a friend is taking some new class at the gym and decides to give it a try, he or she is engaged in ways that characterize the development of a new interest. However, new interests do not always develop. Sometimes, a person's existing interests can be so intense that they may interfere with the development of potential new interests. It is also possible that the learning environment is not presently supporting the development of a new interest, although it could. To illustrate how new interests may or

TABLE 3.1 A Case Example of the Triggering of Interest in Mathematics and Its Development.

During high school, Eva developed an interest in mathematics and completed seven levels of mathematics in four years. However, when she began high school, her only goal was to complete calculus for college applications, and she had little, if any, interest in mathematics.

Eva was the youngest child in a home where she played games that involved problem-solving, such as chess and sliding-block puzzles, and engaged in a lot of open-ended Lego construction. She liked school mathematics assignments when she was working on them but did not look forward to mathematics. She did not realize she was off track in learning mathematics until she was in sixth grade and her parents and a number of the parents of other students got together and demanded that the school teach their children the mathematics they needed for middle school.

In seventh grade, the students were given sixth- and seventh-grade-level textbooks and were expected to work independently to complete them. They were to finish one section of the textbook per week, and could work on any section that they wanted at any time. Eva recalls that her teacher checked to see that students completed the sections assigned the first month and did not check the homework after that. However, Eva's mother would sit with her every day after school and help her to work through problems in the textbooks.

Eva remembers being a little excited when her mother used colored blocks to help her learn positive and negative numbers, but she also reports that any excitement she experienced was short-lived. She was just doing what she was told to do. She did not do any extra work on problems that she did not understand, nor did she think about mathematics in her free time.

In ninth grade, Eva's counselor told her that she needed to take a course in algebra, and preferably a course in trigonometry, in order to go to college. She was initially placed in the second half of algebra, but was dropped back into the first half of the course because she struggled and did not put very much effort into learning the concepts. The first half of algebra was a good fit to Eva's mathematics abilities and the teacher was very welcoming and receptive of her timid questions. In fact, the support and encouragement that she felt led her to enroll in the second half of the course right away, even though she had not planned to take the second half of algebra until the following year.

The next term was pivotal. Eva describes this teacher as making the concepts of algebra "come alive." She appreciated that he provided clear explanations and she knew he liked teaching algebra. He was also the AP Calculus BC teacher, and in the course of teaching, he provided examples of how algebra was used in calculus. Eva describes herself as fascinated by algebra and excited to go to class every day. She also reports that she began feeling confident about her mathematical abilities. By the end of the year, Eva was determined to work her way up to AP Calculus BC. She was curious about calculus, and had come to love the challenges of mathematics. By the time Eva enrolled in trigonometry, she was voluntarily spending extra time on her mathematics homework and thinking about other ways to approach the problems assigned. Outside of school, she started reading articles about mathematics (e.g., about Fibonacci sequences in nature, such as the spirals in pinecones) and played with making circular arcs like the spirals in her artwork. Mathematics had become fun to think about. She observes that she 'sort of forgot' that she was supposed to be completing mathematics classes in order to go to college; it was only on hindsight that she realized that to someone else her interest in mathematics, and the number of courses she completed, might seem extraordinary.

Source: Renninger and Pozos-Brewer 2015: 379–380.
Reprinted with permission from Elsevier.

may not develop, consider the examples of an engineer and his job situation, a middle-school student and her writing assignment, and children at a hands-on museum exhibit.

The Engineer

The engineer works at a firm and has a job with two main components. The first involves solving technical problems and the second is "selling," that is to bring in work for the firm.

> This engineer loves solving technical problems and enjoys the subsequent analysis and testing to determine whether his solutions work. He is willing to work late and independently on these problems and often reaches elegant and cost-effective solutions. He undertakes his work with the highest professional skill, conscientiously, and on time. However, he does not involve himself in selling the services of the company and bringing in clients. Selling involves skills that do not necessarily come with an engineering degree, and he feels he was not prepared for this part of the job. In fact, it is a major challenge for the company to figure out how to interest engineers in the business side of their job. If the engineer is not interested in the development of the firm's business, how can his interest in selling be triggered and maintained? What kind of reward structure needs to be in place?
>
> A simple solution would be to help the engineer understand the significance of selling to the firm's success and to his continued opportunity to work with challenging problems. He may not realize that he will only have work if new projects can be brought into the company, that others in the company do both problem-solving and selling, and that clients enjoy talking with the engineers about their projects and hearing about the kinds of solutions they are considering.
>
> If the engineer were to develop his understanding of the relation between selling and his interest in problem-solving, he might develop a new interest in selling, and this new interest could be its own reward. However, until this new interest develops, it may be that a monetary reward—one that recognizes even incremental efforts to contribute to the selling side of the business—might be appropriate.

The Middle-School Student

Consider another case, this time of a middle-school student who lives in a city and is given an assignment to write an essay about either living in a city or about space travel.[11]

The student chooses to write about space travel but does not write very much. She does not know very much about space travel and does not have much to say. Her interest was triggered by the opportunity to choose a topic for the assignment, and writing about space travel seemed more attractive to her than writing about living in the city.

The problem is that she sees the assignment as writing about one or another topic and does not recognize that if she does not have enough information to write about the topic she picks, she needs to do some research for this assignment before she can successfully complete it. What might have made a difference for her?

The idea of space travel triggered this student's interest. Her situation illustrates the complexity of providing choice when a student does not have enough knowledge of the topic.[12] The teacher who makes the assignment needs to understand this, and so do any adults who oversee her homework completion. If the student had been supported to recognize that she needed more information to focus her writing assignment, she might have searched and found information to include in her essay, or have chosen another topic.

Children at the Museum

Consider now ten-year-old children visiting a hands-on electronics exhibit at a museum.

> One of the children edges ahead of his classmates to grab the empty seat at a table with a boy and a girl from another school; they are already working with connective and insulating dough, piles of batteries, light emitting diodes (LEDs), and motors. There are no directions; the exhibit is intended to give museum visitors a chance to explore electronics and make squishy circuits.
>
> The child first glances at the boy seated across from him who is systematically trying out the different LEDs. He then watches the girl who is working to light an LED by touching the positive and negative leads to corresponding sides of the battery. The child picks up one of the LEDs in front of him, looks back at what the boy and the girl are each doing, puts the LED down, gets up and leaves the table. The girl and the boy continue working.
>
> The girl and the boy are focused, purposeful, and happily engaged. Their science teacher had previously involved them in similar project-based work at school. When they sat down at the table, they recognized the materials and knew that they could use them to make squishy circuits. They not only had some knowledge of what was possible, but had also had previous

opportunities to ask questions, get answers, and explore the same types of materials. They are able to generate challenges for themselves while at the exhibit.

The child who joined them briefly also had his interest triggered by the materials, but he had no prior experience with circuits. Because he really did not know what he could do with an LED or why the other children were doing what they were doing, he got up and left the table. Even though the other children provided models of what could be done at the table, the child who had no previous experience could not make use of this. He needed somehow to learn about the possibilities for working with the materials. If a museum docent or a teacher or one of the children at the table had asked him what he was thinking and shared their own thoughts about the activity, this might have given him some ideas about what he could be doing. Without a set of directions or support from other people, the triggered interest that led him to sit down at the table had fallen off.[13]

Each of these cases illustrates potential difficulties in the development of a new interest. The engineer has a strong existing interest in problem-solving and does not understand the need for selling. Thus his interest in selling could be triggered and then maintained; however, he needs help to understand the relation of selling to problem-solving and to find it rewarding. The middle-school student writer and the child at the museum each have a triggered interest that is not supported and so falls off. The middle-school student has her interest triggered by the topic of outer space but does not understand that even though she would like to write about the topic, she does not have enough information about space unless she does additional research. The child who sits down at the museum electronics project table has a triggered interest in the activity that is not supported by anyone with information about how to participate.

As the cases demonstrate, people need to have enough content knowledge relating to whatever about the content is triggering their attention in order to make a connection and possibly develop a new interest.[14] The cases also illustrate that existing interests (e.g., the engineer's interest in problem-solving, the two children's interest in squishy circuits) are characterized by the frequency and depth of individuals' engagement and by the possibility that they may voluntarily pursue their interest with or without other people.

If the engineer, the middle-school student, or the child with no background in circuitry were determined to learn new content as part of the process of developing a new interest, it would be relatively easy to support them to do so. They would be asking for help and seeking opportunities to think and talk with others. They also could be encouraged to participate in an activity and to develop their knowledge and skills. In such a situation, it is likely that they would also be feeling that they can do the activity (they are self-efficacious), would understand at least implicitly the value of their continued effort, and would be self-regulating, or prioritizing, their activities in order to allow the new interest to develop.

If, on the other hand, these individuals did not think that they needed, wanted, or were capable of developing a new interest (e.g., the engineer does not want to do selling) and/or were missing critical information (e.g., the engineer does not understand the relation between having projects to work on and selling; the middle-school student does not understand that in order to write about a topic you need to have sufficient content knowledge and that she needed to do some research; the child at the circuit table with no relevant background information does not recognize his need for directions), they would be unlikely to seek relevant knowledge and develop their skills by themselves, and they would need external supports to do so. They are also unlikely to have felt capable of seeking information themselves, nor would they be able to self-regulate because they do not have a clear sense of what they are doing.

In addition to active participation, a person needs to be able to find connections between prior experience and the new interest, as well as to continue to deepen this understanding, so that a new interest can be maintained and developed. Moreover, although another individual such as an employer, educator, or parent could change the learning environment and support engagement, it is the person who must be ready to develop their knowledge, although this is not necessarily something about which they may be aware. It is not sufficient (or likely to be effective) to simply tell the engineer that selling is important, or to tell the child all that he might need to know about options at the table on circuitry. An intervention that involves rewards may be effective, but only if it motivates active participation.[15]

The process of triggering interest and enabling a person to engage with new content requires providing opportunities for seeking information and participation in activity. Providing appropriate support requires knowledge about a person's phase of interest. Whether a new interest has been triggered and has begun to develop can be determined by paying attention to changes in at least four behavioral indicators: the person's frequency of engagement with the new content, depth of engagement, voluntary reengagement (wants to reengage and does), and capacity for independent reengagement (does not necessarily need input from others or for others to be involved). These indicators provide the basis for identifying the phase of a person's interest as well as the measurement of interest.

Identifying and Measuring the Phase of a Person's Interest

In our 2011 review of the conceptualization, measurement, and generation of interest, we conclude that conceptualizations of interest need to be aligned with their measurement if they are to be generally applicable and able to inform practice. Here we describe indicators and measures that have been used to assess interest. Identifying what needs to be assessed (indicators of interest) is an essential first step in the measurement process. Only with clarity about which indicators are relevant is it possible to determine what type of measurement will best address study questions. In most situations, researchers need indicators of interest that are behavioral (e.g., observed frequency of engagement), in addition to direct measures (e.g., a question such as "How interested are you in mathematics?").[16] Direct measures assume that a person is in a position to respond to questions; we may assume that most individuals can respond to a question about their interest, but such responses without behavioral confirmation are not likely to distinguish among phases of interest.

Because people engage with their interests similarly, behavioral indicators are simple enough that they can be tools for the researcher and the educator alike. Compared to their other activities, people reengage with their more developed interests:

1. frequently;[17]
2. with understanding or depth of knowledge;[18]
3. voluntarily;[19]
4. independently.[20, 21]

Together, these four behaviors provide reliable information.[22] A person who is interested in something is likely to reengage with it frequently and to do so with increasing depth of understanding, voluntarily, and independently.[23, 24]

The information these four indicators provide may not exactly correspond to what people explain when asked about their engagements. The development of a person's interest is marked by increases in one or more of the four behaviors set out above and not necessarily represented by whether and how much they like the activity. As Ginzberg et al. (1966) observed, interest describes investment (e.g., collecting stamps) rather than preference or liking (e.g., which bowtie to wear): "the individual gains the satisfaction only as a result of effort and output ... Interests imply more differentiation and complexity than preferences" (1966: 244–245 as cited in Hidi and Ainley 2002: 264).

Liking: Only a Rough Gauge of Interest

In everyday use and in some research studies, how much a person likes an activity is considered to be evidence of interest. To some extent, liking may indicate that interest has been triggered.[25] However, evidence from interest research and neuroscience suggests that it is insufficient to measure interest solely on the basis of positive feelings.[26] As mentioned earlier, negative affect may be associated with the experience of interest, especially in early phases of development.[27] In later phases of interest, a person has positive feelings generally and may also have negative affect (e.g., frustration associated with completing a challenging project). However, negative affect for the person with a more developed interest is overcome by the focus and engagement that accompanies well-developed individual interest.[28]

Liking does not necessarily distinguish between less and more developed interest, since liking may characterize both earlier and later phases of interest development. Take, for example, two students who "like" their educational psychology course: there could be differences between a student who likes first-year psychology but has never thought much before about how and why a person learns and another student who also likes the course, has a lot of prior experience working with children, is able to compare what is being explained in the lectures to these past experiences, and has plans for studying psychology in the future. Differences in the two students' phases of interest in psychology can be assessed by looking at their behaviors: How frequently do each of the students involve themselves in psychology, either by seeking additional readings on topics covered or by engaging the professor and peers in discussions about psychology, etc.? How much does each of them know and understand about psychology? Do they each seek additional information because they have to or because they want to? Will they seek information regardless of whether others are also seeking information? Because interest is a variable that develops through phases, its measurement needs to focus on indicators that can recognize interest in each phase.

In neuroscience, liking, wanting, and learning have been identified as distinct physiological correlates of reward processing that may or may not co-occur.[29] This suggests that whether a person likes an activity does not necessarily mean that the person also wants to further engage or learn. Therefore, liking is not a sufficient indicator of interest.

Measuring Interest as a Variable That Develops

There is no one method for assessing interest and its development.[30] Many data sources have been used to collect data on interest. They include:

- facial expressions;[31]
- neuroscientific techniques;[32]
- chronicles of observations (e.g., using continuous or ongoing records such as written notes or video to track activity, questioning, etc.);[33]
- artifact analysis (e.g., student classroom work, responses to ICAN probes);
- class-enrollment data (e.g., whether students elect to reenroll in a psychology course);
- descriptive information about the context (e.g., whether a course that is taken is required of majors);
- descriptive information about participant engagement (e.g., log data from online activity that tracks frequency and depth of resource use in relation

to whether resources were required, patterns of use relative to others in a cohort);[34]

- self-reports (e.g., surveys, interviews).

The most commonly used data source for assessing interest is the self-report. Self-reports may include questions that complement other data sources (e.g., asking participants to rate how much they like science followed by a question that asks what they like about it); surveys that include questions that provide data about behaviors (e.g., forced-choice, Likert ratings asking "How likely are you to do mathematics problems that are not assigned?"[35]); and open-ended free response items (e.g., "Name at least two activities such as tap dancing or reading that you have done for at least three years that you do just because you want to, not because you have to").[36]

Despite the frequency of their use, surveys have potential complications when they are the only source of data employed. Frenzel et al. (2012) pointed to the need for researchers to appreciate that younger and older students may interpret the same survey items differently.[37, 38] They found that younger students tended to respond to items asking about mathematics (e.g., "I like to read books and solve brainteasers related to mathematics," Frenzel et al. 2012: 1082) as addressing experience and value, whereas older students' responses suggested that they interpreted the questions as addressing their desire for more knowledge and autonomy in working with mathematics. These results raise a more general question about how respondents interpret questions on surveys and the benefits of confirming that their responses address the indicators the researcher intends to measure.[39]

Another complication of surveys is that respondents in an early phase of interest development may not be in a position to respond to questions about the level of their interest; they may not be conscious that their interest has been triggered, and, as such, they are not in a position to report on it. In such instances, triangulation of results may be advisable (e.g., by comparing survey responses to data that capture engagement such as that provided by observations or log files).[40] In contrast, people who have had prior experience with a content of potential interest (e.g., undergraduates who declare their intention to major in a science, technology, engineering, and math (STEM) discipline in college, students who are taking advanced literature courses, members of a law review, an ice-skating club, or a design team of a software company) are likely to knowingly prioritize their interest and are in a position to report on their interested activity when asked about it. Collecting additional data from sources that can provide confirmation for survey responses (e.g., open-ended items in a large-scale, forced-choice survey, or interviews with a subsample of those surveyed) can be used to offset potential complications, as participants may vary in their abilities to respond to surveys. They can vary in their meta-awareness of their interest, and consequently their readiness to work with survey items that ask them about their interest.

If one recognizes that interest is a variable that develops, then measurement needs to use indicators that reflect the potential for interest to develop and/or address participants' activity with the content of interest over time. However, the four behavioral indicators described above may need to be modified based on factors such as the content, the context of activity, and the age of participants.[41, 42] Two additional and distinct issues that are frequently raised in relation to measuring interest as a variable that can develop include (1) how long it might take interest to develop and (2) when researchers can simply focus on relatively earlier and later (less and more developed) interest, as opposed to identifying all four phases of interest.

The development of interest is idiosyncratic, and, as mentioned at the beginning of this chapter, people have multiple interests. In measuring the development of interest, assessment needs to address characteristics that are common across types of interest and responsive to differences among people in the focus, breadth, and depth of their interest(s) at the time of measurement. Thus, although people are all similarly hardwired to develop interest (even multiple interests), the content that is of interest to one person is often different from what is of interest to the next (e.g., mathematics versus bridge). In addition, people who share the same interest may connect to different aspects of that content. For example, two people with an interest in bridge may differ such that the first will look for and read books describing bids and how hands can be played and another may, instead, spend time playing and rethinking how bids were made and/or could have been made. It is these idiosyncrasies that can make interest appear to be complex. It is the regularity of the rewards that accompany seeking and related positive feelings that make interest predictable.

The development of interest may involve slow and steady change (research has recorded as many as four years for a shift from a triggered to a maintained situational interest) or it may be relatively quick to develop, given repeated opportunities to engage.[43] It is very unlikely that the initial triggering of interest will become fully developed in a single sitting, however. Take a young girl's heightened excitement at being included in a critical moment that involves saving someone's life during an after-school program's visit to a hospital emergency room. Her excitement may appear to include the forms of developing knowledge and valuing that are characteristics of more developed forms of interest. One visit to an emergency room could be a powerful trigger that could result in sustained engagement. However, whether the girl's interest goes beyond the heightened excitement of initial triggering relative to her other activities must also be considered. In order for the girl to move from an initial triggering through the phases of interest development, she would need to make connections to the disciplinary content that then led her to seek related activities and opportunities that would enable the deepening of her content knowledge.

It is easy to distinguish between this girl's developing interest in health care and another student who, although he also experienced the hub of activity in the emergency room, only wanted to get back to his video game, once the excitement waned. The girl might be described as having more developed interest than the boy. We do not have enough information to begin to map out whether the girl had a maintained, an emerging, or a well-developed interest, but we do have enough information to recognize that the two youths' interest levels differ and to know that they would need different supports in order to seriously reengage with emergency room care in the future.

In such a case, it would be most useful for the after-school coordinator to focus on whether the youths' interest is developing by looking for indicators that can be observed and by using the two broad categories of earlier and later or less and more developed interest. Working with the broader categories to describe phases of interest development can also be useful for researchers who are conducting large-scale studies with a very large sample size; in such cases more precise consideration of the interest trajectory may not be needed (depending on the research questions), and/or it may not be possible to collect enough sources that could validate survey responses because additional data would be too difficult to collect.

For some research purposes, more fine-grained tracking of interest is warranted.[44] Efforts to identify all four phases of interest prospectively have been undertaken in domains as far reaching (and specific) as second-language learning of challenged college learners,[45] the extracurricular interests of juvenile delinquents,[46] engineering students' work with a discrete task,[47] developing STEM interest in middle-school students in a community-supported context, and middle-school student writers.[48] For example, in order to target sources of second-language learning remediation for challenged college-age students, Cabot (2012) used Hidi and Renninger's (2006) description to develop survey items specific to each of the four phases of interest. These items were vetted by two external judges with expertise in motivation and then distributed to ninety-eight students. The items were found to reliably identify learners in the first three phases of interest development but not the fourth, well-developed individual interest. Given the characteristics of the learners studied (the students are in remedial classes and the second language is challenging for them), it is not surprising that she was not able to use the survey to identify students with a well-developed interest. They may not have existed in the populations studied.

Phases of interest were identified using the indicators of frequency, depth, voluntary engagement, and independent engagement in studies of writing and science, two of which are described briefly here. Both of these studies provided data about various phases in the development of interest, allowed consideration of the development as well as the falling off of interest, and provided insight about the students' perceptions of their experiences working with particular content. In each, an initial between-person analysis of all data sources was used to provide baseline understanding of what might be generally expected of participants at the given age, in the given context. Following this, within-person analysis of participants' individual activity was undertaken.

In the first study, Lipstein and Renninger (2007b) studied seventy-two middle-school students (thirty-eight boys, thirty-four girls) and their interest in writing, using a combination of forced-choice and open-ended survey items. The survey data together with the students' responses to in-depth unstructured interviews was then used to develop composite portraits of students in each phase of interest. Each portrait represented the data of multiple students and provides representative detail about students in each phase of interest, including their disciplinary knowledge, goals, strategies, effort, self-efficacy as writers, and feedback preferences.[49] In addition, the retrospective interviews enabled changes in interest to be tracked and linked to the students' perceptions of their experiences in working with the content.[50]

In the second study, Renninger and Riley (2013) used behavioral indicators to identify interest and changes in eight (three male and five female) participants' interest over four years. Coding of continuous written records collected daily during the five weeks of an out-of-school workshop provided the basis of this multi-year assessment and enabled the tracking of change over time. Interviews with participants at three time points each year (pre-, post-, and five weeks following conclusion of the workshop) were used to confirm findings from analysis of the written records.

Concluding Thoughts

People are hardwired to have interests and to be able to develop new interests. Existing interests can be studied either as particular topics (e.g., plants, cells) or more generically at the level of the domain (e.g., science), depending on how this information is to be used. For new interest(s) to develop, a person needs to have enough knowledge of or value for a domain to find seeking information rewarding. People who have more developed interest can be recognized by their repeated engagement with particular content, the depth of this engagement, and the likelihood that they will opt to engage with that content voluntarily and independently. Those with less developed interest do not reengage with content in this way.

Notes

1 Travers (1978) suggested that it is a sign of pathology (e.g., depression) when a person does not have an interest. It should be noted that there is a distinction between Travers' assessment and the tendency of a young person to report boredom. In such cases, the young person is likely to have an interest in other contexts (e.g., videogames).
2 Fryer 1931.
3 See Renninger 1992.
4 See Krapp and Fink 1992.
5 For example, Bathgate et al. 2013.

6 See www.onetcenter.org/reports/IPSF_Psychometric.html (accessed August 28, 2015).

7 Assessing interest using an inventory that is limited to a listing of topics is subject to complications, such as what the rating means and whether it means the same thing for each participant (Frenzel et al. 2012), whether the participant has had prior experience with the topics that they rate highly, and so forth. (This will be discussed later in this chapter.)

8 Since Bandura and Schunk's (1981) publication, the term "intrinsic interest" has been recognized as misleading, as it sets up an expectation of "extrinsic interest," which is a nonexistent term (see discussion in Hidi 2000). Instead, we refer to interest.

9 See also, Deci 1975; Ryan and Deci 2012.

10 Bjork and Hommer's (2007) and Zink et al.'s findings (e.g., Zink et al. 2003; Zink et al. 2004) point to the connection between active participation and rewards.

11 Hidi and Anderson 1992; Hidi and McLaren 1990, 1991.

12 Flowerday and Schraw (2003) found that knowledge development is important for the ability to make a choice; with the development of knowledge, feelings, and value for a given subject, people are better able to work with the choices they are offered within that subject. Without some knowledge of the content(s) about which they are offered choice, people are not able to make informed choices and can only pick haphazardly (see review in Katz and Assor 2007).

13 Kirschner et al. (2006) discuss the needs of learners in open-ended situations; Maltese and Harsh (2015) suggest that the structure of open-ended, project-based settings such as the LED table at the museum might need to differ depending on the phase(s) of interest of the participant(s).

14 It is possible to have enough knowledge of the content triggering attention to develop interest without being reflectively aware of that knowledge.

15 For example, Bjork and Hommer 2007; Zink et al. 2003; Zink et al. 2004.

16 Interest differs from most other motivational variables in that a person may not be in a position to accurately report on their interest in the earliest phases of interest development, when they may not even know that their interest has been triggered. Interest is not a belief; rather, in our conceptualization, interest is a psychological state during an engagement and also a cognitive and an affective motivation to reengage with particular content. Direct measures of interest, such as asking a person how interested they are in something, do not provide information about the distinction between different phases of interest.

17 Frequency of engagement can be assessed in a number of ways—for example using running records (e.g., that allow consideration of consecutive and distributed engagement over time), log files of participant work online (e.g., that allow tracking types and frequency of participation), and surveys that include ratings of a participant's activities in relation to each other (see Renninger and Pozos-Brewer 2015).

18 Depth of participant engagement can refer to comprehensive reading of a text (e.g., Schiefele 1999, 2001), or exploration (e.g., exploration associated with problem solving, such as a preschooler working to figure out when a block will slide down the roof of a building she is constructing), accuracy, and/or complexity (e.g., sophistication of strategies employed in problem-solving) (see Renninger and Pozos-Brewer 2015).

19 Voluntary engagement as a behavioral indicator refers to the choice to engage with the activity when it is possible, but not required. Such data can be collected using running records, log files (e.g., tracking participant engagement in discussions, or their use of online resources), and on surveys asking questions about how likely they are to engage in [or with] particular activity outside of school, etc. (see Renninger and Pozos-Brewer 2015).

20 If a person is interested in a collaborative activity, this clearly changes the ease of assessing independent engagement. If, on the other hand, the interest is in mathematics,

which can be undertaken collaboratively or independently, the choice to work mathematics problems independently some of the time would be useful confirmation of developing interest, because it would distinguish the more intensely interested from those for whom it was more of a social endeavor.

21 Independent reengagement can be assessed using video and running written records of free play (e.g., by identifying consecutive and distributed instances of engagement with different play objects), and online using log files that allow tracking the type of engagement (e.g., discussion, use of resources, etc.). On surveys, independent reengagement can be determined by using Likert-scale or open-ended questions that ask about study contents (e.g., for a study of undergraduate students using an online environment to write mathematics, it might be useful to ask an open-ended question about the different types of software with which they are familiar; whereas, for middle-school students in an integrated social-studies, science, and language arts program, asking about extracurricular activities could help to clarify what they are doing in addition to the work that they are assigned in school) and also about contrasting activities, and/or direct inquiry about whether the respondent is likely to engage with the activity independently (see Renninger and Pozos-Brewer 2015).

22 Collecting data on as many indicators as possible is recommended, although sometimes not all of the indicators are able to be assessed. The number of times a person does something does not provide enough information to be an indicator of interest.

23 See Renninger and Pozos-Brewer 2015; Renninger and Schofield 2014; Renninger and Su 2012; Renninger and Wozniak 1985.

24 Evidence for this assertion is provided by Renninger et al.'s (2011) study of 741 teachers' work with an online professional-development module focused on teaching mathematics. Using multiple methods, they found that rate of participation based on logfile data did not predict either interest or learning. Continued participation was dependent on the way in which the teachers worked with the structure and content of the modules. Some teachers engaged in thinking with others about approaches to setting up problems in the online discussions, whereas others did not discuss mathematics at all and instead talked about management problems such as whether everyone got to class on time.

25 Liking is an indicator of positive affect that may or may not be related to an interest.

26 Berridge et al. 2009; Ernst and Spear 2009; Harackiewicz et al. 2002; Silvia 2006.

27 Ainley 2007; Bergin 1999; Hidi and Harackiewicz 2000.

28 Kim et al. 2009; Renninger 2000.

29 Berridge et al. 2009.

30 See Murphy and Alexander 2000.

31 As Ainley and Hidi (2014) point out, using facial expressions as behavioral measures of interest is complicated because of variations across individuals, social groups, and cultures. More specifically, whether facial expressions can be used to reliably identify interest has produced contradictory findings. Some findings indicated that facial expressions have to be monitored for several seconds to provide information on interest association (Reeve 1993) and that coherent clusters of interest-indicating facial displays may in fact not exist (Reeve and Nix 1997). According to Scherer (2009), the facial expressions associated with specific feelings reflect a dynamic process of reappraisal. Subsequently, Mortillaro et al. (2011) investigated four positive affective states: pride, joy, interest, and sensory pleasure. Importantly, they provided specific definitions for each affect. For example, interest was described to the actors as "being attracted, being fascinated, or having one's attention captured," and joy was described as having a "feeling of great happiness caused by an unexpected event" (Mortillaro et al. 2011: 263; cf. Ainley and Hidi 2014). Although judges were able to classify the set of expressions reliably, the

findings indicated that expressions of interest and joy were both specific and over-lapped and pointed to the need to focus on the temporal sequence of facial expressions.

32 The most frequently used neuroimaging technique by psychologists is the fMRI scan-ner. The scanner uses blood flow and oxygen metabolism to track signals throughout the brain. Typically, the participant lies in the scanner and is presented with either auditory or visual stimuli that induce brain activity. fMRI scanning is not invasive and does not involve radiation. It has excellent spatial and good temporal resolution. (See Gruber et al. 2014.)

33 Renninger and Hidi (2011) reviewed methods of collecting observational data on interest, noting a range of data types, including ethological running records (e.g., Renninger and Bachrach 2015; Renninger and Wozniak 1985) and video footage that allows micro-analysis (e.g., Azevedo 2006; Barron et al. 2009; Pressick-Kilborn 2015; Pressick-Kilborn and Walker 2002). They point out that a combination of observa-tion and self-report has been used in learning environments such as museums and classrooms. For example, Falk and Adelman (2003) used entry-exit interviews and unobtrusive tracking to assess visitors' interactions with exhibits at an aquarium. In classroom research, Nolen (2007b) used self-report data, observation, and artifact analy-sis to track interest in a short-term longitudinal study of primary-school children in two classrooms. The multiple data sources in this study allowed description of peda-gogical variations that contributed to or hampered the children's developing inter-est for writing. Similarly, Pressick-Kilborn and Walker (2002; see also Presick-Kilborn 2015) mapped individual trajectories of interest development using a combination of field notes, informal interviews during lessons, and semi-structured interviews with selected students at three points.

34 Online assessment of interest has included studies of participation in coursework and software specifically designed to allow monitoring of participant behavior. Sansone et al. (2011), for example, studied anticipated interest for beginner-level learning in modules for a computer-science course, and its relation to participants' patterns of engagement (e.g., total frequency of accessing an optional example and exercise links, or incidental recognition of words appearing on those pages) and patterns in self-reported interest for learning.

The Between the Lines software developed by Ainley and her colleagues (e.g., Ainley et al. 2002; Graham et al. 2008) captures participants' responses during their work with tasks. This method archives information about participants' choice of text, their perseverance, and goals, as well as their responses to questions asking them to rate their affect.

Ely et al.'s (2013) MINE tool has been used with troubled adolescents who might not take traditional self-report measures seriously. It provides respondents with a pool of sixty potential interests and collects information about the cognitive and affective dimensions of their interest experience using an interactive interface. Preliminary find-ings support the validity of the MINE tool and also indicate that it allows participants to explore, trigger, and discover new interests.

35 This item is an adaptation of an item employed by Renninger and Schofield 2014.

36 This item comes from a survey distributed to middle-school students (Renninger et al. 2002).

37 Examples of surveys that either focus on or include items used to assess interest include those developed by Bathgate et al. 2013; Chen et al. 1999; Dawson 2000; Eccles et al. 1993; Ely et al. 2013; Haüssler and Hoffmann 2002; Jenkins and Pell 2006; Linnenbrink-Garcia et al. 2010; Marsh et al. 2005; OECD 2007; Rotgans and Schmidt 2011; Schiefele et al. 1993; Vollmeyer and Rheinberg 2000.

38 In their review of interest measures, Renninger and Hidi (2011) explain that self-report measures include tools such as questionnaires, interviews, and reporting from experience-sampling (in which participants are asked to rate or comment on the level

of interest that they experience at particular times, or in a given situation). Items vary from asking about interest (e.g., "How interested are you in mathematics?") to asking about components of interest (e.g., "How likely are you to do a mathematics problem that is not assigned by the teacher?"). As Renninger and Hidi also noted, the content of items used to assess interest in self-reports tends to vary. Researchers who consider the affective component central tend to employ items that address feelings (e.g., Alexander et al. 1995; Tobias 1994) or value (e.g., Chen et al. 1999; Linnenbrink-Garcia et al. 2010; Schiefele et al. 1993). Those who include knowledge as a component of interest use assessments of feelings and value and add items assessing knowledge (e.g., Haüssler and Hoffmann 2002; Renninger and Schofield 2014), or they make use of existing items to create a knowledge assessment. In their study of data from the Programme for International Learner Assessment survey (OECD 2006), Ainley and Ainley (2011) used items in the assessment that allowed them to assess learners' interest in finding out more about specific topics as well as learners' reactions to the specifics of the topic on which they were working.

For purposes of understanding the relation of interest to other motivational variables, or understanding the trajectory of interest development, multiple sets of items can provide more information. For example, Haüssler and Hoffmann (2002; see also note 10) administered their survey of twenty-one items to study three dimensions of interest (individual interest for the domain of physics, interest in the topic, and interest in the activity with the topic) at three times. Data from each allowed tracking of change in each type of interest. In their work with MINE, Ely et al. (2013) were able to track individual students' varying levels of interest for different activities, providing interest profiles. Multiple sources of input can also provide useful information. (See interviews with participants and parents in McHale et al. 2009; see also OECD 2007; Renninger et al. 2008.)

Varying forms of in-depth retrospective interviews with individuals (e.g., Azevedo 2013b; Barron et al. 2014; Fink 1998; Gisbert 1998) and experience sampling methods (e.g., Krapp and Lewalter 2001; Schiefele and Csikszentmihalyi 1994; Shernoff 2010; Shernoff et al. 2003) also provide rich sources of information about interest.

39 Frenzel et al. (2012) point to the importance of cognitive validation, that is, confirmation that the questions posed by the researcher are the same as the questions answered by a respondent. See also discussion in Karabenick et al. 2007.

40 See discussions in Renninger and Bachrach 2015; see also Renninger et al. 2011.

41 It is expected that behavioral indicators are appropriate for differences among studies based on content and context of the activity and age of participants. See related discussion in Renninger and Pozos-Brewer 2015.

42 Renninger and Hidi (2011) point to gaps between conceptualizations of interest and methods that are used to study it (Krapp and Prenzel 2011). The mismatch is attributable to a number of factors, among them differences in conceptualizations of interest that are not recognized, and research questions that may address interest as both a dependent and an independent variable. Unfortunately, empirical reporting does not typically include description of the relation between the conceptualization and the choice of measures.

43 See Renninger and Riley 2013.

44 In such cases, it would be useful to distinguish a person's interest in terms of the four phases in order to map the trajectories of individuals being studied. Such an undertaking ideally would involve considering how the four behavioral indicators of interest (frequency, depth, voluntary, and/or independent participation) apply in the settings and for the population of students being studied.

For example, in order to study developing interest in STEM-related professions such as emergency-room care, it would be important to know about the kinds of behavioral data that could realistically be collected in that setting. A person whose interest in emergency-room care was triggered by a visit to the emergency room might or might not be able to return to the hospital to watch, assist, and ask questions that allowed addressing frequency, voluntary, and/or independent behaviors. Alternatively, how might a person with developing interest in emergency-room care gather such information? Are there resources (e.g., online) that can provide them with information and/or resources about emergency care—and, if so, do they voluntarily seek to use them? In addition, in order to assess the depth of knowledge (and possibly the focus of interested engagement) a researcher needs to consider the nature of relevant content knowledge and what its consolidation and development would look like. What type of activity is a person able to do? It probably is not possible for youths to voluntarily go to the emergency room to observe and ask questions. If a person from the hospital is slated to give a talk at a local library, does the youth opt to attend? What is the quality of their attention? What does the participant notice and wonder about? What would participants at this age and with the same background notice and wonder more generally?

45 Cabot 2012.
46 Ely et al. 2013.
47 Michaelis and Nathan 2015.
48 Dierking et al. 2014.
49 Renninger, Kensey et al. 2015 reported similar findings in a cross-sectional, short longitudinal study of middle- and high-school students in which students were identified as having more or less developed interest in science. The study included quantitative and qualitative data and provides portraits of two students in the same science class, one with less and one with more developed interest in science.
50 These data were reported in Renninger and Lipstein 2006.

4

INTEREST, MOTIVATION, ENGAGEMENT, AND OTHER MOTIVATIONAL VARIABLES

What is the relation between the development of interest and other motivational variables?

Interest is always motivating and engaging; the presence of a developing interest ensures that motivation and engagement are meaningful.[1] However, the presence of motivation and/or engagement does not necessarily indicate that a person has interest, or that engagement is meaningful. How interest develops, as well as whether it develops, depends on the alignment between a person's learner characteristics (e.g., prior experience, personality) and the triggers that the environment or other people provide (either knowingly or unconsciously). This alignment sets the stage for motivation and engagement to potentially develop. For example, as Emma's interest in photography develops, her goals are modified, her feeling of self-efficacy (knowledge that she can engage and learn) improves, and her ability to self-regulate (initiate and moderate engagement) increases.[2]

In this chapter, we first clarify what the terms "motivation" and "engagement" mean and consider their links to interest. Following this, we describe findings from research on interest suggesting that in earlier phases of interest, interest and different types of motivational variables (goals, self-efficacy, and self-regulation) are distinct, whereas in later phases of interest they are more likely to be coordinated, develop reciprocally, and be mutually supportive.[3]

Motivation and Engagement, and Their Links to Interest

Motivation and engagement each describe the way in which a person interacts with the environment. In everyday conversation, the terms "motivation" and "engagement" are often used interchangeably with interest, even though this is not always accurate. Motivation refers to the desire or will to do something and may or may not be due to a developing interest. Engagement refers to a person's or a group's involvement in a particular context (e.g., the classroom, the family) that also may or may not include interest.[4]

Motivation and Interest

Motivation is beneficial or productive when it is accompanied by developing interest. However, motivation and interest are distinct concepts. Goals,[5] achievement motivation,[6] expectancy-value,[7] self-efficacy,[8] self-regulation,[9] flow,[10] and grit[11] may be called motivational variables[12] that could be but are not necessarily studied in relation to interest and a particular content such as learning Hungarian, mathematics, etc.[13, 14] When studied in relation to particular content, being motivated to seriously engage is something that a person is believed to be aware of and, as such, to be able to describe well enough to answer questions on surveys or in interviews. It is also expected that a person's motivation reflects decisions about how to engage with the content and that these decisions can be changed or reversed.

To illustrate the potential distinction between motivation and interest, consider a person who is motivated to learn Hungarian in order to honor the request of a beloved grandmother, although he has no interest in actually knowing the language. For this grandson, given the amount of time it requires, learning Hungarian is a very difficult task. It would require a great deal of self-regulation, and learning Hungarian would be more difficult for him than it would be for a linguist who is interested in establishing relations among various language groups, such as Hungarian and Finnish. The person with nothing more than the support of someone's wish may be motivated to engage, but is unlikely to be in the position to think about the similarities and differences between his native language and Hungarian, to pay attention to the role of inflection and its meaning, and so forth. The linguist might still be challenged by the difficult task of learning Hungarian, but would be differently energized by the challenge because her goal was informed by her existing interest in languages.[15]

Interest is not a belief. Instead, interest refers to the psychological state of a person during engagement as well as the cognitive and affective motivational disposition of that person to reengage with particular content (e.g., Hungarian) over time. Although people are likely to have beliefs about their interest(s), they are not necessarily conscious of their interest during engagement. More specifically, those in the earlier phases of developing an interest may not recognize that their interest was triggered or be in a position to address this. They might not even think that they could develop such an interest at any point in time. Those in later phases of interest development, on the other hand, might be able to acknowledge and describe their interest or their intention to pursue their interest, although they also may be caught up in the activity that this involves and not be in a position to reflect on their behaviors.

Differences between motivation and interest may seriously affect the experience of practitioners: educators, employers, and the like. It is a problem when those working with learners who are high in one type of motivation (e.g., goals to achieve) do not recognize when some of these learners' interest is low. Students who have low interest need a different kind of support than those with developed interest.[16] Students who want to achieve and get good grades but have little interest in learning Hungarian, understanding mathematics, and so forth need support to start making connections to the disciplinary content of Hungarian, mathematics, etc., if interest is to develop.

Ideally, through the triggering process a student with little interest will be supported to start making connections to the content that she is expected to learn. This is essential for interest to develop. When learners have no prior experience or formal training in a discipline, the triggering of interest may involve the educator, parent, or employer sharing the connections that they have made to the content. In this way, they can provide learners with an understanding of the possibilities for making connections, in turn encouraging them to want to know more about content.[17] This type of triggering can lead learners to generate, find, and see the relation between what they already know and the knowledge and skills of the content to be learned.

If educators or the environment (e.g., software or tasks) provide support for continued and deepening engagement through triggers that are aligned to learners' present understanding, they optimize the likelihood that interest is supported to develop.[18] The process of triggering interest and supporting learners to make connections needs to enable them to develop enough knowledge about the content to be learned to lead to engagement.[19] Sansone et al. (e.g., 1992) have demonstrated that external supports to trigger interest may not always be required; they found that learners themselves can generate their own support to even engage in boring tasks. As Renninger et al. (2004) noted, it is also likely that this type of self-generated triggering of interest can be expected of learners once they are young adults. Children can only be expected to self-generate triggers for content that is already a developing interest.[20]

In order to support learners to make connections to mathematics, for example, work on a project such as raising money to build a tree house could be used. Such a project involves multiple opportunities for students to make connections between what they already know about mathematics and project work. In particular, students would identify calculations that are needed and "matter."[21] Once the students decided to sell cookies as a fundraiser (a decision which has already involved discussion and tallying of ideas and votes for one or another money-raising strategy), recipes could be gathered and tested, for which the proportions need to be calculated, the ingredients need to be bought at the best price, and the cooking needs to be organized and executed. At the same time, the students might be planning the tree house, including its design and construction, length and size of needed boards, numbers of nails, any preassembled windows, and so forth. Another example of support for mathematical connection-making is a class assignment that asked students to identify all of the types of mathematics in one of the activities that they had been engaged in for at least three years and to share this with their classmates.[22] A student who had been doing English country dancing provided the following example: the geometric figures and formations of the steps, the symmetry or parity of turn-taking, the need to fit a standard figure to different tempos or meters (dances in three beats or footfalls per measure instead of two or four), and the permutations of sets and progression through the dance.

Possibly the most important step in the process of supporting learners to make connections is the expectation that they will think about the connections they are making. They also need to be given time to do so.[23] Reflecting on what they are learning and opportunities to explore new ideas are critical—what differs may be the nature of the connections that a learner can be expected to make: in earlier phases of interest these may focus on the learner's experiences outside the given discipline and on the discipline, such as making connections between cooking and mathematics; whereas for learners with more developed interest, the connections are more likely to be more specifically about the content itself, such as making connections between addition and multiplication.[24] Reflection provides learners with a basis for subsequent knowledge development and the possibility of identifying the value of it. A context that engages the learner in reflecting is one in which interest can be supported to develop.

When a teacher, parent, tutor, employer, etc., incorrectly assumes that a person's motivation also includes interest (e.g., due to eye contact or head nodding, or inquiry about performance), they may respond to questions or feedback that would be more appropriate for a person with developed interest (e.g., suggesting another way to approach the problem or explaining the way in which the mathematics that they are working on is related to an advanced mathematics concept that the student has not heard of). If, on the other hand, teachers correctly identify that students have a developing interest in mathematics, they can provide support by encouraging them to think about how the problems could be related to other problems—see the case presented in Table 3.1. In such a case, the trajectory of the students' developing interest would be similar to that of Emma's developing interest in photography.[25] Interested students would be likely to ask questions if they do not fully understand the links that their teachers are making. They would increasingly have the ability to set goals for developing understanding and might work on these independently and voluntarily outside of class assignments.[26]

For the students who have not yet had their interest triggered by mathematics, having to think about more than the problem to be solved and how to approach it could be overwhelming, and may intensify feelings that they cannot complete the work at hand or engage with mathematics more generally. In such a case, they may only return to doing more mathematics if required to do so.[27] If, instead of providing information and expecting students to ask questions, the teacher were to ask them what they noticed about the problem (explicitly about how it could be solved), the teacher and the student could together use what they noticed to then begin talking about how to approach solving the problem.[28] In this case, the teacher would lead the explanation, facilitating the discussion to draw on the students' contributions and underscoring those ideas that the students need for further developing their understanding. Facilitation of this sort is likely to lead students to ask questions, enable them to begin making connections to the mathematics, and could trigger their interest. Project work and conversations that involve thinking together can provide support for continued and deepened thinking about content for all learners.

Engagement and Interest

Engagement, like motivation, is beneficial and productive when it is accompanied by interest. A person whose interest is developing is a person who is meaningfully engaged.[29] However, it is possible for a person to be engaged but not interested (as in the case of the student who is only striving for a grade). It is not possible to have a developing interest and not be engaged given the opportunity, unless there are competing motives (e.g., when you want to continue reading a book but have a chemistry test the next day).

The research literatures on engagement and on interest are almost completely distinct, although they each consider cognitive and affective involvement in some context.[30] Whereas earlier discussions and research on engagement focused on cognitive, affective, and behavioral aspects as distinct from each other, more recent discussions have begun to point to overlaps among them.[31] They also point to the critical importance of the learning environment, or context, as influencing the quality of the person's activities.

Engagement research was initially undertaken to address disengagement that can lead students to drop out and not complete school, and disengagement, rather than interest, continues to be a focus of engagement research.[32] Nevertheless, as Azevedo (2015) notes, engagement can be overgeneralized.[33] We suggest that articulating the synergy between interest and engagement could be particularly useful for researchers and practitioners alike. Interest research foregrounds the psychological state and motivational disposition of a person in order to better understand "how," "why," and "when" engagement persists and makes an impact. As such, these studies typically target the impact of interest on a discrete set of variables (interest as an independent variable[34]), although some interest research considers how interest can be elicited (interest as a dependent variable[35]). In contrast, studies of engagement typically focus on detailed examination of the "what" of engagement and "for whom" it makes a difference (engagement as a dependent variable). They describe the school environment, or context (including the family, classroom, teacher, and/or peers), in relation to the students' cognitive (e.g., perceived relevance of school work, goals), affective (e.g., autonomy, school connectedness), and/or behavioral (e.g., attendance, participation in school activities) activities.[36, 37]

On the basis of extensive study of students in classrooms, and using experience-sampling methods,[38] Shernoff et al. (2003; see also Shernoff 2013)[39] have reported that when students experience both academic intensity (challenge, concentration, and interest) and positive emotional responses (enjoyment, esteem, and intrinsic motivation), engagement was meaningful. However, Shernoff (2013) was also careful to note that academic intensity and positive emotional responses are independent of each other, and that student experiences often lack one or both. Based on his work in schools, the educator Schlechty (2011) has suggested that meaningfully engaging tasks:

- are novel and authentic;
- provide affirmation and choice;
- include provisions for students to learn what they need to know to effectively complete assignments;
- include opportunities for collaboration and/or consultation with others;
- involve students in working with substantial content;
- are organized to enable the student to engage in making a product;
- have clear standards for task completion.[40]

Interventions such as Christenson and colleagues' (e.g., Appleton et al. 2008)[41] Check and Connect Intervention[42] enable schools to support disengaged K–12 students to develop adaptive behaviors.[43] Check and Connect is used to target and then provide support to grade K–12 students who show signs of disengagement (e.g., poor attendance, behavioral issues, low grades) and who may be at risk for dropping out. Students are identified for support on the basis of their behaviors in school (e.g., attendance) and their responses to a survey with items asking about feelings about and goals in school. The interventions are carefully sequenced and individualized. A Check and Connect trained mentor collaborates with individual students, their teachers, and parents to identify changes needed for school success and to monitor each student's progress.

Implicit in this type of intervention is the expectation that the students receiving it are or can be made aware of their challenges, the need for changed behavior, and the importance of setting goals. In other words, the students need to be committed to do what is necessary to change their behaviors. In addition, there is an expectation that the mentor and other adults will be involved in ongoing monitoring and recognition of students' successes. The design of the intervention draws on findings from studies of motivation generally, and more specifically from research on goals, self-efficacy, and self-regulation (reviewed in relation to interest in the next section of this chapter).[44] The intervention also emphasizes the importance of social relatedness (the connection to the mentor and to other adults who are collaborators), and the students' feelings of competence and autonomy.[45]

Research on engagement has focused almost exclusively on how the environment can be made to support engagement, with little direct consideration of how and what interest may be contributing to this process.[46] However, there are some notable exceptions. Larson (2000), for example, did not cite interest specifically but described initiative as including behaviors that characterize interest development, and positive outcomes that are also associated with studies of interest: improved attention, strategy use, and learning. Other work has pointed to interest as emerging in studies of engagement. For example, Shernoff (2013) summarized his and his colleagues' findings as having identified interest as a characteristic of meaningful engagement. On the strength of these findings, Larson (2014a) drew on the four-phase model of interest development to provide a basis for sustaining engagement in literacy activities.

Both interest and engagement focus on the processes of a person's engagement with the environment.[47] However, in interest research, affect and cognition are considered to be coordinated in their development, meaning that one does not occur without the other,[48] whereas engagement research typically lists cognition and affect as two of the different (and distinct) dimensions of engagement.[49] Reschley and Christenson (2012) described the relation among the dimensions of engagement (affect, cognition, behavior, academic engagement) and suggested that cognition and affect might be considered primary and coordinated: "We speculate that … engaging or disengaging students cognitively and affectively precedes changes in students' behavior and academic engagement" (2012: 9; as cited in Renninger and Bachrach 2015: 59). Their hunch, as Renninger and Bachrach (2015) pointed out, has now been confirmed by interest research. Research on interest always presumes the coordination of affective and cognitive components and provides explanations of which characteristics make a task "engaging" and why meaningful engagement includes intensity as well as positive enjoyment.[50]

Given Larson's (2014a, 2014b) findings, it seems likely that clarifying the contribution that student interest makes to engagement, and, in particular, to the ability to benefit from an engagement intervention, could inform understanding of engagement more generally.[51] For example, information about students' phase of interest for a given discipline would allow those implementing interventions to distinguish among students who could benefit from being supported to begin developing their interest and those who have already done so. Use of information about the phase of students' interests in designing and implementing interventions might result in students being positioned to be actual partners in interventions instead of being recipients who are supposed to be partners.

Interest, Goals, Self-Efficacy, and Self-Regulation

In earlier phases of interest development, interest may be triggered, and it may or may not be sustained. However, if a triggered interest is supported to develop and is sustained, then as interest continues to develop, the person will be both motivated and meaningfully engaged. In later phases of its development, interest involves a more sophisticated form of seeking, one that involves substantive or deep engagement, wanting to understand and learn.[52, 53] More developed interest of this type has been found to be coordinated with other motivational variables, such as goals,[54] self-efficacy,[55] and self-regulation.[56] As interest develops, its relations to these motivational variables are increasingly mutual. These relations can also be referred to as reciprocal. For example, interest development can influence how self-efficacious one becomes, and self-efficacy can influence interest development. It is only in later phases of development that goals, self-efficacy, and self-regulation become coordinated with interest. Moreover, the relations between phases in the development of interest and motivational variables such as goals, self-efficacy, and self-regulation have received substantial attention from motivation researchers.[57] This research indicates that persons in earlier phases of interest may not have enough experience or knowledge to be in a position to set goals, feel self-efficacious, or self-regulate and prioritize work on content that could develop into an interest, because they do not have enough experience or knowledge to do so.[58]

For example, encouragement and a mandate for the engineer to learn how to "sell" his services to potential clients could provide him with enough information to understand the need for selling, as well as support for acting on this new information that, in turn, would support the development of his feelings of self-efficacy and his self-regulation. These developments would help him to become involved in selling and, possibly, he would come to understand that selling is an element of the problem-solving that has been his interest all along at the firm. Similarly, Emma's noticing and then reading the directions that were in the bottom of the camera case enabled her to continue to develop her interest in photography and, subsequently, her ability to set goals for herself, to feel self-efficacious, and to self-regulate. Importantly, the variables of interest, goal setting, self-efficacy, and self-regulation are each distinct concepts that become increasingly coordinated as interest develops. In this section of the chapter, we review findings that provide a basis for describing interest as having a reciprocal relation with other motivational variables.

Interest and Achievement Goals

Both interest and goals have energizing effects on learning.[59] Whereas interest refers to both a psychological state and also to a motivational predisposition to reengage with particular content, goals refer to the object of engagement. Many investigations of each of these variables have been undertaken independently;[60] some researchers have also suggested that interest and goals may not be separate entities and should, instead, be viewed as related concepts.[61]

Achievement goals have been the focus of an extensive literature.[62] Ames (1992) defined achievement goals as integrated patterns of beliefs or attributions that reflect the purpose of achievement behavior (to succeed: to do well compared to other people) and influence individuals' responses to achievement tasks. Accordingly, goals have been presumed to guide people's thoughts, feelings, and performance as they approach academic activities.[63] Here we focus on the relation between interest and two of the most frequently studied achievement goals, mastery and performance-approach goals.[64] Students with mastery goals aim to develop new knowledge and skills. In contrast, students with performance-approach goals strive to demonstrate their competence relative to others. Researchers have tended to consider interest to be more aligned with mastery goals than with performance goals, presumably because when they use the term "interest," they are focused on interest that has already been developed, rather than interest that could be developed or that is in the process of developing. However, Hidi and Harackiewicz (2000), among others, have pointed out that "successful" students hold both types of goals.[65]

In their review, Hidi and Harackiewicz further noted that the relation between interest and mastery goals could be elaborated. They argued that, on the one hand, learners who are interested in a particular subject or topic are especially likely to adopt mastery goals in courses that address that subject or topic and, on the other hand, learners who enter a course with a more general mastery orientation are also likely to develop interest as they work on improving their knowledge and skills. Harackiewicz et al. (2002) reported on a longitudinal investigation that examined the dynamics of college students' individual and situational interest in conjunction with their achievement goals and academic performance. Seven semesters following enrollment in an introductory psychology course, the number of psychology courses the participants took, their recorded major, and two long-term academic performance measures were collected. Study findings confirmed that interest and mastery goals were reciprocally related over time. Interest at the beginning of the course was found to predict mastery goal adoption and situational interest during the course, as well as interest measured seven semesters later. Moreover, the effect of initial interest on continued interest was partially mediated through mastery goals, suggesting that a mastery-goals approach facilitates interest development as students become more engaged with course material.

Subsequently, many achievement goal researchers have reported that whereas performance-approach goals have positive effects on grades at high school and college levels, mastery goals have positive effects on these students' interest.[66] Harackiewicz et al. (2008) concluded that these findings support a multiple goal perspective according to which both mastery and performance-approach goals can promote beneficial but distinct educational outcomes.[67] They also reported that in studies that demonstrated positive association between mastery goals and interest, the results indicated that adoption of mastery goals in courses predicted subsequent interest—findings that led to the assumption that interest was an outcome of mastery goals.[68] However, Harackiewicz et al. further noted that goal researchers have not examined how initial levels of interest predict the adoption of mastery goals and rather than a one-directional causality between mastery goals and interest, we must consider a reciprocal effect of mastery goals and interest. They concluded that mastery goals could be viewed as both products and predictors of interest. In their words:

> When individuals enter a situation with interest in the topic, they may be motivated to learn more about it (i.e., adopt a mastery goal), and they may develop more interest when they approach a task with a mastery goal. ... Our findings suggest that interest must be conceptualized as an ongoing process and studied over time to elucidate the processes through which initial interest affects goal adoption and continued interest, as well as the processes through which goal adoption influences the development and deepening of interest.
>
> (Harackiewicz et al. 2008: 117–118)

Harackiewicz et al. (2008) also reported on the reciprocal effects of interest and performance: early interest predicted exam performance and grades, and early exam performance predicted subsequent interest.[69] The researchers interpreted these findings as demonstrating both that students perform well on tasks that they find interesting and that they become more interested in activities as they perform well.

Renninger et al. (2008) provide further details about differences between the goals of learners in earlier and later phases of interest. They observed that even though the middle-school-age learners they studied in both earlier and later phases of developing science interest could be excited, attentive, and asking questions, only those in later phases of interest were likely to have the kind of goals that might be considered to reflect achievement motivation—conscious goals to achieve success by meeting other people's expectations about what school success involves, such as completing assigned work to receive high grades. They found that the learners who had less developed interest were not motivated to achieve because they had little if any knowledge of and value for science.

Renninger et al. (2008) found that learners with less developed interest are not yet in a position to independently set domain-based goals for themselves that can be realized. Instead, opportunities to experience setting and realizing present goals (e.g., looking inside a worm) triggered their interest. They described such experiences as potentially essential for developing the kinds of connections to science that could eventually lead to asking questions, reflecting, and seeking answers. They also suggested that coupling this type of experience with proximal goals that could support the learners to feel successful might trigger continued development of their interest in science.

In a set of follow-up studies, Renninger et al. (2014) described differences in the goals, or purposes, of those with more developed interest and those with less developed interest; for example, they reported differences in the behaviors of participants during a mink dissection:

> At the beginning of the session that included the mink dissection, AR, a participant whose initial interest in science was more developed, immediately began working to identify different organs, wanting help to use the scalpel, and asking focused questions about topics such as whether the thickness of the mink's neck helped it wrestle with and tear apart prey. In contrast, N, a participant with less developed initial interest in science, excitedly ran from table to table to see what the minks at the other lab tables looked like. He was one of the first to get a probe and to ask to see the mink's brain. During the dissection he identified many similarities between the mink's body and a human's body. AR's interest appeared to be triggered by the novelty of the connections she made first in identifying organs and getting a closer look at them, and consideration of the mink's physical characteristics and their implication for its survival, whereas N seemed to respond to the novelty of the dissection activity itself.
>
> (Renninger et al. 2014: 120)

The researchers found that AR, the participant representative of those with more developed interest, had more knowledge to work with and was also more focused in her approach to dissecting, and that N, the participant with less developed interest, sought to inform himself about dissections at a more general level, before he was ready to focus on the activity. The researchers also raised a question about whether either of the participants had articulated goals for their workshop engagement, and concluded that the participants' behaviors suggested that the goals that they set and reset for themselves were related to their respective phase of interest.[70]

Lipstein and Renninger (2007b) similarly reported differences in the goals of middle-school writers and their phase of interest in writing and pointed to the implications of these differences for instruction. Based on survey and semi-structured in-depth interview data, they confirmed that the learners' phase of interest was reciprocally related to their goals, and noted that the relation between the learners' interest and their goals pointed to forms of feedback on writing with which the students were ready to work.[71] Those with less developed interest often simply wanted to finish assignments and/or to please their teachers, and needed discrete information that supported them to think about their writing, whereas writers with more developed interest wanted to know what others thought about their ideas and sought out and were in a position to consider feedback on their writing and engage in discussion about it.

In two different studies of undergraduate students in STEM majors, Renninger and her colleagues (Renninger and Nam 2012; Renninger and Tibbetts 2010) further suggested that those with less developed interest had more pronounced achievement goals than those with more developed interest. They found that with more developed interest in their STEM major, undergraduate students were likely to be more focused on content and less encumbered by the need to achieve than were those with less developed interest. Although students with more developed interest achieve, they do not focus on achievement. Instead, because of their developed interest, they focus on continuing to develop their disciplinary content knowledge, and thus they also achieve. These findings support the association of interest and mastery goals.

Based on survey data and follow-up semi-structured interviews, Renninger and colleagues reported that the undergraduates with a developed interest assumed that they would be pursuing graduate work and did not worry about their grades as long as they were doing well enough in their courses (80 percent or better). When involved in summer research, the students were animated in talking about the content of the research on which they were working (e.g., for a person conducting research in a physics lab: what they were learning about heat shock) and made no mention of its importance for subsequent pursuits such as graduate school. By contrast, students with a less developed interest in their majors were concerned more about their performance in the same courses as those with more developed interest (wanting grades of 92 percent or better). Moreover, when these individuals were involved in a summer research program, they described summer research as essential for developing their résumés so that they could go to graduate school. If the particulars of their research program were mentioned, they were not detailed.

In describing the reciprocity of interest and goals, Harackiewicz et al. (2008) noted that when students perform well in exams, their increased sense of competence—self-efficacy—may also lead them to increasingly value and enjoy the activity. In other words, they pointed to the reciprocity of the relation between interest and self-efficacy, the topic that we consider next.

Interest and Self-Efficacy

Self-efficacy is a cognitive construct that refers to individuals' beliefs about their ability to successfully produce outcomes,[72] and is typically linked to perceptions of ability for the task generally (e.g., how well you can throw darts), rather than the skills it may require (e.g., the skill of throwing a dart).[73] The term "self-efficacy" is sometimes referred to as ability beliefs,[74] self-concept of ability,[75] or competence.[76] We use the term "self-efficacy" to refer to individuals' beliefs about their own abilities, because this is the term most often used in the research on this topic as it relates to interest. We acknowledge and appreciate that there are differences of emphasis represented by the other definitions.[77]

People who have high self-efficacy for a task are more willing to engage, work harder, persist longer, and have fewer adverse reactions when they encounter difficulties than people who doubt their own capabilities.[78, 79] Both self-efficacy and interest are domain-specific and draw on similar information about a person's participation; however, self-efficacy is a motivational variable that is based on a belief and is therefore different from interest. As with goals, self-efficacy and interest are distinct in earlier phases of interest and are reciprocally coordinated in later phases. There is also evidence suggesting that interest needs to be triggered in order for the reciprocal relation of interest and self-efficacy to unfold.[80]

Hidi et al. (2002) were among the first to note that interest and self-efficacy ratings are correlated in tasks across a variety of domains, for example mathematics tasks,[81] motoric learning tasks (dart-throwing),[82] writing revision tasks,[83] and science-related expository writing tasks.[84] The link is particularly strong in the domains of science and mathematics.[85] Interested engagements were found to lead to improved performance when accompanied by increased self-efficacy. Research findings from these studies have demonstrated that interest-driven learning tends to be focused and persistent and to include positive affect, especially when individuals perceived themselves as being capable of working on a task.[86] As Bandura (1997) explained, individuals' self-efficacy can be improved though feedback from their own activity or from others. Thus, once interest has begun to develop, engaging in interesting activities can naturally provide individuals with the feedback that they need to persevere in their work with tasks even when the tasks are challenging.

Bandura and Schunk's (1981) study of proximal goal-setting was one of the first studies to investigate the link between goals and interest, and pointed to their importance for self-efficacy.[87] They hypothesized that proximal goals would serve as an effective mechanism for cultivating a student's competence, self-efficacy, and interest. Study participants were elementary-school children who displayed gross deficiencies and had low interest in mathematics. Children were randomly assigned to one of four treatment conditions: proximal goals (they should work to complete six pages of problems during each session), distal goals (they should complete all forty-two pages of the problems by the end of the seven sessions), no goals (they should finish as many problems as they could), and no treatment (no intervening work with goals). The results showed that children in the proximal goal condition made substantial improvements in mathematics, relative to the children in the other conditions. They developed both self-efficacy and interest in the activities for which they had initially had little interest. Subsequent studies have demonstrated that proximal goals are most easily accomplished, and also that the development of interest can lead to changes in a person's goals.

Not surprisingly, Renninger et. al. (2014) also found that the development of interest and self-efficacy were coordinated in their studies, when the middle-school-age youth they were studying were asked to respond to prompts in their lab notebooks that began with I can (ICAN). For example, they found that participants identified as having little interest and low self-efficacy became animated when dissecting owl pellets, or working on surface tension (e.g., a child accidently spilled a water droplet on the table and realized that it looked different than the water on the wax paper he was using, and then proceeded to put a few more drops on the table). The youth wanted to share their discoveries with their lab group, did so repeatedly, and, even if they did not get attention (because the others were similarly captivated by their own experimentation), they continued to work independently. In their lab note-books, the participants' ICAN responses also reflected increasing attention to what they were learning and what they wanted to figure out. The researchers reported that all participants (those with more and those with less developed interest) achieved when they worked with prompts encouraging them to reflect on science content. Moreover, the more ICAN prompts the youths responded to, the more they learned and the more their interest and self-efficacy developed, regardless of the level of their initial interest at the beginning of the workshop.

Renninger et al.'s (2014) findings further suggested that increases in learn-ing and self-efficacy were heightened when the tasks of the workshop were retooled to provide the youth with additional opportunities to make connec-tions to the science content. For example, while participating in a mink dis-section, the youths calculated the length of the mink's intestine relative to the length of its body and compared this proportion to projects about the length of the human intestine relative to the length of the human body. They were sup-ported to see this information in their thinking about the intestine's function. In contrast, youth in a control group merely observed the locations and discussed the functions of various organs. In this example, changing the characteristics of the tasks through integrating disciplinary content in a teacher-guided inquiry context enhanced the workshop participants' ability to make connections to the activities and could do so at the level of challenge that they were each ready to work with. This resulted in gains for both interest and self-efficacy for all work-shop participants—those with less as well as those with more developed interest.

Bong et al. (2015) have also reported a critical link between interest and self-efficacy. In a cross-sectional and longitudinal study of over 7,000 Korean secondary-school students across subject areas, they found that there was a signifi-cantly stronger association of interest and self-efficacy in mathematics and science than in language arts.[88] In addition, their findings indicated that mathematics interest was considerably more stable than mathematics self-efficacy[89] and, con-trary to previous predictions,[90] prior interest was a more powerful determinant of subsequent self-efficacy than prior self-efficacy was of subsequent interest. Their data also suggested that interested engagements led to the development of com-petence. They concluded that the strong tie between interest and self-efficacy in mathematics and science, along with the stronger predictive power of prior inter-est for subsequent self-efficacy than vice versa in mathematics, indicated that at least in these domains, it may be critical for students to become and stay interested in order for them to feel competent.[91]

Kim et al.'s (2015) studies of interest and perceived competence among Korean students provide additional insight. They tested the relations among interest, utility value (perception of usefulness), engagement, and academic achievement in mathematics for a total of 18,907 students in 6th, 9th, and 10th grade. Their results indicated that across all three grades, interest was a stronger predictor than utility value of both classroom engagement and achievement Moreover, the difference in predictive power of interest and utility value became even more pronounced as students moved into higher grades. The predictive power of interest for classroom engagement and achievement increased as the grade level rose, whereas the predictive power of utility value decreased. Multiple group comparison further revealed that the predictive power of utility value decreased only among those who had low perceived competence and remained significant for those with high perceived competence. Taken together, these results suggested that it may be more helpful for educators to facilitate students' interest in mathematics than to emphasize its utility value, especially when students lack mathematical competence.

In other words, students lacking in self-efficacy may need to have their interest in a discipline triggered in order to begin to develop feelings of self-efficacy. The work of Hulleman and his colleagues (e.g., Hulleman and Harackiewicz 2009)[92] has suggested that a value affirmation intervention can provide this type of trigger.[93] They reported that when students were asked to explain the utility of the tasks on which they were working, students with less initial interest developed interest and made gains in performance. Especially for students with less developed interest, it may be critical that the students themselves generate the utility of the content to be learned.

A number of studies have also considered the effect of directly explaining the importance of information (communicated utility) to participants, the way in which such information is typically provided in classrooms.[94] For example, Durik and Harackiewicz (2007) studied the benefit of providing participants in an experimental study with utility-value information about a new approach to solving mathematics problems, and found that participants who had more developed interest benefited from the information, whereas those with less developed interest did not. This is another instance of the reciprocity of interest and motivational variables—in this case, utility value.

Taken together, these studies indicate that there is a close relationship between interest and self-efficacy, and that differences in this relation can be introduced by the nature of the task and its context (whether performance is stressed). However, studies have also shown that self-efficacy may be increased or decreased in relation to increases and decreases in interest,[95] and that high levels of self-efficacy may not always be associated with high levels of interest.[96] The two variables do differ; it is possible for them to be mismatched and/or for the process of their coordination during development to be gradual. Renninger et al. (2011), for example, reported that mathematics teachers who had high self-efficacy and low interest for mathematics appeared unable to engage in discussions of mathematics even when online teacher professional development modules with which they were working provided support for them to do so at a level that they could manage. Figuring out how to support the development of coordination between interest and self-efficacy appears to be needed. For example, for the teachers who were challenged learning online, Renninger et al. (2011) pointed to the possibility of retooling the design of the teachers' initial work online to enable them to choose the level of problem difficulty with which they would work, in turn also providing them with a cohort of teachers with whom to work who were ready to engage at the same levels of challenge.

Self-efficacy is a belief and, as such, is based on cognitive evaluation, and may be influenced by the feelings and valuing that accompany developing competence.[97] Interest is not a belief; rather, it is a psychological state as well as a motivational variable with affective and cognitive components. The development of interest includes three components: feelings, value, and knowledge. These together are considered to provide a basis for developing feelings of competence.[98] Evidence points to reciprocal development of interest and self-efficacy. However, given that interest has a physiological basis, it is also assumed, as suggested by the study of Korean students in mathematics, science, and language arts classes (Bong et al. 2015) and the data from study of science workshop participants (Renninger et al. 2014) that the initial development of interest typically precedes the development of self-efficacy, following which, there is a continued reciprocal relation between the two.[99]

Interest and Self-Regulation

As Sansone et al. (2015) pointed out, self-regulation is only a problem in learning, in the workplace, on the playing field, and so forth, when a person does not have interest. Self-regulation refers to the way in which individuals control their own thoughts and actions. More specifically, self-regulation of learning refers to those self-generated actions that focus on acquisition of academically relevant knowledge and skills.[100] Research on self-regulation has included investigations of the relation between goal attainment and interest development, as well as of individuals' abilities to be active participants in their own behavioral, cognitive, and motivational processes, in order to regulate affect.[101]

Most of the earlier empirical investigations of self-regulation and interest considered either one or the other of these variables; more recent work has pointed to several links between the two variables. On the one hand, findings from interest research have demonstrated that self-regulation is an integral part of interest development.[102] On the other hand, a number of investigators focused on self-regulation have concluded that interest can be a motivational factor that facilitates development and maintenance of self-regulation.[103]

In their self-regulation of motivation model, Sansone and her colleagues (see Sansone et al. 2015 for an overview) have described how the experience of interest is linked to self-regulation.[104] In ground-breaking research, Sansone et al. (1992) demonstrated that interest can be enhanced by intrapersonal (intra-individual) self-regulation. They found that as individuals start to participate in an activity, they make judgments about their level of interest in the activity, and these judgments determine whether they continue their participation. A person might decide to discontinue the activity if his or her interest level is low. Alternatively that person might try to generate more interest by modifying the activity or related goals, and such modifications require self-regulation. In their research, Sansone et al. focused on the kind of self-regulatory mechanism that may be required for such activities. In two of three related studies, they compared college students' responses to novel tasks that had to be performed repeatedly but that varied in how interesting they were. In a third study, the students' beliefs about motivating strategies for everyday and leisure activities were examined. The combined results of the three studies indicated that the students recognized regulatory processes that could increase their interest and contribute to their continued engagement.

In addition to focusing on how individuals are able to self-regulate to increase their interest, interest researchers have argued that as interest develops in an activity, self-regulation also develops as an integral aspect of performance, and that interest is a mediator of self-regulatory processes.[105] More specifically, as described in the four-phase model of interest development, self-regulation, accumulation of more information, and increased valuing lead to self-generated reengagement, which is an important aspect of both emerging and well-developed interest.[106]

As noted above, Renninger et al. (2004) have pointed to the ability of children to self-regulate when they are interested; they also explained the difficulties associated with teaching self-regulation to youth. For example, Renninger and Leckrone (1991) described children's persistent and focused reengagement that only occurred with toys that the children were interested in. Nolen (2001) noted that children as young as kindergarten may attempt to regulate their interest to avoid boredom, and Meyer and Turner (2002) found that fifth graders intentionally increased the challenge of writing tasks to make them more interesting.

Similarly, Renninger and Hidi (2002) described Sam, a middle-school-age student, and his self-regulation of his more and less developed interests. Sam was identified as having a well-developed interest in soccer (football) and was observed to self-regulate related activities. He could be found juggling balls with his feet around the house, and if there were a possible game, that was where he wanted to be. He regularly sought out opportunities to play and even rigged his own lighting so he could practice his kicks after dark with his father after he returned from work. He clearly self-regulated his activities related to soccer. His interest for science was less developed, and so was his self-regulation of activities related to science. That is, he only did what he needed to do on science assignments until his interest was triggered by the presumed death of the turtle (the turtle was hibernating because of the cold weather) that he was to care for and observe over a weekend as part of his science assignment. His triggered interest led him to attend to the turtle, and to begin developing assessments of the turtle's abilities to move forward (not unlike a soccer player). As Sam's case illustrates, interest is a mediator of self-regulatory processes.[107] The development of interest is accompanied by the activity of self-regulation that is integral to performance.

Zimmerman (2002) has described self-regulatory processes as including three successive phases, of forethought, performance, and self-reflection, and each of these phases as characterized by sub-processes. The forethought phase has two major categories, one of which includes variables that self-regulation researchers have referred to as self-motivational beliefs. The constructs included in this category are self-efficacy, outcome expectations, goal orientation, and interest.[108] Zimmerman concluded that when there is interest, activities or skills are valued for their inherent properties, and that students who are interested in an activity are more likely than those without interest to become motivated to plan and use learning strategies than persons without interest in the activity. Similarly, Pintrich and Zusho (2002) reported that individuals who were more interested in an activity or task perceived the task to be more valuable, important, or useful, and so were more likely to use self-regulatory strategies.

Concluding Thoughts

We have explained that the presence of a developing interest indicates that a person's abilities to set and meet goals, feelings of self-efficacy, and abilities to self-regulate are also likely to develop and become increasingly coordinated. Once interest begins to develop, a person's motivation and engagement also are both positive and beneficial and will lead to developed understanding and achievement. The learning environment and tasks or activities more specifically can be adjusted to support people to make connections to them. Moreover, it can be expected that different things will trigger interest in each phase of interest. Triggers for interest that are aligned with the level of a person's interest (e.g., the possible death of the turtle was aligned with the low level of Sam's interest) might be expected to support the development of associated motivational variables (e.g., self-regulation to monitor the turtle's needs).

Notes

1 As we saw in the last chapter, curiosity defined as a knowledge gap is also motivating.
2 Lipstein and Renninger 2007b.

3 Reciprocal, as it is used here, is not a mathematical reference but rather a description of the different relation that exists between variables at different points in their development. Thus, as Harackiewicz et al. (2008) point out, for example, learners with less developed interest are not as able to set goals and follow through to realize them, as are those with more developed interest. This relation is explained in more detail later in this chapter, and other examples of the reciprocal relation between interest and motivational variables are provided.

4 Christenson et al. 2012b; Fredricks et al. 2004. In explaining the relation of these three components of engagement, Reschly and Christenson (2012) speculated that changes in student behaviors are linked to changes in their cognitive and affective engagement—we describe this as interest (see Renninger and Bachrach 2015 for further discussion of the links between interest and engagement).

5 Goals describe plans for activity and can include either longer range (distal) or shorter-term (proximal) outcomes (see Senko et al. 2011).

6 Achievement motivation refers to the motivation to be successful (see Wigfield et al. 2006).

7 Expectancy-value refers to the appraisal of possibility (e.g., Eccles et al. 1983; Wigfield and Eccles 2000, 2002).

8 Self-efficacy refers to a person's belief about their capacities. Various research groups have studied this variable somewhat differently; see, for example, Bandura 1997; Eccles et al. 1993; Schunk and Usher 2012.

9 Self-regulation refers to the ability to follow through to accomplish planned goals (e.g., Hidi and Ainley 2008; Zimmerman and Cleary 2009).

10 Flow refers to the psychological state of engagement during which a person is so focused on an activity that they may lose track of time (e.g., Csikszentmihalyi 1990; Jackson 2012).

11 Grit refers to the determination to master content, especially when interest and its facilitating effect on effort is not present (e.g., Duckworth et al. 2007).

12 Assessments of expectancy-value, flow, and grit include ratings for interest; goals, achievement motivation, self-efficacy, and self-regulation do not, although each of these variables has a reciprocal relation to interest, described in more detail later in this chapter.

13 Motivation is usually studied more generally, not in relation to particular content, although calls for this focus have been made (e.g., Urdan and Schoenfelder 2006).

14 On the other hand, Ainley (1998) has pointed to interest as also having a more general aspect. Her discussion is similar to discussions of "openness," one of the factors of the Big Five personality traits described in social psychology (McCrae and Costa 1992).

15 Hidi et al. 2002; see also Walkington and Bernacki 2014.

16 Durik et al. 2015; Jones et al. 2015; Renninger 2010; Renninger, Kensey et al. 2015; Sansone et al. 2015.

17 See example provided by Larson (2014a) in the context of ninth-grade students' language and vocabulary learning.

18 See related discussion in Järvelä and Renninger 2014.

19 See Azevedo 2006; Linnenbrink-Garcia, Patall et al. 2012; Renninger 2010.

20 There are a number of studies in which the triggering process has been documented. Renninger and Hidi (2002) provide examples and discussion of the triggers of a middle-school student's interest for three different domains (reading, science, and soccer). Pressick-Kilborn (2015) describes the changing triggers that characterize the developing interest of a middle-school student's interest in science over time. Azevedo (2013a, 2013b) provides detailed discussions of the role of triggers as supports for the continuing engagement of a person who has a well-developed interest.

21 This is a project that Lisa Morenoff and Grade 5/6 students at the School in Rose Valley (Rose Valley, Pa.) took on one spring. Other examples of projects such as this

include those described in Levy's (1996) *Starting from Scratch*. The interested reader is pointed to integrated-science, social-studies, and language-arts curricular content described in Mark Springer's (1994, 2006) descriptions of the Watershed and the Soundings classrooms.

22 This is an assignment that Art Mabbott, a teacher in a Seattle public school, has productively used for years with his students. See also Chazan (2000).

23 See Azevedo 2006.

24 Support for reflection is basic to learning (Boscolo and Mason 2001; Bruner 1966; Chi et al. 1989; Chi et al. 1994) and is frequently the one aspect of pedagogy that educators (parents, employers) overlook in their planning either because of time it may take, and/or the assumption that the learner is doing this reflection. As will be discussed later in this chapter, when learners with little prior knowledge and no formal experience with science are supported to reflect as part of the ICAN Intervention, the amount of reflection that they do predicts changes in their learning during inquiry activities as well as in the development of their interest in science (see also Renninger et al. 2014).

25 See Renninger and Pozos-Brewer (2015) for additional discussion of case material presented in Table 3.1 about the development of interest in mathematics.

26 As will be discussed later in this chapter, students' feelings of self-efficacy and self-regulation would also continue to develop along with their interest. See related discussion in Renninger 2010.

27 As will be discussed later in this chapter, such a student is also likely to have low self-efficacy and little ability to self-regulate.

28 Noticing and wondering are techniques for engaging learners in mathematics that have been developed and refined by members of the Math Forum (see http://math-forum.org/workshops/universal/documents/notice_wonder_intro.pdf). See also Ray 2013.

29 Shernoff (2013) built on the work of Rathunde (1998), Dewey (1913), and Csikszentmihalyi (1990) to describe meaningful engagement as including elements of work and play; he also explicitly acknowledged the role of interest in this type of engagement. In identifying responses to learning tasks, Schlechty (2011) also pointed to meaningful engagement as a goal for educators, and further clarifies that other less-productive forms of engagement include strategic compliance, ritual compliance, retreatism, and rebellion.

30 The interested reader is pointed to Ainley's (2012) chapter in the *Handbook of Research on Student Engagement* in which she pointed to the importance of person and environment alignment and to shared concerns of research on engagement and research on interest. Shernoff (2013) also included a section on interest in his volume, *Optimal Learning Environments to Promote Student Engagement*. He explained that interest conceptualized as a variable that develops focuses on the interaction between the person and the environment and noted that because of this, interest is a motivational variable that is particularly relevant to discussions of engagement. However, he did not elaborate on the implications of research on interest for engagement research or on the relation between studies of interest and studies of engagement. In his research, he and his colleagues (Shernoff et al. 2003; Shernoff and Hoogstra 2001; Shernoff and Schmidt 2008) pointed to interest as an emergent aspect of meaningfully engaged behavior.

31 Christenson et al. 2012a; Fredricks 2014; Fredricks and McCloskey 2012; Shernoff 2013.

32 See Christenson et al. 2012b; Fredricks et al. 2004.

33 It is useful to note Azevedo's (2015) observation that the research on engagement is wide, varied, and of differing levels of granularity. He wrote that "engagement is one of the most widely misused and overgeneralized constructs found in the educational, learning, instructional, and psychological sciences" (2015: 84). We add to these

comments that the concerns of engagement researchers are those of practice, and it may be for this reason that the literature draws on multiple constructs. Furthermore, we suggest that articulating the synergy between interest and engagement would be particularly useful for researchers and practitioners alike.

34 In research, an independent variable is a variable that is examined as a possible influence on some other variable. For example, interest might be studied as an influence on learning, in which case interest would be the independent variable and learning would be the dependent variable.

35 In research, a dependent variable is the target variable under study. Interest or change in interest could be a dependent variable in studies of interest.

36 See Christenson et al. 2012b; Fredricks et al. 2004.

37 In the engagement literature, the notion of "changed engagement" has begun to be extended beyond indicators such as student attendance and grades to include commitment, investment, identification, and belonging (http://checkandconnect.umn.edu/model/engagement.html).

An example of items related to workplace (as opposed to school) engagement can be found at http://thebuildnetwork.com/team-building/employee-engagement-tool.

38 Experience sampling is a research method in which participants systematically report on their behavior at requested intervals.

39 See also Shernoff and Hoogstra 2001; Shernoff and Schmidt 2008.

40 See discussions and models in Fredricks 2014; Schlechty 2011; and Shernoff 2013.

41 See also Appleton 2012; Christenson and Reschley 2010.

42 See checkandconnect.umn.edu.

43 Another approach to counteracting student disengagement is provided by organized programming to promote positive youth development (PYD). Positive youth development refers to the supports (resources, opportunities) for young adults to develop the knowledge and skills (the ability to assume leadership, to take initiative) that are needed in order to make positive transitions to adulthood. It is expected that communities and organizations have a critical role in providing such supports. See Heck and Subramanian 2009; Lerner et al. 2005; Small and Memmo 2004.

PYD focuses on organized support (e.g., from the community or government agencies) to encourage the "5 Cs"—competence, confidence, connection, character, and caring—which, when in place, enable youth to be in a position to make positive contributions (Lerner et al. 2005; McKay et al. 2011). For example, Larson (2000: 170) pointed to the need to support youth to take initiative (being "motivated from within to direct attention and effort toward a challenging goal") and suggested that supports for taking initiative may be most effectively provided in structured voluntary activities outside of school (e.g., sports, arts, organizations such as 4-H and scouting; see also Fredricks and Simpkins 2013 for a review of out-of-school activities and programming).

44 Shernoff (2013) describes each of these motivational variables as contributing to engagement; he also describes interest as contributing to engagement, although he does not go on to discuss the implications of these contributions.

45 Feelings of competence and autonomy are tenets of self-determination theory. Self-determination theory is a theory of motivation developed by Deci and Ryan (see Ryan and Deci 2012) that focuses on a person's personal growth and fulfillment.

46 For a review of measures to assess engagement, see Fredricks et al. 2011. Studies in which interest is conceptualized as a value, belief, or propensity generally locate interest in the person (e.g., Deci and Ryan 2000; Eccles et al. 1983; Schiefele 1991). In such studies, interest is often assessed on the basis of liking, or positive emotion, although, as indicated in Chapter 3, these measures alone are no longer adequate for explaining the motivating power of interest. In some of these models, value and feelings are sole indicators; in others, such as the expectancy-value model, interest is one source of value that is analyzed along with importance, utility, and cost (see discussion in Sansone 2009).

Eccles et al. (2015) have pointed out that studies of expectancy have not focused on the development of interest but rather on its presence (or absence) and its implications for student decision-making at a given time. They suggested that expectancy–value theory provides a complement to the four-phase model because it provides information about the beliefs (particularly expectancies) that are associated with interest. Further work to understand when and under what conditions expectancies do develop could be particularly important for purposes of practice, in particular (see discussion in Renninger and Hidi 2011).

In their theoretical work on self-determination theory, Ryan and Deci (2012) also consider interest to be a value, and describe interests along with proclivities and curiosities as examples of intrinsic motivations that interact with "social pressures, constraints, and reward contingencies" (2012: 227) beginning at an early age. Rather than focusing on the implications of beliefs, however, they focus on the conditions that can support interest development and maintenance; they describe autonomy, competence, and social relatedness as necessary. Ryan and Deci (2000) refer to Krapp (2002a) as suggesting early experiences are important to the development of later, career-related identities (see also Krapp 2007). This conceptualization of interest differs from research findings that informed development of the four-phase model.

In the four-phase model, it is understood that interest can develop at any age. Thus, rather than conceptualizing interest to be an outcome of autonomy, competence, or social relatedness, the relation between interest and each of these is considered to be reciprocal. As Hidi and Renninger (2006) point out, engaging content that is of interest may lead to an increased sense of competence and/or autonomy.

47 See discussions of engagement research in Gresalfi 2009, as well as discussions of the focus of interest research in Renninger and Su 2012. See also Renninger and Bachrach 2015.
48 See Renninger 1990, 2000; Renninger and Su 2012. As interest develops, so does knowledge and value. Just as knowledge enables the development of value, so developments in value lead to search for additional knowledge (or understanding).
49 For example, Reschley and Chistenson 2012; Fredricks et al. 2004; Fredricks and McCloskey 2012.
50 See discussion in Renninger 2000.
51 Such suggestion is consistent with Larson et al.'s (2015) description of directions for future study of effective practices in youth development.
52 Berridge et al. 2009.
53 We intentionally do not use "meaningful" here, although it certainly could also be used as a descriptor. However, in earlier phases of interest, as a person is developing their understanding of a content, their present understanding may be already meaningful to them, however much more substantive and deep it will be as their interest continues to develop.
54 For detailed reviews and discussion of the achievement goal literature, see Harackiewicz et al. 2008; Hidi and Harackiewicz 2000; Senko et al. 2011.
55 Bong et al. 2015; Kim et al. 2015; Nieswandt 2007.
56 Hidi and Ainley 2008; Sansone 2009; Sansone and Thoman 2005.
57 Harackiewicz et al. 2002; Harackiewicz et al. 2008; Hidi and Ainley 2008.
58 See related discussion in Renninger 2010.
59 Tobias 1994.
60 Hidi and Harackiewicz 2000.
61 Murphy and Alexander 2000.
62 See discussions in Harackiewicz et al. 2002; Harackiewicz et al. 2008; Senko et al. 2011.
63 Hidi and Harackiewicz 2000; Hulleman, Schrager et al. 2010.
64 Senko et al. (2011) noted that achievement-goal theory has been one of the most prominent theories of motivation in educational research. Originally, the theory focused on mastery goals aimed at developing one's competence, and performance goals aimed

at demonstrating such competence by outperforming others (e.g., Ames and Archer 1988; Dweck 1986). Furthermore, the prevailing assumptions were that mastery goals had more educational benefits than performance goals. More specifically, as Hidi and Harackiewicz (2000) summarized, "Mastery goals are predicted to orienting people toward acquiring new skills, trying to understand their work, and improving their level of competence. Other positive aspects of behavior attributed to mastery goals have been persistence in the face of difficulty or failure, the achievement of self-referenced standards, and the recognition that effort and risk-taking are elements of achieving success. In contrast, performance goals are postulated to lead individuals to seek positive evaluations of their ability and avoid negative ones, to try to outperform others, and to consider ability, rather than effort, the cornerstone of successful performance" (Hidi and Harackiewicz 2000: 160–161).

Whereas research in the 1980s and 1990s supported positive consequences of mastery goals and maladaptive consequences for performance goals, with the publication of an article by Harackiewicz and Elliot (1993), a shift in perspectives occurred. The researchers emphasized that both mastery and performance goals can have positive outcomes. Eventually, the two-goal model developed into a multiple-goal model, including approach and avoidance aspects to both goals.

65 Dweck 2002.

66 See Harackiewicz et al. 2008.

67 For example, Harackiewicz et al. 2008; Pintrich 2000.

68 Tanaka and Murayama (2014) investigated the relations among situational interest, boredom, task-specific perceptions (expectancy, utility, and difficulty), and achievement goals. They conceptualized interest and boredom as achievement-related emotions. The study used within-person interest, boredom, and perception measurements—an important and not frequently used methodology—and hierarchical linear modeling. The researchers reported several findings on how individual differences in approach goals influence emotions and perceptions of participants. More specifically, the findings showed that higher interest and lower boredom were associated with higher perceptions of expectancy and utility and lower perceptions of difficulty. In addition, achievement goals influenced the within-person measures.

69 Harackiewicz et al. (2008) distinguished between two phases of situational interest as "catch" and "hold." These terms were first formulated by Dewey (1913) and were subsequently used by Mitchell (1993). We have suggested using the terms "triggered" and "maintained situational interest" to describe situational interest, corresponding to catch and hold. As Hidi (2000) explained, "catching" suggests the interpretation that the interest has already been elicited and is then diverted to a stimulus or activity; the term "triggering" can describe interest that is being newly elicited, even from a state of lacking interest.

70 See related discussion in Renninger et al. 2008.

71 See also Lipstein and Renninger 2007a, and Renninger and Lipstein 2006.

72 Bandura 1977; Zimmerman 2000.

73 Zimmerman and Kitsantas 1996, 1997, 2002; Zimmerman and Schunk 2004.

74 See discussions in Dweck 2002; Wigfield and Eccles 2002; and Wigfield et al. 2012.

75 See Bong et al. 2015; Bong and Skaalvik 2003; Denissen et al. 2007; Durik et al. 2015.

76 See Harackiewicz and Sansone 1991; Sansone et al. 2015.

77 See discussions in Bong and Skaalvik 2003; Pintrich 2003; Wigfield et al. 2012.

78 See reviews in Bandura 1997; Pajares 1996.

79 Both general ability and age have been reported to influence the accuracy of learners' perceptions of their likelihood of success. Ability seems to be positively correlated with the accuracy of judgments, whereas age is a negative factor. That is, younger children tend to have more positive perceptions of their ability to achieve than older children. (See discussions in Dweck 2002 and Wigfield et al. 2012.)

80 For example, Zimmerman (2000) reported evidence that self-efficacy was predictive of whether students would choose to engage in challenging academic tasks, as measured by their rate of performance and expenditure of energy as well as by the quality of their performance, implying that self-efficacy develops prior to interest.
81 For example, Bandura and Schunk 1981; Bong et al. 2015; Kim et al. 2015.
82 For example, Zimmerman and Kitsantas 1996, 1997, 1999.
83 For example, Schunk and Zimmerman 2007; Zimmerman and Kitsantas 2002.
84 For example, Bandura and Schunk 1981; Hidi et al. 2007; Kim et al. 2015; Zimmerman and Kitsantas 1997, 1999.
85 Bong et al. 2015.
86 See discussions in Barron et al. 2014; Lipstein and Renninger 2007b; Renninger 2010.
87 Task-related goals are examples of proximal goals, whereas the longer-range goal to understand mathematics is a distal goal.
88 The findings also showed that boys had significantly higher mean levels of interest and self-efficacy in mathematics and science than did girls.
89 The stability coefficients of interest ranged between .62 and .65 from Year 1 to Year 4, whereas those of self-efficacy ranged between .37 and .40 for the same period.
90 Bong et al. (2015) noted that a number of researchers' work (e.g., Bandura and Schunk 1981; Bergin 1999; Eccles and Wigfield 1995; Harter 1982) indicated the presumption that perceived competence (self-efficacy) precedes interest.
91 Moreover, girls tend to rate their competence lower than boys (e.g., Bong et al. 2015; Eccles et al. 2015).
92 See also Hulleman, Godes et al. 2010.
93 For an overview of the intervention, see discussion in Harackiewicz et al. 2014.
94 In follow-up work, Durik et al. (2014) further explored the impact of participants' self-assessment of competence, or perceived competence, on communicated utility in two studies. They replicated results that were earlier reported by Durik and Harackiewicz (2007) but found that the moderating effect of interest was weaker. They attributed this to the strong relation only between more developed interest and perceived competence. Participants who had lower perceived competence about mathematics and received directly communicated utility information showed less interest in the new technique once they learned of its utility whereas participants with higher levels of perceived competence had increased interest in the mathematics technique after receiving the utility intervention. They also solved more math problems correctly. In a second study, the researchers also established that expectancies have a critical role in how participants responded to communicated utility value. They found that with additional encouragement about their expectancy (an expectancy boost), those with lower perceived competence had improved performance and those with higher levels of expectancy did not. This set of studies underscores the differences among individuals in their readiness to work with tasks as well as the importance of how they understand themselves in relation to tasks that they are assigned. It also points to the role of task perceptions in participants' perceptions of their own abilities (see Durik et al. 2015).
   In an earlier study of the effects of competence and interest on how people receive feedback, Sansone (1986) had addressed the relation between students' perceptions of the task and their perceptions of their abilities. She reported that interest in the task deepened when competence was not a salient characteristic of the feedback they received.
95 For example, Niemivirta and Tapola 2007.
96 For example, Carmichael et al. 2010; Renninger et al. 2011.
97 Renninger 2010.
98 Renninger 1990, 2000.
99 Hidi and Ainley 2008.
100 Schunk and Zimmerman 1994, 2007; Zimmerman and Bandura 1994.

101 Boekaerts 1997, 2006; Pintrich and Zusho 2002; Sansone et al. 2015; Zimmerman and Bandura 1994.

102 For example, Sansone and Thoman 2005.

103 For example, Pintrich and Zusho 2002.

104 See also Sansone and Harackiewicz 1996; Sansone and Smith 2000; Sansone and Thoman 2005.

105 See Sansone 2009; Sansone et al. 2015.

106 See Hidi and Renninger 2006; Renninger and Hidi 2011.

107 See Sansone 2009; Sansone and Thoman 2005; Sansone et al. 2015.

108 It should be noted that in Zimmerman's work (e.g., Zimmerman 2000), interest has been defined as a belief—primarily a cognitive evaluation. If interest is defined as a belief, it is presumed that a person needs information that can be evaluated before interest can develop. Research such as that describing Sam indicates that he is not in a position to describe his triggered interest in the turtle. He would not, if asked, express a belief that he had interest in the turtle, or in science more generally. However, his behaviors suggested that his interest was triggered, and developing, and that he was increasingly self-regulated as a result.

5

INTEREST AND CONTENT

Is it a paradox that interest declines as subject matter gets more developed?

What is "interest-driven learning"?

Does it matter if interests are taken up in rather than out of school?

How different is an interest in one versus another subject matter or domain?

Given that content knowledge is essential to the development of interest, it could seem paradoxical that declines in student interest are repeatedly chronicled as students move into secondary school, a time when disciplinary content typically becomes the focus of academic work. Similar declines in interest have also been noted in out-of-school settings, beginning when children are about eight to ten years of age and their social development leads them to begin comparing their own abilities to those of others.[1]

In this chapter, we provide a context for thinking about declines in interest. We first consider how interest is related to content knowledge as well as the relation between interest and identity. We clarify the meaning of interest-driven learning and explain that interest can be supported to develop in a variety of settings.[2] Following this, we review findings from studies of interest conducted both in and out of school, organized by subject matter, or domain: reading, writing, second-language learning, history, science, mathematics, art, music, and physical education. In concluding the chapter, we suggest that declines in interest may not be paradoxical even though they may appear to be so.

Interest and Content Knowledge

The development of content knowledge is essential for interest development and is also an outcome of interest development. Leslie (2014) also recognized the importance of content knowledge that can be provided to learners by parents and teachers. He noted that "knowledge gives curiosity power" (Leslie 2014: 180), and recognized the role of knowledge in initiating and maintaining the search for more information, an explanation which is consistent with the coordination of developing interest (and knowledge) in the four-phase model.[3]

Consider briefly the following comments from Steve, who stopped working on a research proposal he was writing in order to figure out how to unstick the blade in his kitchen blender. In this case, the content is mechanical and the problem is concrete: the alignment of a blade either needs adjustment or the blender needs to be replaced. Asked in an email how he would describe his interest in fixing the blade and his decision to work on it, he responded:

> In some ways working on the stuck blade is similar to those metal manipulation puzzles. It
> - is a problem to work on that is mechanical/physical;
> - provides the satisfaction of figuring out something about how things work;
> - also gives me the opportunity to be clever and have an insight.

He continues:

> But it is also different from those puzzles. I'd be more likely to work on something that needed to be fixed than one of those puzzles because it:
> - involves doing something worthwhile, so it allows me to do something that otherwise would feel indulgent;
> - allows understanding how the systems around us work and not feeling out of touch, ignorant, and dependent;
> - might be the quickest way to having a working device, and I don't like having things that don't work. I like to have things in good working order and to contribute to that;
> - saves money.

Then, reflecting further, Steve observed:

> I will avoid tinkering if it:
> - seems too difficult or dangerous and I don't have a readily available way to figure it out, or I am worried about irreparably breaking it;
> - doesn't seem like there is anything interesting to be figured out or learned and the fix isn't that useful or effective or important (gluing stuff we don't really care about, etc.).

Steve has a developed interest in what he variously describes as "metal manipulation puzzles," "mechanical/physical" things, and, more generally, "how things work." In his response, one can hear the expectancies he weighed (e.g., previous experiences working with similar problems, an appreciation for the present problem and its potential complications, a desire for time invested to be worthwhile), as well as a question about whether he stands to gain more content knowledge (i.e., learn more about how things work) by working to unstick the blade.[4] His behavior and self-description point to his having a developed interest in this type of problem: he has prior experience, deep knowledge, and a willingness to independently engage. He also thinks the misaligned blade represented an opportunity to learn something new. It would be rewarding to further develop his understanding of this type of problem. Despite his interest, he says he would not have interrupted what he was doing to work on the blade without the promise of new understanding.

Emma's developing interest in photography (see Chapter 1) provides another, slightly different look at interest and content knowledge. Recall that when she first received the camera, she was not told much (if anything) about how to use it, and she did not look for instructions. She had some basic understanding that people take pictures with cameras and began taking pictures of flowers. However, she read the directions when she found them, which happened to have coincided with some spare time to explore and practice using the camera. The camera directions contained specific information about considering light and shadow when shooting pictures. She already had some sense that this was something she wanted to know more about; it corresponded to the way she had been organizing the photos in her album. Emma read the directions carefully and then began attending photography club meetings so she could learn more. The continued development of her interest in photography reflected the opportunities she both saw and took advantage of. As Emma's interest in photography developed, the opportunities to develop her understanding of photography increasingly informed her activity.

Further insight about the relation between interest and content knowledge is provided by the data from the study of the undergraduate students doing summer research in STEM disciplines (described in Chapter 4). Whereas these data suggest that content knowledge alone is not an adequate indicator of interest, they also indicate that interest supports the acquisition of more content knowledge. Students with less developed interest had sufficient skills and content knowledge to continue to major in a STEM discipline; however, they differed from students with more developed interest in their purpose, focus, and in the content of their skills and knowledge.[5] Those with less developed interest in their STEM major described the summer research as necessary for their résumé, whereas those students with more developed interest described their summer research experience in terms of the specific information they were acquiring (e.g., a physics student talked about what he was learning about heat shock and what he was trying to figure out). Those with less developed interest were concerned about their performance and about getting into graduate school. Those with more developed interest assumed that they would be pursuing graduate study and were focused instead on continuing to deepen already existing content knowledge. This meant that the summer research experience was preparing them for subsequent research opportunities, including graduate study, and it was also enabling them to deepen their understanding of disciplinary content. Those with less developed interest were acquiring skills and content knowledge, but had not yet made connections to the content of the research questions being addressed in the laboratory research.

It is possible that the experience of the students with less developed interest could have been different, especially since interest can be supported to develop. The students' professors might have helped them to develop their interest in the work of the laboratory. If the students with less developed interest had an understanding that developing their own interest was both possible and would be beneficial, they also might have worked to focus more specifically on developing connections to the content of the research themselves.[6]

To recap, the above examples highlight continued development of new understanding as rewarding. In the first, Steve was willing to invest time because fixing the blade offered the opportunity to continue to learn; otherwise, he was not interested in the activity. In the second, Emma was ready to take on additional information when she found, read, and then acted on the directions; she had enough content knowledge to make use of the more specific information about light and shadow and was ready to work with this new information. In the third example, the undergraduate students differed in their phase of interest for their STEM majors and in the opportunities they saw in their summer research; these differences affected the way that they participated in and gained experience from the summer research. Of note, the students with less developed interest had sufficient content knowledge of the discipline; however, because they had less developed interest, they would have benefited from support to engage the content of their work in the laboratory.[7]

Interest and Identity

People typically associate themselves as well as others with the content of their existing interest(s) (e.g., I am a mathematician; she is a bridge player), meaning that in everyday discussion interest is often used to describe identity. However, the association of interest and identity only applies to people in relation to their developed or known interest(s) and does not hold for interests that are in the process of developing, the potential of new interests to develop, or the malleability of interest (i.e., an existing interest may develop further, decrease, or go dormant).[8]

As people develop their interest in a particular content, they increasingly come to associate themselves with that content.[9] Conversely, early in the development of an interest, it is unlikely that a person would identify with that object (event or idea) as an interest, even when interest has been triggered. Take Emma, for example. When Emma first received her camera, it is unlikely that she expected to develop an interest in photography, join a photography club, or identify as a photographer. Similarly, the students with less developed interest in their STEM majors harbored doubts about whether they would be admitted to graduate school, and did not yet associate graduate study with the pursuit of disciplinary questions like those undertaken in laboratory research. Rather, they explained their participation in summer research as necessary for admittance to graduate school, and implied that this would determine whether they continued in the discipline. Despite the fact that the two groups of students had similar achievement profiles on entering college, students with less developed interest did not make the same connections to the content as their peers with more developed interest, and so they were not in a position to work with content in the same ways as their more interested counterparts.

Interest-Driven Learning

Interest-driven learning typically refers to learning driven by interest that has already developed; it is most often used to describe the kind of involvements that are possible in online environments in which learners make a decision to continue to work, play, etc., and their interest can be said to fuel their reengagement.[10] Curwood et al. (2013) describe fan-based affinity groups that, for example, use movies such as *The Hunger Games* as a basis for writing and role-playing that is shared with, and informed by, others, their interests, and their participation. Similarly, in massively multiplayer online games, participants might be involved in helping to construct a world in which they have a role that they develop in relation to their interest(s) and on which others come to rely (e.g., *World of Warcraft*).[11]

Interest can be triggered and supported to develop both in and out of school, and advanced training in a sport, music, art, drama, or writing is an example of interest-driven learning that when undertaken outside of school can complement, provide enrichment, or even be a replacement for schooling. Renninger, Kensey, et al. (2015), for example, cite the example of a high-school student who explained that participation in the extracurricular Science Olympiad program made the difference for her; Science Olympiad made it possible for her to sustain her interest in science and to plan to pursue it in college, even though she found her high-school coursework wanting.

Out-of-school (or extracurricular) activities can have similarities to the formal instruction of schools in that they (a) often include designed or programmed activity, (b) may have clear bars for achievement, and (c) are explicitly designed to be opportunities for participants to continue to develop new skills and understanding. However, out-of-school contexts also typically differ from the school context in at least one critical way. Participants in out-of-school settings usually have or want to have a developed interest in the setting; if they did not, they would not be participating. There could be exceptions to voluntary participation, for example, if a parent enrolls his or her child in piano lessons or a robotics club without consent.

The quality of teaching/facilitation/coaching in schools and in out-of-school contexts can vary, and it may or may not support the development of students' or participants' interest.[12] An educator who understood the power of interest could adjust the learning environment for participants by providing different amounts of structure (e.g., specific feedback about what needs to be done rather than more general admonitions such as not using so many words when writing). Students/participants with less developed interest are likely to need more structure, whereas students/participants with more developed interest may need less.[13] Providing more structure for a student/participant also involves considering the person's potential to implement change and what needs to be said, modeled, and/or practiced in order for change to occur. A basketball player who has a less developed interest may not implement the techniques learned during practices and get blocked during a game, whereas players with more developed interest are more able to figure out what could be different and to draw on the techniques they have learned as a repertoire of strategies during games. The player with less developed interest is also by definition a person whose interest has the potential to develop; he or she can be supported to make use of the strategies learned during practice and become a more effective player but may need support from other people to do so.

Educators wishing to support interest to develop in a topic, activity, or domain need to determine whether those with whom they are working understand the related content and, if so, what kinds of connections they have made to it. Armed with this information, they can then support continued and meaningful engagement by facilitating the development of additional connections or by providing opportunities for reflection and practice.[14]

As Järvelä and Renninger (2014) noted, interactions with content and support from others (or the design of the environment, exhibit, text, etc.) to engage content in new ways is essential for the triggering and sustaining of interest, and can be expected to positively influence motivation and engagement. Both in- and out-of-school contexts can incorporate design elements that explicitly support students to make connections to content and develop their interest. Such connections will support them to continue to reengage, to do so with increasing depth, to opt to engage when they have the opportunity, and to do so whether they are working independently or with others. Pressik-Kilborn (2015) highlights the teacher's role in this process of structuring the environment. She notes that the decisions that the teacher makes—whether or not they are intentional—either contribute to or limit the development of student interest. Such decisions include the focus of the content covered, the types and sequencing of tasks, the opportunity for group and individual work, the inclusion of bulletin boards that display related content, and the allocation of time.

Similarly, Azevedo (2006) pointed to software features and the flexibility of the environment as enabling participants in a computer-based visualization project to develop feelings of confidence, and meeting the students' additional needs to have enough time to think on and explore ideas they were generating. In another study detailing a participant's developing interest in model rocketry, Azevedo (2011) further explained that the nature of the activity, or practice, is not simple repetition but rather an incremental and recursive process through which people both reinforce and stretch their present understanding based on what they bring to situations and the presenting characteristics of the situation. It is a process that involves a succession of ongoing triggers for interest, many of which are self-generated once the learner has a more developed interest. However as Turner et al. (2015) reported, teachers (and educators more generally) sometimes need to be reminded or helped to understand why motivation is important, and that their role in triggering and supporting interest to develop is critical. Hidi (2000) has further suggested the importance of recognizing that interests, extrinsic motivation, and performance goals have complementary roles in making tasks more rewarding for those who are unmotivated.[15]

Students need to know that they can work with content. They need the kind of repeated activity (practice) that enables them to extend what they know in new ways and also positions them to develop value for the content, feelings of self-efficacy, and abilities to self-regulate. In addition, they need activities or opportunities that are discrepant enough that they are forced to take stock of what they have known and are supported to work with it in new ways.[16]

Interest by Domain

In this section, we summarize a selection of relatively recent studies of interest that have been conducted both in and out of school, and we consider their implications for supporting learners to build their understanding of and value for content.[17] In a few cases, earlier studies have been included in this review because of the perspective they provide. We have also made an effort not to repeat the presentation of studies that have already been described in this volume. We primarily draw on studies in which less developed and more developed interest have been clearly distinguished, because the way in which interest is assessed influences how the findings can be interpreted.[18] Differences based on identifiable demographic characteristics are noted.

Reading and Text Features

Studies of reading date back to the early 1900s when educators began using interest inventories to determine which topics might be most effective for supporting their students' engagement in reading texts,[19] not only for reading instruction, but for instruction in other subject matter domains as well.[20] Findings from these studies pointed to demographic differences such as gender and geographic location (e.g., rural farming communities, cities) as indicators of which topics are likely to be of interest to students.

Importantly, giving a story about baseball to students who are interested in baseball may increase the likelihood that they will read the story.[21] However, providing the students with a single text about baseball is not likely to immediately support them to develop interest in reading without repeated work with texts that are interesting and/or instruction to develop their skills as readers.[22] Rather, providing learners with texts that address their interests can provide an effective context for supporting them to read, and for providing them with reading instruction.

Even if reading materials are challenging, students may want to continue to read about topics that are of interest to them.[23] For example, Larson (2014a, 2014b) used information about phases of learner interest as a basis for motivating literacy instruction in biology classes and found that it was positively associated with developments in students' conceptual understanding. Similarly, when participants engage with content that triggers their interest such as reading/writing fan fiction, listening to podcasts, remixing video, or engaging in digital activities with other participants who have similar interests, their understanding has been shown to develop.[24]

In addition to the role of topics as a source of interest, research on reading has addressed: (a) the features and structure of texts,[25] multimedia presentations,[26] and games[27] that can trigger and possibly sustain interest,[28] as well as (b) the relation between interest and other variables in learning from text. Findings from such studies were reviewed in Chapters 1 and 2 of this book. To recap briefly, high-interest stories have been found to lead to more effective and longer-term recall than low-interest stories.[29] Readers can be expected to immediately recognize that information is interesting without having to compare it to prior understanding; thus, for example, asking them whether a task is of interest to them is different than asking them whether the task is important. A reader is likely to find it relatively easy and fast to attend to and process information that is of interest, but it is a different task if the person is also working to learn new information and/or to determine its importance. In the latter case, the learner may need to take more time with the task.[30]

In a related line of analysis, it has also been found that although the features and structure of text typically enhance learning, seductive details,[31] also described as distractors or decorative illustrations,[32] can enhance presentation of text and possibly learning from it, but also may derail learners. For example, placing a picture of a frog in the lower corner of a science textbook page may mean that the reader pays attention to the frog rather than to the information on the page. In fact, as Wade (1992) pointed out, students in the United States often know the seductive details about their former president, Abraham Lincoln. They tend to know that he had a top hat and a beard but, despite the fact that texts address his role in the emancipation of all slaves following the Civil War, this information is not readily recalled. Magner et al. (2014) subsequently reported similar differences depending on the phase of learner interest. Decorative illustrations triggered situational interest but did not maintain it, and, for students with less developed interest, they derailed learning.[33, 34]

Consistent with findings from the studies of interest and other motivational variables reported in Chapter 3, moreover, studies of interest in reading suggest that interest has a mediating effect on reading comprehension, recall, and motivation. For example, Unsworth and McMillan (2013) found that high topic interest was correlated with lower rates of mind-wandering and thus also improved reading comprehension.

Writing

Although frequently considered together in academic settings, writing and reading are different in their relations to interest. Writing involves generating both content and written text, and the writer may have interest in one but not the other. When reading, the content is provided and the reader may or may not have an interest in reading and/or in the topic of the text.

Individuals who have an interest in writing are likely to be predisposed to want to write and to receive feedback—to engage in conversation about their writing and the ideas that are being expressed—that will allow them to develop their texts.[35] Learners with less developed interest may be able to make connections to writing instruction if the topic is one in which they are interested; being interested in the topic, however, does not mean that a learner has already developed an interest in writing.[36] As a result, feedback to writers with less developed interest is more likely to be valuable when it is brief, specific, and constructive.[37]

For learners with less developed interest in writing, the possibility of writing about topics of interest to them does appear to make the work more manageable and meaningful. McCarthey et al. (2004) reported that the second-language learners they studied were (with one exception) resistant to writing but successfully worked within a structured and not entirely supportive writing curriculum by writing about topics that were of interest to them: their holidays, families, and activities outside of school.[38] For participants in online affinity groups who collaborate together to write, edit, and/or design and share information about their interests, writing is the means for communicating, and they do a lot of it; as

Curwood et al. (2013) have suggested, teachers who are not making use of this type of digital opportunity to engage their students in writing should consider this evidence.[39]

Nolen (2007a, 2007b) has detailed the positive ways in which the classroom community can support the development of children's writing, as well as some of the unintended consequences of teachers' behavior. As her research indicated, whether interest was supported to develop in the classrooms studied depended both on what the children brought to the classroom, and on the kind of support that they found for developing their interest in writing.

Consider again the example (presented in Chapter 3) drawn from Hidi and McLaren's (1990) studies of middle-school students who were given the choice of writing about space travel or life in the city.[40] The students with a triggered interest in space travel chose to write about this topic even though they had almost no knowledge about space travel and lived in the city. This instance demonstrates that students may not have enough content knowledge to write about a chosen topic of triggered interest; this may affect how developed and/or effective the writing can be. From the students' perspectives, it may seem sufficient if they write about what they are interested in. However, if a developed essay is the expectation, students who write about a triggered interest without doing additional research to acquire more knowledge are at a disadvantage. The choice may affect not only their grades on an assignment but also their sense of identity as developing writers. Another finding from these studies pointed to the increased ease of writing when a person has related knowledge.

Given that the interestingness of themes and topics is found to influence comprehension in reading, it had been initially hypothesized that interest would be a positive influence on writing. It can be. That is, for interest to be a positive influence on writing, sufficient knowledge about the topic is necessary. Findings such as those from the Hidi and McLaren's (1990) study just described, together with those that indicated that interest in writing was complex, have pointed to the role of developed knowledge about writing as a positive influence on the production of content associated with writing.[41] Findings have also demonstrated the benefits of instruction on interest in specific genres, including argumentation, narration, and reporting, as these are related to meaningful classroom activity.[42]

Second-Language Learning

As with the studies described in the sections on reading and writing, second-language learners have been found to draw on their own interests as a way to make tasks meaningful. To date, there have been only a few research studies of interest and second-language learning. Cabot (2012) provided insights about the triggering and sustaining of interest in French language learning using an interdisciplinary intervention. She drew on materials from a psychology of sexuality course in order to trigger the interest of a group of native English speakers, and studied their work to learn French as a second language in relation to their phase of interest in learning French. A control group of students worked with traditional course materials. Those who received the intervention were found to have higher levels of situational interest than the control group, higher school engagement (more student–student interactions, use of reference materials, and class participation), and higher achievement. She also reported that relative levels of engagement and achievement of target group participants reflected expected differences based on their phases of interest. In other words, those with less developed interest were outperformed by those with more developed interest. However, compared to the control group, Cabot also found that even those with less developed interest in the target group continued to pursue and be successful in subsequent course work, suggesting that just the triggering of situational interest in the target group predicted increased continued enrollments and success in subsequent course work.

Technology can be a forum for triggering and supporting interest in second-language learning. A number of studies have been undertaken in which web-based or computer-based instruction has been used to support learners' interest in learning English as a second language, for example in China[43] and Saudi Arabia.[44] These studies reveal positive effects on both the development of interest and achievement.[45] Some examples of this type of intervention include multi-sensory delivery of instruction that involves participants in simultaneously seeing, hearing, and doing work with the second language,[46] computer-assisted language learning that uses software to support vocabulary building,[47] blended learning in which in-class learning is supplemented with a web-based teaching platform,[48] and blog writing.[49] In these studies, other research questions have also considered the role of stories[50] and dramatization[51] as effective entry points for English language learning.

History

The role of triggering an interest in historical reasoning has been examined. Logtenberg et al. (2011), for example, conducted a study to examine the basis of students' abilities to "problem find," or question, in historical reasoning. Not surprisingly, they found that those in the high-interest/knowledge group did the most historical reasoning and made the most connections to the text, while those in the low-interest/knowledge group did the least historical reasoning and made the fewest connections to the text. They also found that although the middle interest/knowledge group asked more content questions, there were no differences between the groups in terms of the topic or type of questions posed, suggesting that all groups were in a position to ask questions if so supported. The researchers pointed to the importance of supporting students to contextualize, or make connections, to what they have read.

Other studies have assessed the effect of activity type as a support for student interest in history. Examples include digital mapping of local history,[52] integrated curricula,[53] and simulations to support students' developing abilities to engage in social perspective taking (e.g., represent one country and take another country's perspective during a treaty negotiation).[54] In studying social perspective taking in the *GlobalEd* simulation, for example, Gehlbach et al. (2008) found that increased interest was related to greater ability in social perspective taking. However, in the Gehlbach et al. study, they found that whereas the use of the simulation to trigger interest for social studies increased interest, it did not extend to developing interest for social studies more generally. It seems that additional scaffolding to sustain the initial triggering of interest was needed.

Science

Understanding student interest has been a particular concern in the sciences (general science, biology, chemistry, computer science, engineering, and/or physics[55]) for several reasons.[56] Science education has taken on greater importance as developments in advanced technologies have become the standard in research and its application. For example, if students are planning to pursue biomedical research or medicine, it is not enough for them to simply complete prerequisite courses; they need to be able to deeply understand the information so they can apply their knowledge in the workforce.[57] This situation points to the importance of supporting students to develop enough interest so that they retain what they have learned for subsequent use. Those with less developed interest in physics have been found to succeed in developing their interest and improve their performance when the physics they are learning is embedded in life-science content (e.g., optics of vision, cell-membrane potential).[58]

Another reason that student science interests are important to the sciences is that attrition rates from the sciences are very high, even among students whose scores, classroom performance, and original intention to pursue a science major suggest that they should be successful.[59] As school subjects, the sciences are demanding at least in part because the hierarchical structure of their content means that missed or misunderstood coursework needs to be mastered before students are ready to learn new content.[60, 61] Becher and Trowler (2001) have observed that clarifying ways in which students can be supported to make connections to science is essential, as is the need to support them to sustain these.[62]

Studies of interest and science have most often addressed which science topics are of interest to students' instructional practices as supports for interest, and the relation of interest to other variables, in particular the development of self-efficacy.[63] Specific science topics (e.g., owl pellets and the food chain) have also been studied as a potential source of interest in studies of reading[64] and/or writing.[65]

As described in Chapter 3, Bathgate et al. (2013) reported that an interest in specific science topics (e.g., cells, plants) is highly correlated with an interest in science more generally. As such, depending on the question to be addressed, it might be appropriate to focus on specific topics and/or the more general category of science when assessing interest.[66] Information about topics that can be used to trigger the interest of students, and ways in which information about topics of interest might be used to provide the context of instruction, have particular relevance for practice. Details about individual students' development of interest in science, on the other hand, can provide a nuanced understanding of how the process of interest development unfolds.

Gender differences in science interest have been repeatedly identified,[67] although it should also be noted that Randler and Bogner (2007) reported that when a topic of study such as ecology is of interest to both males and females, this negates the effect of gender on achievement. Renninger, Kensey et al. (2015) also found that when females had more developed interest in science, there were few gender differences in their sense of their possibilities to pursue science, whereas when females had less developed interest in science gender differences were more pronounced. With the exception of biology in which females are overrepresented, males are more likely to continue to pursue coursework in the sciences.[68] Hagay and Baram-Tsabari (2011) have described a general disconnect between students' interests in biological topics and the topics addressed in their biology curriculum. They suggested that schools use students' interests and information to retool the curriculum.[69]

Out-of-school opportunities to engage in science have been used to provide support and access to science content.[70] They have been found to support interest development through projects, exploration of media, structured learning opportunities, and mentoring.[71] Out-of-school science opportunities have also been found to predict continued coursework in the sciences.[72]

A number of interventions have been undertaken with mixed results. These include:

- Out-of school summer STEM programs and extracurricular activities that provide particular benefits to underrepresented groups and have been found to close the gender gap.[73]
- Increasing the relevance of content (e.g., by introducing scientists through their struggles rather than just their achievements, or using life-science examples in physics courses for nonmajors), which has proven to increase achievement for students with less interest.[74]
- A laboratory intervention during the electromagnetism section of a traditional introductory course that resulted in positive changes in topic interest but had no effect on general physics interest or gender differences in interest.[75]

- An after-school computer-science program for low-income Latino students that supported the development of language proficiency and technological fluency.[76]
- An after-school club designed to use gaming, specifically *World of Warcraft*, as a basis for helping adolescent males develop an interest in effective school-related behaviors. This failed; the males' disinterest in game-related instruction led to what the researchers referred to as the "Let me know when she stops talking problem"—in other words, the youth wanted to be able to play the game, were not paying attention to the information that they were being given, and were just waiting until the information stopped so that they could play.[77]

In discussing students' likely situational interest in technology in general, and its potential use in classroom learning, Philip and Garcia (2013: 316) cautioned that:

> The just-add-technology-and-stir fallacy is especially problematic …
>
> When teachers and administrators explore the use of technologies in the classroom, they must be doubly cautious that they are not assuming that student interest is inherent to a gadget like a smartphone or that the instrument will transform learning and schooling to more equitable ends, particularly for students in urban schools. Relevance and transformation emerge through the interaction of texts, tools, and talk. Supporting teachers in these interactions to enable rich learning is a difficult task, layered at the classroom, institutional, and societal levels.

Technology can trigger interest; however, as Philip and Garcia (2013) have suggested, more support needs to be in place for triggered interest to enable learning. Specifically, learners need time invested in the work (e.g., the work of the teacher to scaffold instruction based on students' strengths and needs, as well as the work of the student on tasks and with text) and interactions that enable learners to seriously engage content.

Hoffmann and Häussler and their colleagues (e.g., Häussler and Hoffmann 2002) have suggested it may not be the topic of interest, per se, but the context (e.g., the curriculum, the instructional practice, the gender composition of the classroom) that warrants our attention.[78] In a series of studies, they have reported that 80 percent of the variation between males' and females' interest in physics was due to the context in which physics was introduced. For example, females were more interested in learning about how pumps move blood through an artificial heart than they were in learning about how pumps extract gasoline from great depths. Häussler and Hoffmann (2002) found that females were interested in natural phenomena, mankind, social issues, and practical applications. They also found that all of these topics were of interest to males as well, although not all of the topics that were of interest to males were of interest to females. Additionally, their findings indicated that the best predictor of interest in physics was the students' confidence in their own performance.

On the basis of these findings, Hoffman and her colleagues designed and developed a comprehensive intervention to support seventh-grade students to develop their confidence and increase their general interest in physics. They developed curricular materials that were structured to support females' interest in physics by focusing on the context in which the physics concepts were taught, provided teacher training sensitive to females' needs, and explored promotion of potential gains for females in different classroom configurations (e.g., partial and whole classes of single-sex instruction and coeducational classrooms, half versus whole-class instruction). Hoffmann (2002) reported that the new curriculum positively influenced the achievement of both males and females, and that students (especially the females) in the part-time single-sex half classes experienced the greatest gains. Their findings indicated that when supports for interest and self-concept were provided, learning occurred and interest could be expected to develop.

In the context of a ninth-grade chemistry classroom, Nieswandt (2007) reported on the relation among situational interest, self-concept, and attitude in the development of conceptual understanding. She found that initial situational interest positively influenced self-concept and conceptual change. She also suggested that initial interest had only short-term effects on conceptual change, and that situational interest that goes beyond the initial triggering of interest was needed in order to promote longer-term conceptual change. In related work focused on engineering, Dohn (2013) pointed to the potential that sources of situational interest, together with addressing students' needs for self-efficacy, provide as supports for learning. Dohn described inventions as a source of situational interest for middle-school students, and pointed to trial-and-error experimentation, the invention's functionality (whether it worked), and collaboration as either contributing to or possibly derailing students' interest. He reported that although students' interest was triggered during the design phase, and some students were able to self-regulate and sustain interest when their designs did not work, it was essential to provide instruction and guidance for sustaining student interest for students who were not yet ready to provide this for themselves.

Nieswandt's findings that suggested a complex relation between conceptual change and interest were subsequently supported and explained by Linnenbrink-Garcia, Pugh et al.'s (2012) study of ninth and tenth graders' understanding of natural selection. In their study, Linnenbrink-Garcia et al. studied changes in students' conceptual understanding of natural selection in relation to their interest for biology, academic self-efficacy, and prior knowledge of evolution. Grouping students based on their levels of interest, self-efficacy, and prior knowledge, they found that patterns in the students groups' conceptual understanding indicated that for both males and females, interest and self-efficacy were reciprocally related. Those with more developed interest also had more developed self-efficacy and experienced more change in understanding than those with less developed interest.[79]

Mathematics

Interest has been studied as a variable that can support mathematics learning and for addressing concerns that many students (especially females and underrepresented minorities) do not pursue advanced mathematics coursework.[80] Unlike in the sciences, the topics of interest identified in mathematics are typically not directly related to the content of mathematics. They focus on topics such as basketball and music rather than fractals or nonroutine challenge problems. For example, Walkington et al. (2013) reported that students with less ability improved their performance on more difficult problems when the algebra problems they received had their out-of-school interests inserted as problem contexts.[81] However, they also found that this type of personalization served to distract more able students when they worked on easier problems. Findings from their work further suggested that students thought that the more interesting contexts enabled improved engagement and attention.

In a related, earlier study, Renninger et al. (2002) had found that level of interest for mathematics was not necessarily correlated with standardized achievement scores. They also reported that the individualized insertion of topics of more developed interest into mathematics word problems could increase student comprehension (even for learners with less developed interest). Because the problems also accounted for individual students' level of ability in problem solving, the researchers further determined that it is likely that even if students with less developed interest in mathematics do not get the problems correct, when the problem addresses their interests they are led to thinking about mathematics. The Renninger et al. findings suggested that although interesting problem contexts may feel distracting to the student as Walkington et al. (2013) indicated, they actually challenged the more able students to focus on the meaning of the problem (the relation between the content and the problem context), rather than simply applying an algorithm.

Interest as the context for problems has also been used in intelligent tutoring systems such as those that allow middle-school students to personalize aspects of instruction to their own interests (e.g., Carnegie Learning Systems' Grade 6–8 MATHia software).[82] In fact, Walkington and Bernaki (2014) observed that use of individual interests as problem contexts may be most effective for individualized scaffolding in tutoring situations, whereas more generic age-related or shared interests are more effective for online tutoring systems and in classrooms where individualizing problems could be a challenge for the teacher.

Research has also examined influences on the relation between interest and other motivational variables (e.g., self-efficacy) in mathematics learning. Upadyaya and Eccles (2014), for example, reported that teachers' beliefs about children's effort and potential performance positively predicted children's interest in mathematics in primary school. They suggested that the teachers' beliefs influence the feedback that children receive and the way in which teachers work with them. These findings complement those describing moderate to strong correlations between early math skills and interest, and that this early interest was sustained over time.[83] Harackiewicz et al. (2012) also demonstrated that perceptions of mathematics could be influenced by the type of information and interactions that students received.[84] They found that when parents of students in grades 8, 9, and 10 were provided with (a) an understanding that mathematics and science courses were useful in everyday life and for career opportunities, as well as (b) suggestions about how to talk about these topics with their children, this had a beneficial impact on the students' interest and performance. The intervention increased the parents' perceptions of the usefulness of mathematics and science, promoted more discussions between parents and their children about the importance of mathematics and science, and resulted in the children enrolling in significantly more (and advanced) mathematics and science courses.

Information that is provided to students based on the structure of assignments has also been found to vary in its effect on student interest in mathematics depending on the students' level of interest. Schukajlow and Krug (2014) reported that prompting students to construct multiple solutions (as opposed to single solutions) for real-world problems increased their interest. In contrast to the research-ers' expectations, however, only a tendency for competence to influence interest was identified, and there was no influence of autonomy on interest. They speculated that this could be because of the different levels of experience and achievement in the participant group; students' achievement levels may influence the amount of autonomy they want or are ready for. The researchers' findings could be interpreted as pointing to the kind of reciprocal relation for both competence and autonomy that characterizes the relation between interest and both self-efficacy and self-regulation. In other words, asked to construct multiple solutions, students with more developed interest were likely to have more competence and ability to work autonomously, whereas students with less developed interest were likely to have less competence and readiness for autonomy. These results point to the association of competence and autonomy development with interest development, as suggested by Hidi and Renninger (2006).

A number of studies have more specifically explored interest in mathematics in relation to other motivational variables. Durik and Harackiewicz (2007), for example, determined that participants with differing levels of interest for mathematics responded to triggers for interest differently. Those with less developed interest responded to more superficial "interest-enhancing" triggers involving color, whereas those with more developed interest were more likely to respond to challenge. Seemingly consistent with these findings, Tulis and Fulmer's (2013) study of changes in affect during work with a challenging mathematics problem revealed that students who persisted with the tasks even through failure exhibited no decreases in interest, whereas those who did not persist reported lower levels of interest in the task.

In a short-term study of changes in students' interest and self-efficacy while working on a complex computer task, Niemivirta and Tapola (2007) found that interest and self-efficacy profiles varied, levels of interest and self-efficacy were associated, and changes in each were related to changes in the other (a reciprocal relation). They found that (a) prior mathematics achievement predicted initial levels of interest and task-related self-efficacy but had no effect on change in these variables during the task, (b) final task performance was predicted jointly by initial self-efficacy and degree of change in interest, and (c) positive change in interest had an independent effect on performance.

Music

Research on music and interest has addressed problems of school instruction (e.g., music at home being associated with enjoyment and music at school being associated with information)[85] and conditions that can promote positive perceptions of opportunities to listen to and make music.[86] In their study of Australian six- to seventeen-year-olds' perceptions of participating in music, Barrett and Smigiel (2007) identified five characteristics that were found to sustain participation in music:

1. love of performance;
2. shared purpose;
3. a desire for challenge and professionalism;
4. quality in the relationships developed;
5. opportunities for growth.

Sosniak (1990) further elaborated on the conditions that characterize and may influence the development of an interest in music in his study of the development of musical talent.[87] He described the process of developing an interest in music as including shifts from more external to more internal forms of support over time.[88] He noted that such shifts unfolded through three "periods" and that the process was idiosyncratic in that it varied in its rate and details. In the first period, early opportunities to explore music without the need to be particularly systematic or skilled were typical. Often the initial triggering of interest in music was a natural part of living with a family member who valued and had an interest in music. Sosniak described those with early talent as listening to music and learning to identify composers and pieces as early as they could remember. He reported that they recalled their first teachers as enthusiastic, warm, and aware of their early and undeveloped interests in and involvement with music.

In what Sosniak (1990) labeled a second period, musicians' relationships to their teachers could be described as shifting from love to respect. Their instruction at this time was characterized by the need to build skills and attend to detail.

In the third period, moreover, their relationship with their teacher could become strained because their teachers often did not know what to do when their pupils' interest wavered. In this period, music students were expected to: begin to identify as musicians, to consider music a field of expertise, and to make adjustments to fit music into their lives. Sloboda (1990), who has also described the development of interest in music, detailed a very similar trajectory. He added, however, that if students felt uncomfortable or threatened, they were unlikely to be capable of experiencing and developing interest.

In their study of 625 eighteen-year-old black South African male and female students, Marjoribanks and Mboya (2004) corroborated and extended Sosniak's (1990) and Sloboda's (1990) findings, indicating the critical role that caring and supportive teachers play in the development of an interest in music. They have also added more explicit information about the role of the learners' goals and needs for support from the learning environment to this finding; they found that when differences of family background and goals were controlled, students' perceptions of the school learning environment (e.g., the care and support provided by teachers) predicted their interest in music.[89]

Other research relating to music interest has reported that adults tend to prefer receiving instruction in piano, voice, and guitar; performing as members of choral organizations; and taking coursework in music history or aural analysis.[90] Such information is not available about children's preferences. Redundancies in rhythmic sequences have also been studied as influences on interest in composition.[91]

Art

The research literature has included relatively few studies of the development of interest as it relates to art (in contrast to studies of appraisal). Descriptions of art education echo Sosniak's (1990) descriptions of music education, with a period of initial exploration followed by expectations for attention to detail (Gardner 1990; Read 1958), and declines in interest in art as children move into middle school have been documented. Two approaches to art with implications for interest development have been described: manga (a highly artistic form of Japanese comics) and the maker movement. Toku (2001) has explained that Japanese children typically deviate from what might be the expected declines in an interest in art because of manga; they continue to develop their visual narrative skills as they produce manga. As evidence of their interest, Toku pointed to the numbers of Japanese youth involved in the creation of manga, comic books that are developed graphic narratives, and their related involvement in amateur publishing ventures to distribute them.[92] Toku cited their complex representations of the inner and outer self and the role of manga in Japanese culture (they may date to the twelfth century) as two likely explanations of why Japanese youth, in contrast to youth in other countries, are positioned to continue developing their interest in art.

Halverson and Sheridan (2014: 496) described the maker movement broadly as including anyone who "is engaged in the creative production of projects such as making books, or wearable electronics, or squishy circuits in their daily lives and who find physical and digital forums to share their processes and products with others." (See the case of children at the museum project table in Chapter 3.) The researchers distinguished between the process of *making* as activity, *maker-spaces* as locations (e.g., museums, libraries, schools) and communities in which making takes place, and *makers*, those who identify as engaged in making. The New York Hall of Science (NYSCI) (2013) symposium, Making Meaning (M2), for example, provides case studies of young makers indicating that they come from a wide range of racial, ethnic, and socioeconomic backgrounds. All of the youth had a developed interest in what they were making. Their interviewers noted that even among children who had been retained in elementary school, their abilities to collaborate, use effective strategies, and respond to feedback in the context of the making space were superior. The descriptions also pointed to ways in which the opportunity to participate in maker activity was seeding the development of an interest in one or more of the sciences.

Physical Education

Chen et al. (2014) described the goal of physical education to develop "physically literate individuals" who are positioned to have an active lifestyle. Research on physical education and interest has addressed the topics in which participants are interested as well as the role of situational interest in triggering and then supporting the development of interest in some aspect of physical education. Kahan (2013), for example, reported on a study of the interests of 701 urban seventh-grade students that suggested differences based on gender and ethnicity. He found that males were more interested in football than were females; females were more interested in volleyball, yoga, and jump rope. Hispanic students were more interested in soccer than were Asian students; and Hispanic, Black, and Asian students were also interested in ethnocentric games and dance activities.

Savage and Scott (1997), on the other hand, studied a total of 722 rural students and found that both males and females reported preferences for active team sports such as volleyball, football, softball, as well as individual activities such as weight training, biking, and swimming. Christiana et al. (2014) provided further detail about the interests of rural youth who have low levels of fitness and less developed interest in physical activity. These youth were more interested in non-competitive activities and selected activities based on the availability of equipment, previous participation in an activity, parental and peer influences, time spent out of doors, and enjoyment.

Zhu and his colleagues (e.g. Zhu et al. 2009) have worked to clarify how students can be supported to seriously engage their interest in physical activity. They have verified five sources of situational interest in elementary and middle-school physical education:

1. novelty;
2. challenge;
3. attention demand;
4. exploration;
5. instant enjoyment.[93]

The studies suggest that situational interest can be short-lived,[94] may have a positive effect on physical activity,[95] and may be dependent on the expectations of the student and the type of tasks with which they are engaged.[96]

One way in which Zhu and his colleagues (e.g., Zhu et al. 2009) have explored supporting sustained student interest in physical education involved using a workbook as part of instructional practice. The idea was that the workbook would provide students with the expectation that they were learning during instruction in physical education: "Using the workbooks as a curricular intervention created a learning environment in which students expected learning to take place with physical movement. This integrated learning experience contributed to their overall fitness knowledge" (Zhu et al. 2009: 227). Furthermore, Zhu et al. (2009) reported that skipped workbook tasks contributed to decreases in students' knowledge gains. In discussing the ICAN intervention in Chapter 3, we described similar findings in the use of written reflection in an out-of-school science workshop. We have suggested that this kind of written reflection may be essential for participants to consolidate their learning. It may be that using the workbooks in the physical education context enabled students to understand that what they were learning was significant content that they should remember; it may also be that the process of writing provided an opportunity for students to reflect on this information and to consolidate their understanding.

Summary

The research reviewed reveals that although individuals may differ in their interests across domains, interest functions in the same way regardless of the domain. Interest can be developed in or out of school and in various settings. Interest-driven learning occurs when a person continues to reengage. Interest has a uniformly beneficial effect on motivation, engagement, and learning. However, interest needs support from other people or available tasks, activities, or opportunities in order to be triggered and continue to develop, even though individuals may or may not be aware that they are receiving support, such as living in a home with a musician, or having received problem contexts that are matched to their level of difficulty and interest. Triggers that are simply situational, such as personalizations, might not enable a person to seriously engage the content of a discipline.

Declines in Interest

Students' declining interest in school subjects as they move into secondary school has been repeatedly noted,[97] particularly in mathematics and science.[98] Similar declines have also been reported in out-of-school contexts such as piano instruction.[99] As Hidi (2000), Krapp and Prenzel (2011), and Potvin and Hasni (2014) have noted, there are many reasons that declines in interest could be expected. Explanations have included:

- The increasing complexity and hierarchical nature of the content to be learned (e.g., disciplines may become more difficult, and are particularly difficult if students are missing one or another core concept).[100]
- Changes in instructional practice associated with advanced work (e.g., project-based work is replaced by demonstrations and lectures).
- Increases in pressure to be successful, and have strong records.[101]
- The onset of adolescence and accompanying physical and social changes, including awareness of other people's opinions.
- The need of older students to recognize the connections between course work and their possible career pathways.

On teacher recommendations and school profiles, Csikszentmihalyi et al. (1993) explained that they identified 208 outstanding students to track as "talented" youth. They observed that a large number of them abandoned pursuit of their talent during high school; they considered this as wasted talent. They noted that it was possible the youth went on to use their talents in other pursuits, but did not have an explanation for this effect.[102] Based on their data, they pointed to a number of factors that allowed the talent of the students they studied to be realized, factors that echo the data presented in our overview of interest research. Csikszentmihalyi et al. reported the following as necessary for talented individuals to realize their talent:

- recognition of talent;
- ability to concentrate and be open to new experiences and habits, or self-regulation to think ahead, persist, and experience the rewards;
- support and challenge from families and teachers;
- resulting optimal experiences, or flow.

They implied that without the presence of most of these factors, it was likely that talent would be wasted.[103]

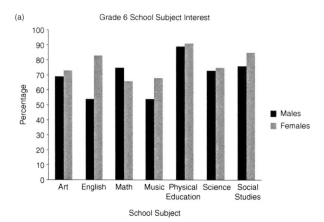

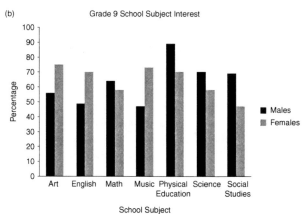

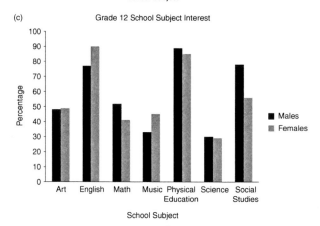

FIGURE 5.1 Percentage of Students Responding with Identified Interest for Each Subject, Cohort by Gender. Bars Depict Second Year Interest for Each Cohort.

Source: Renninger, Kensey, et al. (2015: 99).

Csikszentmihalyi et al.'s (1993) findings point to the importance of interactions with others and the environment more generally (e.g., the nature of the tasks, resources for learning), interactions that interest researchers have described as supports for triggering and sustaining interest.[104] Consider the data presented in Figure 5.1. They describe declines in the interests of students in grades 6, 9, and 12 from one working-class school district, as reported in Renninger, Kensey, et al. (2015). They showed the expected declines in interest in each of the different subjects from grade 6 through 12; however, they also indicated that within grade level, these declines vary by subject matter. This finding suggested that the students responded to their different classes on a subject-by-subject basis and that interest in some subjects increased; in other words, the students' interactions with each of the different subject matters varied and there were increases as well as decreases in their interest for the different subjects. The researchers' analysis of these data pointed to student perceptions of their classroom experiences (including instructional practices) as influencing their level of interest for their different subjects.

Kunter et al. (2007) pointed to students' perceptions of their classrooms as accounting for whether students' interest increases or decreases. They have suggested that students' responses to classrooms were related to their experiences—for example, whether they felt they understood what was expected of them or had a teacher who was responsive.[105] Renninger, Kensey, et al. (2015) reported similar findings in the case analyses that accompanied the presentation of Figure 5.1. They also noted that students with different levels of interest—even when matched on achievement—would describe the same flaws in instructional practices (e.g., a dry lecture), but they responded to them differently. The student with more developed interest focused on all of the information that was being addressed, whereas the student with less developed interest was not willing to even try to pay attention.

Concluding Thoughts

Given that interest requires some form of support, it may be that declines in interest are to be anticipated and are not paradoxical. The development of interest involves work on the part of the individual as well as others, such as the educator, parent, or employer. That is, a person needs support to want to work, to understand content, and to find working with content rewarding. This can involve interactions in which they think together with others about the content and/or the design and provision of tasks, activities, and opportunities.

Notes

1 Renninger (2009) has linked Harter's (2006) detailing of age-related shifts in the development of children's perceptions of others to the development of their identification with and phase of interest for particular content.

2 Interest-driven learning describes learning that is driven by interest that has already developed; it is most often referenced in online environments in which learners make a decision to continue to engage (see Barron et al. 2014; Gee 2004; Illeris 2007, Ito et al. 2010; Lammers et al. 2012).

In their *Interest-Driven Design Framework*, Edelson and Josephs (2004) conceptualized interest as a value, or belief, and the importance of utility in designing to support interest to develop, by which they meant supporting triggered and developed interest to continue to be sustained. This point is one Bergin (1999) made as well.

3 In discussing the educational role of the internet, Ben Greenman (September 16, 2010; www.nytimes.com/2010/09/19/magazine/19lives-t.html) concluded that in supplying answers to questions with ruthless efficiency, the Internet interrupted the "productive frustration" that results when questions ripen into genuine interest via deferral. Whereas Greenman did not explicitly discuss the distinction between curiosity and interest, he implicitly acknowledged the developmental aspect and importance of interest.

4 Steve's comments provide an example of how expectancies play an important role once a person has a developed interest, as described by expectancy-value theory in terms of utility, importance, task interest (liking) and its cost in relation to its benefit (see Eccles et al. 1983; Wigfield and Eccles 2002).

5 Renninger and Tibbetts 2010.

6 Interest in disciplinary content should not be confused with an interest in the grades associated with learning (or performing) the content, or with the potential of the content in question to garner entry to graduate study, a better job, and so forth. Such associated attainments may accompany the development of interest, but interest itself is content-specific.

7 It should be noted that support could also come from the way in which the laboratory experience was structured. Students with less developed interest in the discipline may need a more structured experience such as described in Chapter 4. In Chapter 6, we further discuss the importance of content for interest development.

8 Bergin 1999; see Renninger and Lipstein 2006, for description of data specific to this; see also Azevedo 2011, 2013a, 2013b.

9 Renninger 2009. See also discussions of the development of identification provided by Krapp (2005, 2007).

10 See Barron 2014; Gee 2004; Illeris 2007; Ito et al. 2010; Lammers et al. 2012; Renninger and Bishop in press.

11 Curwood et al. (2013) describe the fan-inspired writing and role-playing as transforming or extending elements of the movie (e.g., its characterization, themes, plot, and so forth).

12 See discussion in Bevan and Michalchik 2012.

13 Although they do not specify differences among students/participants based on interest as a consideration in describing how minimal guidance and/or inquiry is facilitated, both Kirschner et al. (2006) and Furtak et al. (2012) have provided analyses supporting the benefits of providing curricular structure based on student need; we would argue that interest research provides an explanation of why there are differences in students' needs. We note that Maltese and Harsh (2015), Renninger et al. (2014), and Renninger and Riley (2013) have specifically pointed to interest as a basis for this kind of curricular adjustment.

14 See Dohn 2011, 2013; Palmer 2004, 2009; Pressick-Kilborn 2015; Renninger 2010; Zahorick 1996.

15 See Hidi and Harackiewicz 2000; see also Illeris' (2007) discussion of the role and potential of resistance in learning.

16 Pugh and his colleagues (e.g., Pugh et al. 2010; Pugh et al. 2015) detail this type of transformational education and conceptual change in a series of papers. They attribute this kind of triggering to educator activity, although, as Renninger, Kensey et al. (2015) pointed out, it also can be provided either by the design of an exhibit, text, or task and/or

the self-generated triggering of interest based on a person's continued reflection on earlier trigger(s).

17 This overview does not duplicate but is intended to extend earlier reviews provided by Hidi and Renninger 2006; Hidi et al. 2015; Renninger and Hidi 2011; Renninger and Pozos-Brewer 2015; and Renninger and Su 2012.

18 We include findings from studies in which prior knowledge is studied together with value, or in which interest has been assessed as value.

19 For example, Bell and Sweet 1916. See more recent considerations in Fink 2015; Flippo 2014.

20 Baram-Tsabari 2015; Bathgate et al. 2013; Gutherie et al. 2006; Larson 2014a, 2014b.

21 Renninger et al. 2002; Schiefele 1999; Schiefele and Krapp 1996.

22 Tulis and Fulmer (2013) reported that perceived difficulty and reading fluency were predictors of declines in motivation to read and were particularly pronounced when participants began to read a text that they expected to be of interest based on its topic but found that it was difficult.

23 See discussions in Renninger 1992; Renninger et al. 2002; Larson 2014a, 2014b; Paige 2011.

24 For example, Jenkins 2009; see also New London Group 1996; Reid 2011.

25 For example, Hidi and Baird 1986, 1988.

26 For example, Mayer et al. 2008.

27 For example, Magner et al. 2014.

28 See reviews by Hidi 2001; Hidi and Berndorff 1998; and discussion in Magner et al. 2014.

29 For example, Dixon and Bortolussi 2013.

30 See reviews in Hidi 1995; Hidi and Berndorff 1998; Hidi 2001.

31 Garner et al. 1989; Garner et al. 1992; Wade 1992.

32 Magner et al. 2014.

33 Magner et al. (2014) studied interest as a value; however, they also included a measure of knowledge in their study. For purposes of the present discussion, we consider the students on whom they are reporting to have less developed interest if they have low interest and low prior knowledge, and those with high interest and more prior knowledge as having more developed interest.

34 Magner et al. (2014) continue to explain that by including an assessment of knowledge, they may be in a position to explain the mixed findings of seductive details described by Rey (2011). They write: "The appearance of the seductive details effect seems to be moderated by the level of the learners' prior knowledge. If students have a high prior knowledge level seductive details might not increase their working memory load to a critical level that hinders learning processes" (Magner et al. 2014: 149).

35 See Lipstein and Renninger 2007b; Renninger and Lipstein 2006.

36 Boscolo et al. 2007.

37 See Lipstein and Renninger 2007b; Renninger and Lipstein 2006.

38 See also Lenhart et al. 2008; Lipstein and Renninger 2007b; Magnifico 2012.

39 See Black 2008; Chandler-Olcott and Mahar 2003; Curwood et al. 2013; Lammers 2013; Thomas 2007.

40 See also Hidi and McLaren 1991.

41 Albin et al. 1996; Benton et al. 1995; Lipstein and Renninger 2007b.

42 Boscolo and Cisotto 1997.

43 Shao 2012; Zhang and Han 2012.

44 Aljumah 2012.

45 It should be noted that Zhang and Han (2012) employed a control group to demonstrate this effect; other studies have more typically focused only on participants' retrospective accounts.

46 Azmi 2013.

47 Shao 2012.

48 Zhang and Han 2012.
49 Aljumah 2012.
50 Mart 2012.
51 Rothwell 2011.
52 Mitchell and Elwood 2012; the interested reader is also pointed to Kayali's (2009) finding that students are positioned to learn about their own regions as a basis for instruction in geography.
53 See Lee 2007.
54 Gehlbach et al. 2008.
55 A more developed review of interest in each of the science domains is provided in Renninger and Talian (in press). For present purposes, the sciences are considered together, with acknowledgment that each differs from the other in addition to having overlap.
56 See Renninger, Nieswandt et al. 2015.
57 For example, Crouch and Heller 2014; Meredith and Redish 2013.
58 Crouch et al. 2013.
59 See Maltese and Tai 2010; Ohland et al. 2011.
60 Hannover and Kessels 2004; Kessels et al. 2006.
61 Bøe and Henriksen (2013) suggested that physics as a field takes pride in being interest-driven and also in being perceived as difficult and demanding. They observed that this circumstance has served to perpetuate a curricular structure and culture that could be retooled to enable access.
62 See related discussions in Hidi et al. 2015; Renninger, Kensey et al. 2015.
63 For example, Bong et al. 2015; Hoffmann 2002; Linnenbrink-Garcia, Pugh et al. 2012; Nieswandt 2007; see also review by Beier and Rittmayer 2008.
64 For example, Gutherie et al. 2006.
65 Larson 2014a.
66 See Bathgate et al. 2013.
67 For example, Baram-Tsabari 2015; Eccles et al. 1998; Glynn et al. 2015; Hoffmann 2002; Holstermann et al. 2012; Katz et al. 2006; Papastergiou 2008.
68 Hagay and Baram-Tsabari 2011.
69 See also Baram-Tsabari 2015.
70 See Dierking and Falk 2003; Geyer, et al. 2013; Marsh and Kleitman 2002; Schwan et al. 2014.
71 See Barron 2006; Barron et al. 2014; Ito et al. 2010; Lewalter et al. 2014.
72 Sahin 2013.
73 See Dierking and Falk 2003; Marsh and Kleitman 2002; Naizer et al. 2014.
74 Crouch et al. 2013; Hong and Lin-Siegler 2012; see also Reber et al. 2009.
75 Barrett et al. 2012.
76 Zimmerman et al. 2011.
77 Steinkuehler et al. 2011.
78 Hoffmann 2002.
79 It should be noted that interest in this research was studied using the Linnenbrink-Garcia et al. (2010) assessment of feelings and value. The clusters reported couple prior knowledge with this assessment of interest, suggesting that interpreting these findings as reflecting the reciprocity of interest and self-efficacy is appropriate.
80 An overview is also provided in Renninger, Nieswandt et al. 2015.
81 See also Cordova and Lepper 1996.
82 See www.carnegielearning.com (accessed August 20, 2015).
83 Fisher et al. 2012.
84 See also discussion in Harackiewicz et al. 2014.
85 Boal-Palheiros and Hargreaves 2001; Lamont et al. 2003.
86 Lamont et al. 2003.

87 See also Sloboda 1990, 2004; Sloboda and Davidson 1995; Sosniak 1985.
88 See also Bowles 1991; Marjoribanks and Mboya 2004; Sloboda 1990.
89 In this study, family background was defined in terms of both family social status and parents' aspirations.
90 Bowles 1991.
91 McMullen and Arnold 1976.
92 Manga address themes that may, for example, be political, religious, historical, or cultural. In contrast to the two-dimensional characteristics of the visual story in the comic books of other countries, manga includes elements that each have a set of rules concerning descriptions of an inside of the head and an outside of the head story.
93 Sun et al. 2008.
94 Chen et al. 2014.
95 Chen et al. 2001; Chen et al. 2006.
96 Zhu et al. 2009.
97 See discussions in Frenzel et al. 2012; Hidi 2000; Wigfield and Eccles 2002; Zimmerman and Kitsantas 1999.
98 See Bong et al. 2015; Frenzel et al. 2012.
99 Sloboda 1990, 1996, 2004; Sloboda and Davidson 1995.
100 See, for example, discussions in Hidi 2000; Frenzel et al. 2012; Wigfield and Eccles 2002; Zimmerman and Kitsantas 1999.
101 See Bouffard et al. 1998; Jacobs et al. 2002; Wigfield and Cambria 2010.
102 Barron et al. (2014) reported similar drift, or attrition, in the Digital Network Project, but it was limited and not on the same scale as that reported by Csikszentmihalyi et al. 1993.
103 See also Lamont et al. 2003.
104 Renninger and Hidi 2011.
105 See related discussions in Frenzel et al. 2010; Renninger, Kensey et al. 2015; Tsai et al. 2008.

6

DEVELOPING INTEREST

What can we now say about interest, its generation, and development?

What are the implications of knowing that interest can be developed?

What could further research help us to understand?

In this book we have explained that interest develops and that it needs support to develop. The research literature now allows us to provide the coherent explanation that earlier researchers like Allport (1946) and Berlyne (1949) were seeking, but one that was not yet within their reach. We focus on the dynamic and malleable aspects of interest and its potential to change in relation to a person's interactions with environment. Interest is grounded physiologically/ neurologically and has both affective and cognitive components. Research demonstrates that experiencing interest activates the reward circuitry and is therefore rewarding.

In describing Steve's willingness to work to unstick the blade in his kitchen blender (see Chapter 5), we explained that he saw an opportunity to continue to develop his understanding of how things work. This means that Steve needed no rewards other than acquiring new knowledge to work on unsticking the blade. We note, too, that Steve also had an interest in this type of problem-solving. When interest is triggered and sustained, people continue to seek information to develop their understanding. This helps explain the power of interest, not only for motivating engagement, but also for directing and sustaining attention, improving memory, and facilitating learning. Interest invigorates and is beneficial. It makes persistence feel effortless and increases the possibility of achievement and creative contributions. We have discussed how interest differs from other motivational variables. Our discussion confirms that the following three premises are essential to understanding the power of interest:

1.   Interest is a psychological state, and it is also a motivational predisposition to reengage with particular content that can develop.
2.   Making connections to content is essential for such development.
3.   The search for content, which is the basis of interest development, is rewarding.

The first premise is that interest is not a trait, a belief (although learners may have beliefs about their interests), or an emotion that results from cognitive appraisal. Interest is a motivational variable that can develop and is associated with a physiologically/neurologically grounded psychological state.[1] Interest has both emotional and cognitive components and is the outcome of interactions between a person and their environment. Affect is of particular importance in the triggering process, especially in the earlier phases of interest development. We note also that either negative or positive affect can trigger interest in these earlier phases. In later phases of interest development, affect is primarily positive and supports the corresponding development of knowledge and value.

It is critical to recognize that interest is not static but malleable, that it can be less and more developed, and that its development may need external support. Focusing on development allows us to also attend to and support the development of interest for those individuals who may presently have little interest. This approach differs from other approaches to research on interest that do not focus on its developmental aspects.[2]

The second premise is that connections between the individual and content are essential for interest to develop. Content supplies information that provides the basis for further information-seeking/searching to take place. Such connections are basic to interest development and, provided that they are sustained and developed, they lead to knowledge acquisition and the development of value. They have a strong impact on conceptual understanding, and result in increased learning.[3,4] Azevedo (2015), in his studies of interest-driven participation across formal and informal scientific settings, concluded that it is through sustained participation that a person finds "hooks" that enable them to continue to self-trigger and sustain their involvement. Such hooks for subsequent engagement can only develop when a person makes connections to content.

Risconscente (2014) demonstrated that focusing instructional practice on the development of content knowledge yields beneficial outcomes for students' interest, self-efficacy, and achievement. Based on extensive research, Durik et al. (2015) also concluded that learners have to focus on task content in order to develop interest. Perhaps no study in the field of interest research has shown the power of content-related interest more than Fink's (1998) investigation of prominent dyslexic professionals and Nobel Laureates. She reported that despite their perceptual disabilities, the well-developed interests of these individuals enabled them to persist in accurately comprehending difficult text, and to eventually achieve outstanding academic and professional success.

Finally, the third premise links searching for interesting information to the activation of the reward circuitry. It allows us to conclude that searching for content is intrinsically rewarding, a conclusion that does not undermine the role that interventions can play in supporting interest development, especially in its earlier phases. The link between interest and reward circuitry helps us explain why interest has a strong association with attention and memory, as neuroscientific researchers have demonstrated that rewards positively influence attention and memory processes. Investigations also have linked novelty to the activation of the reward circuitry, providing an explanation of why novelty is such an important aspect of triggering interest.[5]

Underlying the information that we have presented about the importance and beneficial effects of interest is the critical question of how to trigger and support interest to develop. Although interest development varies across domains and is idiosyncratic across individuals (see Chapter 5), there are at least six emerging issues and themes to which interest research points. We review each of these and provide some examples for purposes of illustration. Many of these examples are drawn from the classroom, as this is where much of the research has been conducted. However, as it should now be clear, these findings are likely to have implications that extend to other settings, because the presence of interest enhances the learning of all persons similarly, regardless of learning environment.

Emerging Issues and Themes

The Importance of Triggering and Maintaining Situational Interest

Hidi and Harackiewicz (2000) argued that one of the most critical issues in education concerns how interest can be generated to motivate academically unmotivated students. They urged educators and researchers to recognize the potential benefits of externally triggered situational interest.[6] This position is in contrast to the argument that "interest is not a quality waiting around to be excited from the outside."[7] Situational interest is not only relevant to academic interest development but also for interest development related to a wide range of other activities.

One of the first researchers who recognized the importance of situational interest was Mitchell (1993), who investigated how situational interest could be supported in classrooms. He reported that group work, computers, and puzzles triggered adolescents' situational interest in mathematics, whereas meaningfulness (personal relevance of the content) and involvement (the extent to which students were actively participating in the activity) tended to maintain situational interest. Another researcher who has acknowledged the importance of situational interest is Palmer (2004, 2009). He emphasized that multiple experiences of situational interest can develop into long-term interest. In his earlier study,[8] he found evidence that repeated experiences of situational interest in a college-level, science teaching methods class (e.g., hands-on activities, novelty, surprise, and group work) had positive effects on students' enjoyment of and motivation in science.[9]

Subsequently, Palmer (2009) examined the sources of situational interest in ninth-grade biology classrooms and reported that the main source of interest was novelty, although choice, physical activity, and social involvement were also implicated in the generation of interest. Similarly, Chen and colleagues' studies (e.g., Chen et al. 2001) of the cognitive demands in physical-education classes demonstrated that increased situational interest was related to learners' experiences of novelty, challenge, high attention demands, and exploration.[10] A web quest application in mathematics[11] and a web-based simulation in social studies[12] provide further confirmation of the central role of novelty in triggering and maintaining interest over time.

Flowerday and colleagues (e.g., Flowerday et al. 2004) have also documented the educational benefits of situational interest. In one study, their findings showed that situational interest fostered deeper learning, as indicated by better memory for main ideas as well as a more global understanding.[13] Based on a subsequent investigation, the researchers concluded that readers' situational interest—rather than topic interest or choice—promoted their engagement.[14] Furthermore, Baram-Tsabari (2015), whose studies demonstrate that information-seeking is an outcome of the triggering of situational interest, has explained that when students generate questions to which they expect answers, they are engaged and their interests develop.[15]

Educational interventions have begun to demonstrate how individual interest can be used to promote engagement and learning.[16] They also underscore that it is interest in the content that needs to be triggered and sustained, not just superficial connections to the content of one or another task or problem. For the plethora of academically unmotivated students, having support for triggering and maintaining situational interest may prove an effective solution.[17] However, the use of triggers should not simply elicit curiosity that is resolved by the closing of a knowledge gap, but instead should be related to content that yields ongoing inquiry and information search. Such triggers for interest (and complementary supports to increase self-efficacy) would enable learners to make the critical connections to content that are needed for interest to develop. For example, if a person is trying to support an unmotivated learner to start making connections to reading, and the trigger selected is a detective story, the student with less developed interest is likely to stop reading the moment that the killer's identity is revealed. In other words, the reader's knowledge gap is closed. If, instead, the trigger for reading involves a comprehensible (for that reader) and complex storyline with multiple characters, such as in the Harry Potter series, its age identification, intricate themes, and multiple complications of the plot are likely to lead to continued reading of the related text.

The Relevance of Early Childhood Experiences and Parental Support

Several chapters in Renninger et al.'s (2015b) edited volume *Interest in Mathematics and Science Learning* pointed to the importance of early childhood experiences for triggering and maintaining interest in the STEM disciplines.[18] Even though researchers who contributed to the volume were looking at mathematics and science education in particular, their findings have relevance for understanding supports for the development of interest in other domains. These investigators concluded that when young children's experiences include opportunities to engage and reengage with potential contents of interest and when there is support in the family (or the community) for taking up such opportunities, interest is likely to develop.[19] Alexander et al. (e.g., 2015) noted that as early as elementary school, children begin to self-regulate their interest in science in the course of their play.[20] The shift from adults assuming responsibility for young children's interest development to the children themselves beginning to seek out opportunities and resources is an important step in the development of interest.

As Renninger (2009) explained, developing interest prior to eight to ten years of age has benefits that include beginning to develop language related to content and experience working with it, before the person begins to start comparing the quality of his or her engagement with others'. Once such self–other comparisons begin to occur, educators, employers, and so forth should be aware that although interest can still be supported to develop, it is likely that a person will be engaging in self–other comparisions and will need additional support to develop a new interest. For example, support may be needed to discourage comparisons of the work involved in developing a new interest to the effortlessness that can characterize the continued development of already existing interests. Unaddressed, such comparison may preclude a new interest from developing. This situation has led some researchers to suggest that if domain-specific academic interests do not begin to develop by middle school, they become more difficult to trigger and sustain. However, there is always the possibility that a new or even an earlier interest that had waned can be triggered and supported to develop.[21]

The Facilitative Role Teachers Can Play in Supporting Interest Development

During the school years, teachers take over some of the support that parents provide for interest development in early childhood.[22] Triggering and maintaining interest in classrooms can be especially critical since students' motivation, interests, and attitudes toward school in general and towards specific subjects often decline (see Chapter 5). Teachers can make significant contributions to the motivation of their students. An educator's style, instructional technology, and organization of materials may all contribute to learners' interest and performance. For example, they can arrange tasks to actively engage learners, and such enhanced participation is likely to increase students' levels of interest.[23] Teachers can make required content personally meaningful and relevant; they can also include information that is novel, surprising, and complex. Since teachers plan and program curricula, they can improve instruction by sequencing and selecting tasks that enable learners to make and continue to develop their connections to content.[24] Researchers have also reported that human aspects, ethically controversial concepts, suspense, and choice may lead to more sustained student interest.[25]

Weighing the content that might be included to trigger and sustain student interest in relation to the content that has to be taught is often a central concern for educators. Lipstein and Renninger (2007a) summarized conditions that could support students to develop or deepen their interest and abilities to write, and concluded that classroom practices needed to balance the amount/type of guidance students "want" from their teachers with students' "needs" based on teachers' observations.[26] Furthermore, Lipstein and Renninger recommended that in addition to whole-class instruction, writing practices should include individualized feedback and small-group activities that are based on each student's phase of interest in writing.

A number of researchers have pointed to the important facilitating role teachers can have in supporting the development of their students' interest. For example, in interviews with over 250 musicians, Sloboda (1990; see also Chapter 5) found that their first music teacher was similarly described as a person who was friendly, encouraging, and able to convey their love of music (e.g., through modeling or playing an instrument well). Long and Murphy (2005) reported similar findings. Using qualitative and quantitative methods, they reported on the substantial impact of teachers' interests in both the subject matter they taught and in their students as individuals on their students' interest development. Xu et al. (2012) found that among the characteristics that distinguished the performance of the eight exemplary African American teachers they studied, three were related to interest: the teachers had a genuine interest in teaching, in their subject matter, and in providing scaffolds for their students' interest.

In the college classroom, Harackiewicz et al. (2008) found that when situational interest was triggered during an introductory psychology course, course selection seven semesters later could be predicted, regardless of whether the students had an interest in psychology before they started the introductory class. As the researchers noted, the effects of early situational interest and subsequent situational interest point to the importance of external supports for interest. They suggest that educators can influence performance and support interest development through situational interest. Finally, on the basis of a three-year study, Turner et al. (2014) reported that even though teachers can be facilitators of their students' engagement, they may need support themselves to recognize this.

The Benefits and Drawbacks of Working with Peers

With the increase of self–other comparisons that accompany the transition to adolescence, peer influence becomes an important factor. The role of group work has been found to contribute to interest development in several studies.[27] For example, Cartun et al. (2014) examined how peers shape interest development for youth in five geographically distributed sites of interest-powered learning: a youth program for documentary film-making; a school-based community service program; a school where students take such courses as game design, critical research, and entrepreneurship; an after-school program that offers work in the arts and humanities; and a teen program working on designing a new library space rich in technology. They found that peers facilitated access to the learning spaces and also that friendships were important in sustaining interest in activities.

Hidi et al. (1998) used a modified version of a cooperative learning tool called the Jigsaw technique to examine students' activities across formal and informal science education settings.[28] In a Jigsaw, students who are in small groups have opportunities to learn and become experts on a topic. Subsequently, they are encouraged to teach other students by sharing the knowledge they have acquired. The researchers predicted that the Jigsaw method would elicit situational interest in science exhibits in a science center by focusing students' attention and creating a social setting. The participants were sixth-graders, and the exhibits dealt with the topic of gravity. The results revealed dramatic differences between the Jigsaw and non-Jigsaw groups, both in time spent at various exhibits and in the students' emotional responses. Many children at this age have been reported to spend less than a minute per exhibits of this type; however, following the Jigsaw, the children spent ten minutes or more trying to become experts at their designated exhibits. In addition, the children provided positive, unique, and affective descriptions of their participation, suggesting that the activity had triggered and maintained their situational interest and had provided them with a sense of empowerment.

However, differences among students' phases of interest can complicate classroom teachers' plans, depending on the objective for the group work. For example, in their investigation of students' interest for writing, Lipstein and Renninger (2007a) found widespread dislike for peer conferences among students with more developed interest in writing if they were paired with students with less developed interest. Although some teachers had apparently grouped their students with good intentions (so that the students with more developed interest could help those with less developed interest), interviews with the students led the researchers to conclude that grouping in this way was "an unproductive strategy because students in different phases of interest conceive of writing differently and are not likely to be able to discuss their writing in a mutually beneficial way" (Lipstein and Renninger 2007a: 82). Lipstein and Renninger further suggested that pairing students in the same phase of interest for group work might have been more beneficial, as students paired in this way would be able to address each other on an equal level. Such a pairing would also allow the teacher to provide additional support to those with less developed interest in writing). These findings complicate thinking about the use of grouping for academic activities. They also suggest that consideration of students' phase of interest could help maximize the benefits of peer interactions.

The Shift from External to Internal Control and the Self-Generation of Interest

Age may be a critical factor in determining to what extent learners need external support to trigger and sustain their interest; however, the learners' phase of interest is also an important consideration. In their observations of Sam (who was briefly described in Chapter 4)—a middle-school student whose more developed interests included reading, soccer, and his friends—Renninger and Hidi (2002) described Sam's sustained abilities to work at and be challenged by situations that involved his interests. He did not need target goals to be set for him; rather, he seemed to be fluid in his abilities to set challenges for himself. He also reported that these activities felt effortless. However, Sam's involvement with a science project on the box turtle was unrelated to his interests and required support from others including his teacher, peers, and parents. Triggering and maintaining Sam's situational interest in science required considerable external effort and might not have succeeded at all if the turtle had not begun to hibernate, which caused Sam to think it had died under his watch. A major difference between Sam's developed interests and his triggered interest in keeping the turtle alive was his ability to generate questions and consider opportunities for improved performance; despite the triggering of his interest in the turtle, he was not able to engage in this kind of activity for the science project. As this study revealed, differences in Sam's abilities to self-regulate across activities are due to differences in his phase of interest, not his age.

As individuals move into adolescence and adulthood, it can be expected that they are increasingly able to self-generate or seek out ways for making connections to content to be learned. Sansone and colleagues have demonstrated that undergraduates were able to recognize their own boredom and develop strategies to make initially uninteresting tasks more interesting.[29] Subsequently, Sansone (2009) reported that such self-generation of interest was predictive of continued engagement. Others have also reported on the conditions that may facilitate the self-generation of interest (e.g., making connections to content, having time to explore).[30]

Harackiewicz et al. (2014) have pointed out that it is not always possible to support interest to develop by changing the content or the nature of the task or activity, but it is possible to alter the way students think about subjects such as mathematics or science, and this can lead to beneficial outcomes. That is, by changing student perceptions of the value (utility, relevance, importance) of the activities in which they engage, it may be possible for educators to increase students' interest. To investigate this position, Hulleman and Harackiewicz (2009) designed a study in which students were asked to write about the value of the content they are going to be learning.[31] More specifically, students were asked to provide explanations of how the course they were taking could be valuable for them, essentially asking them to self-generate interest by making connections between their own lives and the content of the course. Not surprisingly, this approach made an impact on interest in the course as well as student performance, especially for those who entered the course with less developed interest and low expectations of success. Future research might address how individuals could be trained to self-generate their interest in various academic subjects.

It is important that individuals can be supported to develop interest in content by having their interests triggered and maintained, even if no such interest has existed previously. It should also be noted that students whose interest is already developing may not need external intervention to the same degree as those with less interest; however, learners with more developed interest can benefit from challenge and opportunities to continue to develop what they know.

Choice and Interest Development

To evaluate choice as a source of interest development is not a simple matter.[32] On the one hand, choice has been viewed as the triggering of positive processes such as interest development. When individuals are allowed to make choices, they do not feel controlled and instead experience a sense of autonomy.[33] Some evidence even indicates that choice is rewarding.[34] On the other hand, individuals need to have enough knowledge to make informed choices, and lack of knowledge and uncertainty may negate any positive effect that choice would have on individuals' interest development.[35] Neuroscientific research also suggests that negative outcomes may occur when individuals are asked to make choices without relevant information; the brain may be alerted that such choices could have unknown and potentially dangerous outcomes.[36] Thus, it seems that choice can be either beneficial or detrimental depending on the conditions of the activity.[37]

Patall (2012) has provided a review of studies demonstrating that offering choices about aspects of tasks is most beneficial when individuals feel initial interest for the activity or when tasks are such that they can benefit from opportunities to build interest. However, giving learners choices about whether to engage in activities when they do not have enough content knowledge may impede the possibility that their interest could be triggered and may have detrimental consequences for the potential of developing their interest. For example, as Hidi et al. (2015) argued, it may be problematic to give students choices about whether they will continue taking subjects such as physics when they have had no prior formal exposure to physics. If students were required to take courses that they would not have chosen on their own, then their interest would have the possibility of being triggered by their instructors, the curriculum materials, and/or through interaction with others, resulting in beneficial outcomes.[38]

Future Research

We have provided information about how interest can be supported to develop through interactions with others and through the design of the environment. We have noted that interest can be developed for learners of all ages, across domains both in and out of school. However, such development is contingent on individuals making connections to the content of the domain.

We are now in a position to think about Berlyne's (1949) concerns regarding the measurement of interest and the distinction between interest and curiosity. Neuroscience enables us to clarify that interest and curiosity differ. We have proposed using these two terms in a way that meaningfully distinguishes them. Although the experiences of curiosity and of interest may both be rewarding, interest—unlike curiosity—is malleable, can be supported to develop, and is likely to lead to longer-term engagement. The experience of curiosity is triggered by a knowledge gap that once filled is unlikely to result in further searches of information, unless it is related to the person's individual interest. Being interested in a topic is not limited to looking for a specific answer, and typically involves continued information-seeking. Furthermore, description of curiosity as an aversive state does not characterize individuals who seek more information because they have an interest and want to know more about the content.

Interested individuals may also experience curiosity related to knowledge gaps, and knowledge gaps may lead to the triggering of interest. At the present time, we do not know what the differences are in how people experience curiosity if they have more or less interest for a question, idea, etc., related to their knowledge gap. Clarification of such differences could point to more effective ways for practitioners to work with both curiosity and interest in order to support interest to continue to develop. Future neuroscientific research could target the comparison of brain activation when seeking information to close a knowledge gap, when undertaking a more open-ended search for information related to earlier and later phases of interest, or when the two are related. Such comparisons would allow us to establish with certainty how curiosity and interest are related at the neurological level.

The developmental trajectory of the four-phase model provides behavioral indicators that can be used in the classroom, the workplace, or the office to identify (or assess) levels of interest. Recognizing (and assessing) the differences between earlier and later phases of a person's interest supplies information about how various activities may increase motivation and engagement in learning. If they have not already identified the phase of their students' (players', employees', etc.) interest, those responsible for facilitating learning and/or participation in many situations may find it beneficial to do so. The potential complication lies in ensuring the mapping of the indicators to different learning environments in such a way that researchers can compare findings.

Identifying the phase of a person's interest and then supporting it to develop can make the difference in terms of what is learned or accomplished. However, if the phase of a person's interest is misgauged, the teacher, parent, coach, employer, etc., could provide too much or too little information. Without enough information, a person may not ask questions that could provide clarification and continued triggering of an interest; the person could be overwhelmed by the task and frustrated, and it is possible that whatever interest the person did have would fall off. Similar problems would result if a person were provided with too much unrequested information (e.g., such as in lectures that are inappropriately organized, training sessions that are mismanaged, and staff meetings that are badly structured).

We have explained that as interest develops it is increasingly coordinated with other variables, such as self-efficacy, self-regulation, flow, grit, and identity. We suggest that each of these fields of motivational research might benefit from considering how the variables on which they focus could be affected by information about whether the participants they are studying have more or less developed interest. Not only would information from such studies help clarify the links between the different motivational variables and interest research theoretically, but it may also serve to explain anomalies in data. Recognizing the role (and potential implications) of phases of interest in these fields would benefit applications to practice. For example, Duhigg (2012) has suggested that people who want to change their habits must self-regulate: they need to identify the patterns in their behaviors that comprise their habits, if they want to change them. We have shown that being able to self-regulate is related to (and perhaps even contingent upon) the development of interest. If the educator, parent, or employer would like to support changed habits, considering whether the person with the habit has any interest in changed behavior, and/or determining how to first support the development of an interest, is likely to be improve the chances of success.

Similarly, Duckworth et al. (2007) developed a scale to assess the consistency of individuals' interest and their perseverance of effort, but they have not considered, for example, why students have grit in some contexts but not in others. According to the predictions of the four-phase model, we would expect grit to be significantly correlated with interest development. That is, as interest emerges, people persevere in their activities and develop related goals, suggesting that the link between grit and phases of interest could provide useful information about how grit develops and can be supported. That is, information about whether a person has more or less interest in a specific subject matter would suggest how grit might be most effectively supported to develop.

Flow is another, more focused, aspect of a person's experience whose precise relation to interest has not yet been established. In our conceptualization, flow is a possible outcome of a developing or well-developed interest. There is very little information about how the experience of flow could be supported to develop in academic settings. It does appear that if Csikszentmihalyi et al.'s (1993) study of talent development (discussed in Chapter 5) included a measure of students' interest following their identification of talent, and if the students' teachers had understood how to work with interest, the teachers might have been able to offset the observed "waste" of talent. The teachers would have needed to appreciate that a number of the students were very likely to have less developed interest for their area of identified talent initially. With support to develop their interest, it is likely that more of the students would have persevered.

The potential role of interest as a support for meaningful engagement has begun to be recognized, but no work has yet considered the implications of how interventions such as Check and Connect might work for learners with more or less interest for one or another field of study, or what the implications of starting with what the student is interested in as a basis of an intervention might be. Theoretically, this type of information would further develop understanding of interactions between the person and the environment, specifically the kinds of adjustments that can be made for learners who have differing levels of interest for disciplinary content, and their responses to features of the intervention.

There is also research on activation, affect, appraisal, personalization, play, purpose, relevance, and value in which the triggering and maintaining of interest could be targeted. The relation between interest and each of these variables is not fully understood, but would benefit both theory and practice.

Concluding Thoughts

In concluding, we note that we wrote this book for a wide range of individuals: researchers studying learning and motivation; individuals wanting to know more about the power of their own interests and how to develop them; educators and parents wondering how to facilitate motivation in students; business people focusing on ways to meaningfully engage their employees and associates; and policy-makers searching for ways to effect change in schools, out-of-school learning environments, industries, and businesses. We are certain that given the wide-ranging benefits of developing and/or developed interest, there is power for everyone in leveraging interest for motivation and engagement.

Notes

1 As we explained in the introduction, we acknowledge that the word "interest" is widely used to connote interest as an object (e.g., I have interest in mathematics, playing bridge, etc.). However, this meaning is not the focus of this book. We focus on how such interests develop and how they motivate individuals' activities, engagements, etc.
2 See discussion in Renninger and Hidi 2011.
3 See also Glynn et al. 2015.
4 In an important and controversial article that was cited close to 3,000 times, Kirschner et al. (2006) argued that minimally guided instruction (such as in discovery or constructivist learning) does not work for novice to intermediate learners because rejecting instruction based on facts, laws, principles, etc., that is, on the content of the subject matter, ignores human cognitive architecture in general and the importance of memory in specific. Although Kirchner et al. focused on the cognitive aspects of instruction, their argument corresponds to our position in considering the motivational aspects of instruction. Without exposure to content, interest may not develop.
5 See Hidi 2015 for a review of the neuroscientific literature related to the benefits of rewards, as well as their link to novelty.
6 Hidi and Harackiewicz (2000), in addition to pointing to the benefits of situational interest, argued for the potential benefits of extrinsic motivation and performance goals.
7 This quotation (cf. Schraw and Dennison 1994: 3) was attributed to Dewey by Garner et al. (1991).
8 Palmer 2004.
9 See Schraw and Dennison (1994) who described how various sources of situational interest in text affected perceived interest that, in turn, influenced recall.
10 Chen et al. 1999; Chen et al. 2001.
11 Halet 2008.
12 Gehlbach et al. 2008.
13 Flowerday and Schraw 2003.
14 Flowerday and Schraw 2003; Flowerday and Shell 2015.
15 Baram-Tsabari (2015) described a complex set of studies focusing on learners' questioning, which were conducted in the biology classroom, the online Ask-A-Scientist site, and through Google searches.
16 Barron et al. 2014; Knogler et al. 2015; Linnenbrink-Garcia, Patall et al. 2012; Paige 2012; Palmer 2009.
17 Flowerday and Shell (2015) noted that situational interest has been shown to increase reading comprehension, computer performance, and learning but does not affect shallow processing.
18 Ainley and Ainley 2015; Alexander et al. 2015; Crowley et al. 2015. See also Hidi et al. 2015.
19 Ainley and Ainley (2015) described young children's development of science interest as influenced by family support for opportunities to engage and reengage with contents of interest. Pinkard and Austin (2014) also provide detail about the context of learning that is the basis for the Digital Youth Network, and supports interest development.
20 Alexander et al. (2015) conducted a longitudinal study of young children's science interests. They reported shifting roles of parents and children in the development of science-related interests between pre-school and elementary school. The researchers concluded that parents exert greater influence earlier on, and that their values about the importance of education, science, etc., may create the foundation for their children's science interests to develop. During elementary-school years, however, children take on more responsibility by self-regulating for the maintanance of their science-related interests.
21 Maltese and Harsh 2015; Renninger, Kensey et al. 2015.

22 Wigfield et al. (1997) pointed to an association between children's interests and those of their teachers, across domains.
23 See Durik et al. 2015; Harackiewicz et al. 2014; Pressick-Kilbourn 2015.
24 Pressick-Kilbourn (2015) noted that teachers can make content personally meaningful and relevant by building in surprise, novelty, and complexity; they can also model both a sense of wonder about the content and ways to engage with it.
25 See Glynn et al. 2015; Neiswandt and Horowitz 2015.
26 See also Renninger and Lipstein 2006.
27 Mitchell 1993; Palmer 2004.
28 Slavin 1983, 1991.
29 Sansone et al. 1992; Sansone and Smith 2000.
30 Azevedo 2006; Harackiewicz et al. 2014; Renninger et al. 2014.
31 See also Hulleman, Godes et al. 2010.
32 See Patall et al. (2008) for a very competent meta-analysis of the effects of choice on various aspects of motivation.
33 Ryan and Deci 2012.
34 Leotti and Delgado (2011) reported that choice was associated with increased activity in part of the reward circuitry (ventral striatum), suggesting that choice may function as a reward. However, Murayama et al.'s (2015) findings did not replicate these results as in their study the activation of the prefrontal cortex rather than the striatum was associated with choice.
35 Hidi et al. 2015; Katz and Assor 2007.
36 Hsu et al. 2005; Hidi 2015.
37 See Iyengar and Lepper 1999; Patall 2012; Patall et al. 2008.
38 Azevedo (2015) descibes tailored practice as resulting from the presence of structures that are in place to support development. Requirements for course participation may be necessary to support development.

REFERENCES

Adcock, R. A., A. Thangavel, S. Whitfield-Gabrieli, B. Knutson, and J. D. E. Gabrieli (2006) "Reward-Motivated Learning: Mesolimbic Activation Precedes Memory Formation," *Neuron*, 50 (3): 507–517.

Ainley, M. (1987) "The Factor Structure of Curiosity Measures: Breadth and Depth of Interest Curiosity Styles," *Australian Journal of Psychology*, 39 (1): 53–59.

Ainley, M. (1998) "Interest in Learning and the Disposition of Curiosity in Secondary Students: Investigating Process and Context," in L. Hoffman, A. Krapp, K. A. Renninger, and J. Baumert (eds), *Interest and Learning*, Kiel, Germany: IPN, pp. 257–266.

Ainley, M. (2007) "Being and Feeling Interested: Transient State, Mood, and Disposition," in P. Schutz and R. Pekrun (eds), *Emotion in Education*, New York, NY: Elsevier, pp. 141–157.

Ainley, M. (2012) "Students' Interest and Engagement in Classroom Activities," in S. L. Christenson, A. L. Reschly, and C. Wylie (eds), *Handbook of Research on Student Engagement*, New York, NY: Springer, pp. 283–302.

Ainley, M., and J. Ainley (2011) "Learner Engagement with Science in Early Adolescence: The Contribution of Enjoyment to Learners' Continuing Interest in Learning about Science," *Contemporary Educational Psychology*, 36 (1): 4–12.

Ainley, M., and J. Ainley (2015) "Early Science Learning Experiences: Triggered and Maintained Interest," in K. A. Renninger, M. Nieswandt, and S. Hidi (eds), *Interest in Mathematics and Science Learning*, Washington, DC: American Educational Research Association, pp. 17–31.

Ainley, M., and S. Hidi, (2014) "Interest and Enjoyment," in R. Pekrun and L. Linnenbrink-Garcia (eds), *The International Handbook of Emotions in Education*, New York, NY: Taylor & Francis, pp. 205–227.

Ainley, M., S. Hidi, and D. Berndorff (2002) "Interest, Learning, and the Psychological Processes that Mediate Their Relationship," *Journal of Educational Psychology*, 94 (3): 545–561.

Albin, M. L., S. L. Benton, and I. Khramtsova (1996) "Individual Differences in Interest and Narrative Writing," *Contemporary Educational Psychology*, 21 (4): 305–324.

Alexander, J. M., K. E. Johnson, and M. E. Liebham (2015) "Emerging Individual Interest Related to Science in Young Children," in K. A. Renninger, M. Nieswandt, and S.

Hidi (eds), *Interest in Mathematics and Science Learning*, Washington, DC: American Educational Research Association, pp. 261–279.

Alexander, P. A. (1997) "Mapping the Multidimensional Nature of Domain Learning: The Interplay of Cognitive, Motivational, and Strategic Forces," in M. L. Maehr and P. R. Pintrich (eds), *Advances in Motivation and Achievement*, 10 vols., Greenwich, CT: JAI Press, vol. X, pp. 213–250.

Alexander, P. A., and P. K. Murphy (1998) "Profiling the Differences in Students' Knowledge, Interest, and Strategic Processing," *Journal of Educational Psychology*, 90 (3): 435–447.

Alexander, P. A., T. L. Jetton, and J. M. Kulikowich (1995) "Interrelationship of Knowledge, Interest, and Recall: Assessing a Model of Domain Learning," *Journal of Educational Psychology*, 87 (4): 559–575.

Aljumah, H. F. (2012) "Saudi Learner Perceptions and Attitudes Towards the Use of Blogs in Teaching English Writing Course for EFL Majors at Qassim University," *English Language Teaching*, 5 (1): 100–116.

Allport, G. W. (1946) "Effect: A Secondary Principle of Learning," *Psychological Review*, 53 (6): 335–347.

Ames, C. (1992) "Classrooms: Goals, Structures, and Student Motivation," *Journal of Educational Psychology*, 84 (3): 261–271.

Ames, C., and J. Archer (1988) "Achievement Goals in the Classroom: Students' Learning Strategies and Motivation Processes," *Journal of Educational Psychology*, 80 (10): 260–267.

Anderson, B. A., P. A. Laurent, and S. Yantis (2011) "Value-Driven Attentional Capture," *Proceedings of the National Academy of Sciences USA*, 108 (25): 10367–10371.

Anderson, R. C. (1982) "Allocation of Attention during Reading," in A. Flammer and W. Kintsch (eds), *Discourse Processing*, Amsterdam, The Netherlands: North-Holland, pp. 292–335.

Anderson, R. C., L. L. Shirey, P. T. Wilson, and L. G. Fielding (1987) "Interestingness of Children's Reading Material," in R. E. Snow and M. J. Farr (eds), *Aptitude, Learning, and Instruction*, vol. III: *Cognitive and Affective Process Analyses*, Hillsdale, NJ: Erlbaum, pp. 287–299.

Andre, T., and M. Windschitl (2003) "Interest, Epistemological Belief, and Intentional Conceptual Change," in G. Sinatra and P. Pintrich, (eds), *Intentional Conceptual Change*, Mahwah, NJ: Erlbaum, pp. 173–193.

Appleton, J. J. (2012) "Systems Constellation: Developing the Assessment-to-Intervention Link with the Student Engagement Instrument," in S. L. Christenson, A. L. Reschly, and C. Wylie (eds), *Handbook of Research on Student Engagement*, New York, NY: Springer, pp. 725–741.

Appleton, J. J., S. L. Christenson, and M. J. Furlong (2008) "Student Engagement with School: Critical Conceptual and Methodological Issues of the Construct," *Psychology in the Schools*, 45 (5): 369–386.

Arnold, F. (1910) *Attention and Interest: A Study in Psychology and Education*, New York, NY: Macmillan.

Azevedo, F. S. (2006) "Personal Excursions: Investigating the Dynamics of Student Engagement," *International Journal of Computers for Mathematical Learning*, 11 (1): 57–98.

Azevedo, F. S. (2011) "Lines of Practice: A Practice-Centered Theory of Interest Relationships," *Cognition and Instruction*, 29 (2): 147–184.

Azevedo, F. S. (2013a) "The Tailored Practice of Hobbies and Its Implication for the Design of Interest-Based Learning Environments," *The Journal of the Learning Sciences*, 22 (3): 462–510.

Azevedo, F. S. (2013b) "Knowing the Stability of Model Rockets: An Investigation of Learning in Interest-Based Practices," *Cognition and Instruction*, 31 (3): 345–374.

Azevedo, F. S. (2015) "Sustaining Interest-Based Participation in Science," in K. A. Renninger, M. Nieswandt, and S. Hidi (eds), *Interest in Mathematics and Science Learning*, Washington, DC: American Educational Research Association, pp. 281–296.

Azmi, N. (2013) "Multi-sensory Delivery in EFL 'Smart' Classrooms: Students' Perceptions of Benefits, Limitations and Challenges," *Journal of Educational and Social Research*, 3 (1): 33–41.

Baldwin, B. T. (1910) "Review of the Book *Attention and Interest: A Study in Psychology and Education*, by F. Arnold," *The Elementary School Teacher*, 10 (10): 519–520.

Bandura, A. (1977) *Social Learning Theory*, New York, NY: General Learning Corporation.

Bandura, A. (1997) *Self-Efficacy: The Exercise of Control*, New York, NY: Freeman.

Bandura, A., and D. H. Schunk (1981) "Cultivating Competence, Self-Efficacy and Intrinsic Interest through Proximal Self-Motivation," *Journal of Personality and Social Psychology*, 41 (3): 586–598.

Baram-Tsabari, A. (2015) "Promoting Information Seeking and Questioning in Science," in K. A. Renninger, M. Nieswandt, and S. Hidi (eds), *Interest in Mathematics and Science Learning*, Washington, DC: American Educational Research Association, pp. 135–152.

Barrett, M. S., and H. M. Smigiel (2007) "Children's Perspectives of Participation in Music Youth Arts Settings: Meaning, Value and Participation," *Research Studies in Music Education*, 28 (1): 39–50.

Barrett, S. E., Z. Hazari, B. Fatholahzadenh, and D. M. Harrison (2012) "Electromagnetism Unit of an Introductory University Physics Course: The Influence of a Reform-Based Tutorial," *Journal of College Science Teaching*, 41 (6): 40–46.

Barron, B. (2006) "Interest and Self-Sustained Learning as Catalysts of Development: A Learning Ecology Perspective," *Human Development*, 49 (4): 193–224.

Barron, B. (2014) "Advancing Research on the Dynamics of Interest-Driven Learning," in B. Barron, K. Gomez, N. Pinkard, and C. K. Martin (eds), *The Digital Youth Network: Cultivating Digital Media Citizenship in Urban Communities*, Cambridge, MA: MIT Press, pp. 285–296.

Barron, B., K. Gomez, N. Pinkard, and C. Martin (2014) *The Digital Youth Network: Cultivating Digital Media Citizenship in Urban Communities*, Cambridge, MA: MIT Press.

Barron, B., C. Kennedy-Martin, L. Takeuchi, and R. Fithian (2009) "Parents as Learning Partners in the Development of Technological Fluency," *International Journal of Learning and Media*, 1 (2): 55–77.

Bartlett, F. C. (1932) *Remembering: A Study in Experimental and Social Psychology*. London, UK: Cambridge University Press.

Bathgate, M. E., C. D. Schunn, and R. Correnti (2013) *Children's Motivation toward Science across Contexts, Manner of Interaction, and Topic*, Pittsburgh, PA: Wiley.

Becher, T., and P. R. Trowler (2001) *Academic Tribes and Territories: Intellectual Enquiry and the Cultures of Disciplines*, 2nd edn, Buckingham, UK: Open University Press/SRHE.

Bell, J. C., and I. B. Sweet (1916) "Communications and Discussions: The Reading Interests of High School Pupils," *Journal of Educational Psychology*, 7 (2): 39–45.

Benton, S. L., A. J. Corkill, J. M. Sharp, R. G. Downey, and I. Khramtsova (1995) "Knowledge, Interest, and Narrative Writing," *Journal of Educational Psychology*, 87 (1): 66–79.

Bergin, D. (1999) "Influences on Classroom Interest," *Educational Psychologist*, 34 (2): 87–98.

Berlyne, D. E. (1949) "Interest as a Psychological Concept," *British Journal of Psychology*, 39 (4): 184–195.

Berlyne, D. E. (1960) *Conflict, Arousal, and Curiosity*, New York, NY: McGraw-Hill.

Berlyne, D. E. (1966) "Curiosity and Exploration," *Science*, 1: 25–33.

Berlyne, D. E. (1978) "Curiosity and Learning," *Motivation and Emotion*, 2 (2): 97–175.

Berlyne, D. E. and J. L. Lewis (1963) "Effects of Heightened Arousal on Human Exploratory Behaviour," *Canadian Journal of Psychology/Revue Canadienne de Psychologie*, 17 (4): 398.

Berridge, K. C. (2012) "From Prediction Error to Incentive Salience: Mesolimbic Computation of Reward Motivation," *European Journal of Neuroscience*, 35 (7): 1124–1143.

Berridge, K. C., and T. E. Robinson (1998) "What Is the Role of Dopamine in Reward: Hedonic Impact, Reward Learning, or Incentive Salience?" *Brain Research Reviews*, 28 (3): 309–369.

Berridge, K. C., T. E. Robinson, and J. W. Aldridge (2009) "Dissecting Components of Reward: 'Liking,' 'Wanting,' and Learning," *Current Opinion in Pharmacology*, 9 (1): 65–73.

Bevan, B., and V. Michalchik (2012) "Out-of-School Time STEM: It's Not What You Think," in B. Bevan, P. Bell, R. Stevens, and A. Razfar (eds), *LOST Opportunities: Learning in Out-of-School Time*, New York, NY: Springer, pp. 201–217.

Bjork, J. M., and D. W. Hommer (2007) "Anticipating Instrumentally Obtained and Passively-Received Rewards: A Factorial FMRI Investigation," *Behavioural Brain Research*, 177 (1): 165–170.

Black, R. W. (2008) *Adolescents and Online Fan Fiction*, New York, NY: Peter Lang.

Boal-Palheiros, G. M., and D. J. Hargreaves (2001) "Listening to Music at Home and at School," *British Journal of Music Education*, 18 (2): 103–118.

Boe, M. V., and E. K. Henriksen (2013) "Love it or Leave it: Norwegian Students' Motivations and Expectations for Postcompulsory Physics," *Science Education*, 97 (4): 550–573.

Boekaerts, M. (1997) "Self-Regulated Learning: A New Concept Embraced by Researchers, Policy Makers, Educators, Teachers, and Students," *Learning and Instruction*, 7 (2): 161–186.

Boekaerts, M. (2006) "Self-Regulation and Effort Investment," in R. Lerner and W. Damon (eds), *Handbook of Child Psychology*, 4 vols., 6th edn, New York, NY: Wiley, vol. IV, pp. 345–377.

Bong, M., and E. M. Skaalvik (2003) "Academic Self-Concept and Self-Efficacy: How Different Are They Really?" *Educational Psychology Review*, 15 (1): 1–40.

Bong, M., S. K. Lee, and Y.-K. Woo (2015) "The Role of Interest and Self-Efficacy in Pursuing Mathematics and Science," in K. A. Renninger, M. Nieswandt, and S. Hidi (eds), *Interest in Mathematics and Science Learning*, Washington, DC: American Educational Research Association, pp. 33–48.

Boscolo, P., and L. Cisotto (1997) "Making Writing Interesting in Elementary School," paper presented at the 7th bi-annual meeting of the European Association for Research on Learning and Instruction, Athens, Greece.

Boscolo, P. and L. Mason (2001) "Writing to Learn, Writing to Transfer," in P. Tynjälä, L. Mason, and K. Lonka (eds), *Writing as a Learning Tool: Integrating Theory and Practice*, Dordrecht, The Netherlands: Springer, pp. 83–104.

Boscolo, P., L. Del Favero, and M. Borghetto (2007) "Writing on an Interesting Topic: Does Writing Foster Interest?" in S. Hidi and P. Boscolo (eds), *Writing and Motivation*, New York, NY: Elsevier, pp. 73–91.

Bouffard, T., H. Markovits, C. Vezeau, M. Boisvert, and C. Dumas (1998) "The Relation between Accuracy of Self-Perception and Cognitive Development," *British Journal of Educational Psychology*, 68 (3): 321–330.

Bowles, C. L. (1991) "Self-Expressed Adult Music Education Interests and Music Experiences," *Journal of Research in Music Education*, 39 (3): 191–205.

Bruner, J. S. (1966) *Toward a Theory of Instruction*, Cambridge, MA: Belknap Press.

Bunzeck, N., P. Dayan, R. J. Dolan, and E. Duzel (2010) "A Common Mechanism for Adaptive Scaling of Reward and Novelty," *Human Brain Mapping*, 31 (9): 1380–1394.

Bunzeck, N., C. F. Doeller, L. Fuentemilla, R. J. Dolan, and E. Duzel (2009) "Reward Motivation Accelerates the Onset of Neural Novelty Signals in Humans to 85 Milliseconds," *Current Biology*, 19 (15): 1294–1300.

Byman, R. (2005) "Curiosity and Sensation Seeking: A Conceptual and Empirical Examination," *Personality and Individual Differences*, 38 (6): 1365–1379.

Cabot, I. (2012) "Le Cours collégial de mise à niveau en français: l'incidence d'un dispositive pédagogique d'interdisciplinarité," doctoral thesis, University of Montreal.

Carmichael, C., R. Callingham, I. Hay, and J. Watson (2010) "Measuring Middle School Students' Interest in Statistical Literacy," *Mathematics Education Research Journal*, 22 (3): 9–39.

Cartun, A., B. Kirshner, E. Price, and A. J. York (2014) "Friendship, Participation, and Site Design in Interest-Driven Learning among Early Adolescents," paper presented at the Proceedings of the 11th International Conference of the Learning Sciences, Boulder, CO.

Chandler-Olcott, K., and D. Mahar (2003) "Adolescents' Anime-Inspired 'Fanfictions': An Exploration of Multiliteracies," *Journal of Adolescent & Adult Literacy*, 46 (7): 556–566.

Chazan, D. (2000) *Beyond Formulas in Mathematics and Teaching: Dynamics of the High School Algebra Classroom*, New York, NY: Teachers College Press.

Chen, A., P. W. Darst, and R. P. Pangrazi (1999) "What Constitutes Situational Interest? Validating a Construct in Physical Education," *Measurement in Physical Education and Exercise Science*, 3 (3): 157–180.

Chen, A., P. W. Darst, and R. P. Pangrazi (2001) "An Examination of Situational Interest and Its Sources," *British Journal of Educational Psychology*, 71 (3): 383–400.

Chen, A., C. D. Ennis, R. Martin, and H. Sun (2006) "Situational Interest: A Curriculum Component Enhancing Motivation to Learn," in S. N. Hogan (ed.), *New Developments in Learning Research*, Hauppauge, NY: Nova Science Publishers, Inc., pp. 235–261.

Chen, S., H. Sun, X. Zhu, and A. Chen (2014) "Relationship between Motivation and Learning in Physical Education and After-School Physical Activity," *Research Quarterly for Exercise and Sport*, 85 (4): 468–477.

Chi, M. T. H., M. Bassok, M. W. Lewis, P. Reimann, and R. Glaser (1989) "Self-Explanations: How Students Study and Use Examples in Learning to Solve Problems," *Cognitive Science*, 13 (2): 145–182.

Chi, M. T. H., N. De Leeuw, M. H. Chiu, and C. Lavancher (1994) "Eliciting Self-Explanations Improves Understanding," *Cognitive Science*, 18 (3): 439–477.

Christenson, S. L., and A. L. Reschly (2010) "Check and Connect: Enhancing School Completion through Student Engagement," in B. Doll, W. Pfohl, and J. Yoon (eds), *Handbook of Youth Prevention Science*, London and New York, NY: Routledge, pp. 327–348.

Christenson, S. L., A. L. Reschly, and C. Wylie (2012a) "Epilogue," in S. L. Christenson, A. L. Reschly, and C. Wylie, (eds), *Handbook of Research on Student Engagement*, New York, NY: Springer, pp. 813–817.

Christenson, S. L., A. L. Reschly, and C. Wylie (eds) (2012b) *Handbook of Research on Student Engagement*, New York, NY: Springer.

Christiana, R. W., M. Davis, and M. Freeman (2014) "'I'd Rather Dance Outside': A Phenomenological Examination of Youth Experiences in Outdoor, Noncompetitive Physical Activity," *The Qualitative Report*, 19 (46): 1–16.

Claparède, E. (1905) *Psychologie de l'enfant et pétagogie expérimentale*, Geneva, Switzerland: Kundig.

Cordova, D. I., and M. R. Lepper (1996) "Intrinsic Motivation and the Process of Learning: Beneficial Effects of Contextualization, Personalization, and Choice," *Journal of Educational Psychology*, 88 (4): 715–730.

Costa, P. T., and R. R. Mccrae (1992) "Four Ways Five Factors Are Basic," *Personality and Individual Differences*, 13 (6): 653–665.

Crouch, C. H., and K. Heller (2014) "Introducing Physics in Biological Context: An Approach to Improve Introductory Physics for Life Science Students," *American Journal of Physics*, 82 (5): 378–386.

Crouch, C. H., P. Wisittanawat, and K. A. Renninger (2013) "Initial Interest, Goals, and Changes in CLASS Scores in Introductory Physics for Life Sciences," in P. Engelhardt (ed.), *Proceedings of the Physics Education Research Conference*, Melville, NY: AIP, pp. 105–108.

Crowley, K., B. J. Barron, K. Knutson, and C. Martin (2015) "Interest and the Development of Pathways to Science," in K. A. Renninger, M. Nieswandt, and S. Hidi (eds), *Interest in Mathematics and Science Learning*, Washington, DC: American Educational Research Association, pp. 297–314.

Csikszentmihalyi, M. (1990) *Flow: The Psychology of Optimal Experience*, New York, NY: Harper & Row.

Csikszentmihalyi, M. (2014) *Flow and the Foundations of Positive Psychology: The Collected Works of Mihaly Csikszentmihalyi*, New York, NY: Springer.

Csikszentmihalyi, M., K. Rathunde, and S. Whalen (1993) *Talented Teenagers: The Roots of Success and Failure*, Cambridge, UK: Cambridge University Press.

Curwood, J. S., A. M. Magnifico, and J. C. Lammers (2013) "Writing in the Wild: Writers' Motivation in Fan-Based Affinity Spaces," *Journal of Adolescent and Adult Literacy*, 56 (8): 677–685.

Dawson, C. J. (2000) "Upper Primary Boys and Girls Interests in Science: Have They Changed Since 1980?" *International Journal of Science Education*, 22 (6): 557–570.

Day, H. I. (1982) "Curiosity and the Interested Explorer," *Performance and Instruction*, 21 (4): 19–22.

Deci, E. L. (1975) *Intrinsic Motivation*, New York, NY: Plenum Press.

Deci, E. L., and R. M. Ryan (2000) "Motivation, Personality, and Development within Embedded Social Contexts: An Overview of Self-Determination Theory," in R. M. Ryan (ed.), *The Oxford Handbook of Human Motivation*, Oxford, UK: Oxford University Press, pp. 85–107.

Denissen, J. H., N. R. Zarrett, and J. S. Eccles (2007) "I Like to Do It, I'm Able, and I Know I Am: Longitudinal Couplings between Domain-Specific Achievement, Self-Concept, and Interest," *Child Development*, 78 (2): 430–447.

Dewey, J. (1902) *The Child and the Curriculum*, Chicago, IL: University of Chicago Press.

Dewey, J. (1913) *Interest and Effort in Education*, Cambridge, MA: Houghton Mifflin.

Dewey, J. (1933) *How We Think*, New York, NY: D. C. Heath.

Dierking, L. D., and J. H. Falk (2003) "Optimizing Out-of-School Time: The Role of Free-Choice Learning," *New Directions for Youth Development*, 97: 75–88.

Dierking, L. D., J. H. Falk, N. Status, W. Penuel, J. Wyld, and D. Bailey (2014) "Measuring Children's STEM (Science, Technology, Engineering and Mathematics) Interest Development Longitudinally: The Synergies Understanding and Connecting STEM Learning in the Community Project," poster presented at Current Approaches to Interest Measurement: Meeting of the American Educational Research Association, April, Philadelphia, Pa.

Dixon, P., and M. Bortolussi (2013) "Construction, Integration, and Mind Wandering in Reading," *Canadian Journal of Experimental Psychology*, 67 (1): 1–10.

Dohn, N. B. (2011) "Situational Interest of High School Students Who Visit an Aquarium," *Science Education*, 95 (2): 337–357.

Dohn, N. B. (2013) "Situational Interest in Engineering Design Activities," *International Journal of Science Education*, 35 (12): 2057–2078.

Duckworth, A. L., C. Peterson, M. D. Matthews, and D. R. Kelly (2007) "Grit: Perseverance and Passion for Long-Term Goals," *Journal of Personality and Social Psychology*, 92 (6): 1087–1101.

Duhigg, C. (2012) *The Power of Habit: Why We Do What We Do in Life and Business*, New York, NY: Random House.

Duit, R., and D. F. Treagust (2003) "Conceptual Change: A Powerful Framework for Improving Science Teaching and Learning," *International Journal of Science Education*, 25 (6): 671–688.

Durik, A. M., and J. M. Harackiewicz (2003) "Achievement Goals and Intrinsic Motivation: Coherence, Concordance, and Achievement Orientation," *Journal of Experimental Social Psychology*, 39 (4): 378–385.

Durik, A. M., and J. M. Harackiewicz (2007) "Different Strokes for Different Folks: How Individual Interest Moderates the Effects of Situational Factors on Task Interest," *Journal of Educational Psychology*, 99 (3): 597–610.

Durik, A. M., S. Hulleman, and J. M. Harackiewicz (2015) "One Size Fits Some: Instructional Enhancements to Promote Interest," in K. A. Renninger, M. Nieswandt, and S. Hidi (eds), *Interest in Mathematics and Science Learning*, Washington, DC: American Educational Research Association, pp. 49–62.

Durik, A., O. G. Shechter, M. Noh, C. S. Rozek, and J. Harackiewicz (2014) "What If I Can't? Success Expectancies Moderate the Effects of Utility Value Information on Situational Interest," *Motivation and Emotion*, 39 (1): 104–118.

Dweck, C. S. (1986) "Motivational Processes Affecting Learning," *American Psychologist*, 41 (10): 1040–1048.

Dweck, C. S. (2002) "The Development of Ability Conceptions," in A. Wigfield and J. Eccles (eds), *Development of Achievement Motivation*, San Diego, CA: Academic Press, pp. 57–88.

Eastwood, J. D., A. Frischen, M. J. Fenske, and D. Smilek (2012) "The Unengaged Mind: Defining Boredom in Terms of Attention," *Perspectives on Psychological Science*, 7 (5): 482–495.

Ebbinghaus, H. (1885) *Memory: A Contribution to Experimental Psychology*, New York, NY: Dover.

Eccles, J. S., and A. Wigfield (1995) "In the Mind of the Achiever: The Structure of Adolescents' Academic Achievement Related Beliefs and Self-Perceptions," *Personality and Social Psychology Bulletin*, 21 (3): 215–225.

Eccles, J. S., T. F. Adler, R. Futterman, S. B. Goff, C. M. Kaczala, J. Meece, and C. Midgley (1983) "Expectancies, Values and Academic Behaviors," in J. T. Spence (ed.), *Achievement and Achievement Motives: Psychological and Sociological Approaches*, San Francisco, CA: Freeman, pp. 75–146.

Eccles, J. S., J. A. Fredricks, and A. Epstein (2015) "Understanding Well-Developed Interests and Activity Commitment," in K. A. Renninger, M. Nieswandt, and S. Hidi (eds), *Interest in Mathematics and Science Learning*, Washington, DC: American Educational Research Association, pp. 315–330.

Eccles, J. S., A. Wigfield, R. D. Harold, and P. Blumenfeld (1993) "Age and Gender Differences in Children's Self-and Task Perceptions during Elementary School," *Child Development*, 64 (3): 830–847.

Eccles, J. S., A. Wigfield, and U. Schiefele (1998) "Motivation to Succeed," in W. Damon and N. Eisenberg (eds), *Handbook of Child Psychology*, 5th edn, vol. III: *Social, Emotional, and Personality Development*, New York, NY: Wiley, pp. 1017–1095.

Edelson, D. C., and D. M. Josephs (2004) "The Interest Driven Learning Design Framework: Motivating Learning Through Usefulness," *ICLS 2004: Embracing Diversity in the Learning Sciences*: Proceedings of the 6th international conference on Learning sciences: 166–173.

Ekeland, C. B., and I. T. Dahl (2015) "Hunting the Light Tourism on Board the Coastal Steamer *Hurtigruten*: A Cross-Disciplinary Triangulation Approach to the Dynamics of Interest," unpublished manuscript, Department of Tourism, Uit the Arctic University of Norway.

Ely, R., M. Ainley, and J. Pearce (2013) "More Than Enjoyment: Identifying the Positive Affect Component of Interest that Supports Student Engagement and Achievement," *Middle Grades Research Journal*, 8 (1): 13–32.

Ernst, M., and L. P. Spear (2009) "Reward Systems," in M. De Haan and M. R. Gunnar (eds), *Handbook of Developmental Social Neuroscience*, New York, NY: Guilford, pp. 324–341.

Espay, A. J., M. M. Norris, J. C. Eliassen, A. Dwivedi, M. S. Smith, C. Banks et al. (2015) "Placebo Effect of Medication Cost in Parkinson Disease: A Randomized Double-Blind Study," *Neurology*, 84 (8): 794–802.

Falk, J. H., and L. M. Adelman (2003) "Investigating the Impact of Prior Knowledge and Interest on Aquarium Visitor Learning," *Journal of Research in Science Teaching*, 40 (2): 163–176.

Fareri, D. S., L. N. Martin, and M. R. Delgado (2008) "Reward-Related Processing in the Human Brain: Developmental Considerations," *Development and Psychopathology*, 20 (4): 1191–1211.

Fenker, D. B., J. U. Frey, H. Schuetze, D. Heipertz, H. J. Heinze, and E. Duzel (2008) "Novel Scenes Improve Recollection and Recall of Words," *Journal of Cognitive Neuroscience*, 20 (7): 1250–1265.

Fink, R. (1998) "Interest, Gender, and Literacy Development in Successful Dyslexics," in L. Hoffmann, A. Krapp, K. A. Renninger, and J. Baumert (eds), *Interest and Learning: Proceedings of the Seeon Conference on Interest and Gender*, Kiel, Germany: IPN, pp. 402–408.

Fink, R. (2015) *Reading, Writing, and Rhythm: Content Area Literacy Strategies*, Huntington Beach, CA: Shell Education.

Fisher, P. H., J. Dobbs-Oates, G. L. Doctoroff, and D. H. Arnold (2012) "Early Math Interest and the Development of Math Skills," *Journal of Educational Psychology*, 104 (3): 673–681.

Flippo, R. (2014) *Assessing Readers: Qualitative Diagnosis and Instruction*, London and New York, NY: Routledge.

Flowerday, T., and G. Schraw (2003) "Effect of Choice on Cognitive and Affective Engagement," *Journal of Educational Research*, 96 (4): 207–215.

Flowerday, T., and D. F. Shell (2015) "Disentangling the Effects of Interest and Choice on Learning, Engagement, and Attitude," *Learning and Individual Differences*, 40 (May): 134–140.

Flowerday, T., G. Schraw, and J. Stevens (2004) "The Role of Choice and Interest in Reader Engagement," *Journal of Experimental Education*, 72 (2): 93–114.

Fredricks, J. A. (2014) *Eight Myths of Student Disengagement: Creating Classrooms of Deep Learning*, London, UK: Corwin.

Fredricks, J. A., and W. McCloskey (2012) "The Measurement of Student Engagement: A Comparative Analysis of Various Methods and Student Self-Report Instruments," in S. L. Christenson, A. L. Reschly, and C. Wylie (eds), *Handbook of Research on Student Engagement*, New York, NY: Springer, pp. 763–782.

Fredricks, J. A., and S. D. Simpkins (2013) "Organized Out-of-School Activities and Peer Relationships: Theoretical Perspectives and Previous Research," *New Directions for Child and Adolescent Development*, 140: 1–17.

Fredricks, J. A., P. C. Blumenfeld, and A. H. Paris (2004) "School Engagement: Potential of the Concept, State of the Evidence," *Review of Educational Research*, 74 (1): 59–109.

Fredricks, J. A., W. McCloskey, J. Meli, J. Mordica, B. Montrosse, and K. Mooney (2011) "Measuring Student Engagement in Upper Elementary through High School: A Description of 21 Instruments," *Regional Educational Laboratory Southeast, Issues and Answers*. REL 2011-No. 098.

Frenzel, A. C., T. Goetz, R. Pekrun, and H. M. Watt (2010) "Development of Mathematics Interest in Adolescence: Influences of Gender, Family, and School Context," *Journal of Research on Adolescence*, 20 (2): 507–537.

Frenzel, A. C., R. Pekrun, A.-L. Dicke, and T. Goetz (2012) "Beyond Quantitative Decline: Conceptual Shifts in Adolescents' Development of Interest in Mathematics," *Developmental Psychology*, 48 (4): 1069–1082.

Fryer, D. (1931) *The Measurement of Interests*, New York, NY: Henry Holt.

Fulcher, K. H. (2008) "Curiosity: A Link to Assessing Lifelong Learning," *Assessment Update*, 20 (2): 11–13.

Furtak, E. M., T. Seidel, H. Iverson, and D. C. Briggs (2012) "Experimental and Quasi-Experimental Studies of Inquiry-Based Science Teaching: A Meta-Analysis," *Review of Educational Research*, 82 (3): 300–329.

Gardner, H. (1990) *Art Education and Human Development*, Santa Monica, CA: The Getty Center for Education in the Arts.

Garner, R., P. A. Alexander, M. G. Gillingham, and R. Brown (1991) "Interest and Learning from Text," *American Educational Research Journal*, 28 (3): 643–659.

Garner, R., R. Brown, S. Sanders, and D. J. Menke (1992) "'Seductive Details' and Learning from the Text," in K. A. Renninger, S. Hidi, and A. Krapp (eds), *The Role of Interest in Learning and Development*, Hillsdale, NJ: Erlbaum, pp. 239–254.

Garner, R., M. G. Gillingham, and C. S. White (1989) "Effects of 'Seductive Details' on Macroprocessing and Microprocessing in Adults and Children," *Cognition and Instruction*, 6 (1): 41–57.

Gee, J. P. (2004) *Situated Language and Learning*, London and New York, NY: Routledge.

Gehlbach, H., S. W. Brown, A. Ioannou, M. A. Boyer, N. Hudson, A. Niv-Solomon et al. (2008) "Increasing Interest in Social Studies: Social Perspective Taking and Self-Efficacy in Stimulating Simulations," *Contemporary Educational Psychology*, 33 (4): 894–914.

Gerritsen, C. J., M. E. Toplak, J. Sciaraffa, and J. Eastwood (2014) "I Can't Get No Satisfaction: Potential Causes of Boredom," *Consciousness and Cognition*, 27: 27–41.

Geyer, C., K. Neubauer, and D. Lewalter (2013) "Public Understanding of Science Via Research Areas in Science Museums: The Evaluation of the EU Project Nanototouch," in L. Locke and S. Locke (eds), *Knowledges in Publics*, Newcastle upon Tyne, UK: Cambridge Scholars Publishing, pp. 50–74.

Ginzberg, E., S. W. Ginsburg, S. Axelrad, and J. L. Herma (1966) *Occupational Choice: An Approach to a General Theory*, New York, NY: Columbia University Press.

Gisbert, K. (1998) "Individual Interest in Mathematics and Female Gender Identity: Biographical Case Studies," in L. Hoffmann, A. Krapp, K. A. Renninger, and J. Baumert (eds), *Interest and Learning: Proceedings of the Seeon Conference on Interest and Gender*, Kiel, Germany: IPN, pp. 387–401.

Glynn, S. M., R. R. Bryan, P. Brickman, and N. Armstrong (2015) "Intrinsic Motivation, Self-Efficacy, and Interest in Science," in K. A. Renninger, M. Nieswandt, and S. Hidi (eds), *Interest in Mathematics and Science Learning*, Washington, DC: American Educational Research Association, pp. 189–202.

Goetz, T., and N. C. Hall (2014) "Academic Boredom," in R. Pekrun and L. Linnenbrink-Garcia (eds), *International Handbook of Emotions in Education*, London and New York, NY: Routledge, pp. 311–331.

Gottlieb, J., P.-Y. Oudeyer, M. Lopes, and A. Baranes (2013) "Information Seeking, Curiosity and Attention: Computational and Neural Mechanisms," *Trends in Cognitive Science*, 17 (11): 585–596.

Graham, J., R. Tisher, M. Ainley, and G. Kennedy (2008) "Staying with the Text: The Contribution of Gender, Achievement Orientations, and Interest to Students Performance on a Literacy Task," *Educational Psychology*, 28 (7): 757–776.

Gresalfi, M. S. (2009) "Taking Up Opportunities to Learn: Constructing Dispositions in Mathematics Classrooms," *The Journal of the Learning Sciences*, 18 (3): 327–369.

Gruber, M. J., B. D. Gelman, and C. Ranganath (2014) "States of Curiosity Modulate Hippocampus-Dependent Learning Via the Dopaminergic Circuit," *Neuron*, 84 (2): 486–496.

Gunnar, M. R., and M. De Haan (2009) "Methods in Social Neuroscience Issues in Studying Development," in M. De Haan and M. R. Gunnar (eds), *Handbook of Developmental Social Neuroscience*, New York, NY: Guilford Press, pp. 13–37.

Gutherie, J. T., A. Wigfield, N. H. Humenck, K. C. Perencevich, A. Taboada, and P. Barosa (2006) "Influences of Stimulating Tasks on Reading Motivation and Comprehension," *Journal of Educational Research*, 99: 232–247.

Hagay, G., and A. Baram-Tsabari (2011) "A Shadow Curriculum: Incorporating Students' Interests into the Formal Biology Curriculum," *Research in Science Education*, 41 (5): 611–634.

Halet, E. (2008) "The Effect of Designing Webquests on the Motivation of Pre-Service Elementary School Teachers," *International Journal of Mathematical Education in Science and Technology*, 39 (6): 793–802.

Halverson, E. R., and K. Sheridan (2014) "The Maker Movement in Education," *Harvard Educational Review*, 84 (4): 495–504.

Hameline, D. (2000) "Édouard Claparède," *Prospects: The Quarterly Review of Comparative Education*, 13 (1/2): 159–197.

Hannover, B., and U. Kessels (2004) "Self-to-Prototype Matching as a Strategy for Making Academic Choices: Why High School Students Do Not Like Math and Science," *Learning and Instruction*, 14 (1): 51–67.

Harackiewicz, J. M., and A. J. Elliot (1993) "Achievement Goals and Intrinsic Motivation," *Journal of Personality and Social Psychology*, 65 (5): 904–915.

Harackiewicz, J. M., and C. Sansone (1991) "Goals and Intrinsic Motivation: You Can Get There from Here," *Advances in Motivation and Achievement*, 7: 21–49.

Harackiewicz, J. M., K. E. Barron, J. M. Tauer, S. M. Carter, and A. J. Elliot (2000) "Short-Term and Long-Term Consequences of Achievement Goals: Predicting Interest and Performance over Time," *Journal of Educational Psychology*, 92 (2): 316–330.

Harackiewicz, J. M., K. E. Barron, J. M. Tauer, and A. J. Elliot (2002) "Predicting Success in College: A Longitudinal Study of Achievement Goals and Ability Measures as Predictors of Interest and Performance from Freshman Year through Graduation," *Journal of Educational Psychology*, 94 (3): 562–575.

Harackiewicz, J. M., A. M. Durik, K. E. Barron, L. Linnenbrink, and J. M. Tauer (2008) "The Role of Achievement Goals in the Development of Interest: Reciprocal Relations between Achievement Goals, Interest, and Performance," *Journal of Educational Psychology*, 100 (1): 105–122.

Harackiewicz, J. M., C. S. Rozek, C. S. Hulleman, and J. S. Hyde (2012) "Helping Parents to Motivate Adolescents in Mathematics and Science: An Experimental Test of a Utility-Value Intervention," *Psychological Science*, 20 (10): 1–8.

Harackiewicz, J. M., Y. Tibbetts, E. Canning, and J. S. Hyde (2014) "Harnessing Values to Promote Motivation in Education," in S. A. Karabenick and T. C. Urdan (eds), *Advances in Motivation and Achievement*, vol. XVIII: *Motivational Interventions*, Bingley, UK: Emerald Group Publishing Limited, pp. 71–107.

Harter, S. (1982) "The Perceived Competence Scale for Children," *Child Development*, 53 (1): 87–97.

Harter, S. (2006) "The Self," in N. Eisenberg (ed.), *Handbook of Child Psychology*, vol. III: *Social, Emotional, and Personality Development*, New York, NY: Wiley, pp. 505–570.

Häussler, P., and L. Hoffmann (2002) "An Intervention Study to Enhance Girls' Interest, Self-Concept, and Achievement in Physics Classes," *Journal of Research in Science Teaching*, 39 (9): 870–888.

Hay, I., R. Callingham, and C. Carmichael (2015) "Interest, Self-Efficacy, and Academic Achievement in a Statistics Lesson," in K. A. Renninger, M. Nieswandt, and S. Hidi (eds), *Interest in Mathematics and Science Learning*, Washington, DC: American Educational Research Association, pp. 173–188.

Heck, K. E., and A. Subramaniam (2009) *Youth Development Frameworks*, Davis, CA: 4-H Center for Youth Development, University of California Davis.

Herbart, J. F. (1965) "Allgemeine Pädagogik, aud dem Zweck der Erziehung Abgeleitet," in J. F. Herbart (ed.), *Pädagogische Schriften*, 2 vols., Düsseldorf: Kupper, vol. II, pp. 1–114.

Hetland, A., and J. Vitterso (2012) "The Feelings of Extreme Risk: Exploring Emotional Quality and Variability in Skydiving and BASE Jumping," *Journal of Sport Behavior*, 35 (2): 154–180.

Hickey, C., L. Chelazzi, and J. Theeuwes (2011) "Reward Has a Residual Impact on Target Selection in Visual Search, but Not on the Suppression of Distractors," *Visual Cognition*, 19 (1): 117–128.

Hidi, S. (1990) "Interest and Its Contribution as a Mental Resource for Learning," *Review of Educational Research*, 60 (4): 549–571.

Hidi, S. (1995) "A Re-examination of the Role of Attention in Learning from Text," *Educational Psychology Review*, 7 (4): 323–350.

Hidi, S. (2000) "An Interest Researcher's Perspective: The Effects of Extrinsic and Intrinsic Factors on Motivation," in C. Sansone and J. M. Harackiewicz (eds), *Intrinsic and Extrinsic Motivation: The Search for Optimal Motivation and Performance*, New York, NY: Academic, pp. 311–342.

Hidi, S. (2001) "Interest, Reading and Learning: Theoretical and Practical Considerations," *Educational Psychology Review*, 13 (3): 191–210.

Hidi, S. (2006) "Interest: A Unique Motivational Variable," *Educational Research Review*, 1 (2): 69–82.

Hidi, S. (2015) "Revisiting the Role of Rewards in Motivation and Learning: Implications of Neuroscientific Findings," *Educational Psychology Review*, pp. 1–33.

Hidi, S., and M. Ainley (2002) "Interest and Adolescence," in M. Pajares and T. Urdan (eds), *Adolescence and Education*, Greenwich, CT: IAP, vol. 2, pp. 247–275.

Hidi, S., and M. Ainley (2008) "Interest and Self-Regulation: Relationships between Two Variables that Influence Learning," in D. H. Schunk and B. J. Zimmerman (eds), *Motivation and Self-Regulated Learning: Theory, Research, and Application*, Mahwah, NJ: Erlbaum, pp. 77–109.

Hidi, S., and V. Anderson (1992) "Situational Interest and Its Impact on Reading and Expository Writing," in K. A. Renninger, S. Hidi, and A. Krapp (eds), *The Role of Interest in Learning and Development*, Hillsdale, NJ: Erlbaum, pp. 215–238.

Hidi, S., and W. Baird (1986) "Interestingness: A Neglected Variable in Discourse Processing," *Cognitive Science*, 10 (2): 179–194.

Hidi, S., and W. Baird (1988) "Strategies for Increasing Text-Based Interest and Students' Recall of Expository Texts," *Reading Research Quarterly*, 23 (4): 465–483.

Hidi, S., and D. Berndorff (1998) "Situational Interest and Learning," in L. Hoffman, A. Krapp, K. A. Renninger, and J. Baumert (eds), *Interest and Learning: Proceedings of the Seeon Conference on Interest and Gender*, Kiel: IPEN, pp. 74–90.

Hidi, S., and J. M. Harackiewicz (2000) "Motivating the Academically Unmotivated: A Critical Issue for the 21st Century," *Review of Educational Research*, 70 (2): 151–179.

Hidi, S., and J. McLaren (1990) "The Effect of Topic and Theme Interestingness on the Production of School Expositions," in H. Mandl, E. De Corte, N. Bennet, and H. F. Friedrich (eds), *Learning and Instruction: European Research in an International Context*, 2 (2): 295–308.

Hidi, S., and J. McLaren (1991) "Motivational Factors and Writing: The Role of Topic Interestingness," *European Journal of Psychology of Education*, 6 (2): 187–197.

Hidi, S., and K. A. Renninger (2006) "The Four-Phase Model of Interest Development," *Educational Psychologist*, 41 (2): 111–127.

Hidi, S., M. Ainley, D. Berndorff, and L. Del Favero (2007) "The Role of Interest and Self-Efficacy in Science-Related Expository Writing," in S. Hidi and P. Boscolo (eds), *Studies in Writing*, vol. XIX: *Writing and Motivation*, Oxford, UK: Elsevier, pp. 241–255.

Hidi, S., D. Berndorff, and M. Ainley (2002) "Children's Argument Writing, Interest and Self-Efficacy: An Intervention Study," *Learning and Instruction*, 12 (4): 429–446.

Hidi, S., K. A. Renninger, and A. Krapp (1992) "The Present State of Interest Research," in K. A. Renninger, S. Hidi, and A. Krapp (eds), *The Role of Interest in Learning and Development*, Hillsdale, NJ: Erlbaum, pp. 433–444.

Hidi, S., K. A. Renninger, and M. Nieswandt (2015) "Emerging Issues and Themes in Addressing Mathematics and Science," in K. A. Renninger, M. Nieswandt, and S. Hidi (eds), *Interest in Mathematics and Science Learning*, Washington, DC: American Educational Research Association, pp. 385–396.

Hidi, S., J. Weiss, J., D. Berndorff, and J. Nolan (1998) "The Role of Gender, Instruction and a Cooperative Learning Technique in Science Education across Formal and Informal Settings," in L. Hoffman, A. Krapp, K. Renninger, and J. Baumert (eds), *Interest and Learning: Proceedings of the Seeon Conference on Interest and Gender, Kiel, Germany*: IPN, pp. 215–227.

Hoffmann, L. (2002) "Promoting Girls' Learning and Achievement in Physics Classes for Beginners," *Learning and Instruction*, 12 (4): 447–465.

Holland, J. L. (1959) "A Theory of Vocational Choice," *Journal of Counseling Psychology*, 6: 35–45.

Holland, J. L. (1996) "Exploring Careers with a Typology: What Have We Learned and Some New Directions," *American Psychologist*, 51 (4): 397–406.

Holstermann, N., M. Ainley, D. Grube, T. Roick, and S. Bögeholz (2012) "The Specific Relationship between Disgust and Interest: Relevance during Biology Class Dissections and Gender Differences," *Learning and Instruction*, 22 (3): 185–192.

Hong, H., and X. Lin-Siegler (2012) "How Learning about Scientists' Struggles Influences Students' Interest and Learning in Physics," *Journal of Educational Psychology*, 104 (2): 469–484.

Hsu, M., M. Bhatt, R. Adolphs, D. Tranel, and C. F. Camerer (2005) "Neural Systems Responding to Degrees of Uncertainty in Human Decision Making," *Science*, 310: 1680–1683.

Hulleman, C. S., O. Godes, B. L. Hendricks, and J. M. Harackiewicz (2010) "Enhancing Interest and Performance with a Utility Value Intervention," *Journal of Educational Psychology*, 102 (4): 880–895.

Hulleman, C. S., S. Schrager, S. Bodmann, and J. M. Harackiewicz (2010) "A Meta-Analysis Review of Achievement Goal Measures: Different Labels for the Same Constructs or Different Constructs with Similar Labels?" *Psychological Bulletin*, 136 (3): 422–449.

Hulleman, C., and J. Harackiewicz (2009) "Promoting Interest and Performance in High School Science Classes," *Science*, 326 (5698): 1410–1412.

Illeris, K. (2007) *How We Learn*, London and New York, NY: Routledge.

Iran-Nejad, A. (1987) "Cognitive and Affective Causes of Interest and Liking," *Journal of Educational Psychology*, 79 (2): 120–130.

Ito, M., S. Baumer, M. Bittanti, D. Boyd, R. Cody, B. Herr-Stephenson, H. A. Horst, P. G. Lange, D. Mahendran, K. Z. Martinez, C. J. Pascoe, D. Perkel, L. Robinson, C. Sims, and L. Tripp (2010) *Hanging Out, Messing Around, and Geeking Out: Kids Living and Learning with New Media*, Cambridge, MA: MIT Press.

Iyengar, S. S., and M. R. Lepper (1999) "Rethinking the Role of Choice: A Cultural Perspective on Intrinsic Motivation," *Journal of Personality and Social Psychology*, 76: 349–366.

Izard, C. E. (1977) *Human Emotions*, London and New York, NY: Plenum Press.

Izard, C. E. (2007) "Basic Emotions, Natural Kinds, Emotion Schemas, and a New Paradigm," *Perspectives on Psychological Science*, 2 (3): 260–280.

Izard, C. E. (2009) "Emotion Theory and Research: Highlights, Unanswered Questions, and Emerging Issues," *Annual Review of Psychology*, 60: 1–25.

Jackson, S. A. (2012) "Flow," in R. M. Ryan (ed.), *The Oxford Handbook of Human Motivation XX*, London and New York, NY: Oxford University Press, pp. 127–148.

Jacobs, J. E., S. Lanza, D. W. Osgood, J. S. Eccles, and A. Wigfield (2002) "Changes in Children's Self-Competence and Values: Gender and Domain Differences across Grades One through Twelve," *Child Development*, 73 (2): 509–527.

James, W. (1890) *The Principles of Psychology*, London, UK: Macmillan.

Järvelä, S. and K. A. Renninger (2014) "Designing for Learning: Interest, Motivation, and Engagement," in D. K. Sawyer (ed.), *Cambridge Handbook of the Learning Sciences*, 2nd edn, Cambridge, UK: Cambridge University Press, pp. 668–685.

Jenkins, E. W., and R. G. Pell (2006) *The Relevance of Science Education Project (ROSE) in England: A Summary of Findings*, Leeds: Centre for Studies in Science and Mathematics Education, University of Leeds.

Jenkins, H. (2009) *Confronting the Challenges of Participatory Culture: Media Education for the 21st Century*, Cambridge, MA: MIT Press.

Jepma, M., R. G. Verdonschot, H. Van Steenbergen, S. A. Rombouts, and S. Nieuwenhuis (2012) "Neural Mechanisms Underlying the Induction and Relief of Perceptual Curiosity," *Frontiers in Behavioral Neuroscience*, 6 (5): 1–9.

Jones, B. D., C. Ruff, and J. W. Osborne (2015) "Fostering Student's Identification with Mathematics and Science," in K. A. Renninger, M. Nieswandt, and S. Hidi (eds), *Interest in Mathematics and Science Learning*, Washington, DC: American Educational Research Association, pp. 331–352.

Kahan, D. (2013) "Here Is What Interests Us! Students' Reconceived Physical Education Activity Offerings in an Inner-City Middle School," *Physical Educator*, 70 (3): 243–261.

Kang, M. J., M. Hsu, I. M. Krajbich, G. Loewenstein, S. M. McClure, J. T. Wang, and C. F. Camerer (2009) "The Wick in the Candle of Learning: Epistemic Curiosity Activates Reward Circuitry and Enhances Memory," *Psychological Science*, 20 (8): 963–973.

Karabenick, S. A., M. E. Woolley, J. M. Friedel, B. V. Ammon, J. Blazevski, C. R. Bonney et al. (2007) "Cognitive Processing of Self-Report Items in Educational Research: Do They Think What We Mean?" *Educational Psychologist*, 42 (3): 139–151.

Katz, I., and A. Assor (2007) "When Choice Motivates and When It Does Not," *Educational Psychology Review*, 19 (4): 429–442.

Katz, S., D. Allbritton, J. Aronis, C. Wilson, and M. L. Soffa (2006) "Gender, Achievement, and Persistence in an Undergraduate Computer Science Program," *SIGMIS Database*, 37 (4): 42–57.

Kayali, H. (2009) "Effects of Near-to-Far Principle and Other Factors on Learning and Teaching Some Geography Subjects in the Social Studies Course," *Journal of Instructional Psychology*, 36 (2): 175–182.

Kessels, U., M. Rau, and B. Hannover (2006) "What Goes Well with Physics? Measuring and Altering the Image of Science," *British Journal of Educational Psychology*, 74 (4): 761–780.

Kim, S., Y. Jiang, and J. Song (2015) "The Effect of Interest and Utility on Mathematics Engagement and Achievement," in K. A. Renninger, M. Nieswandt, and S. Hidi (eds), *Interest in Mathematics and Science Learning*, Washington, DC: American Educational Research Association, pp. 63–78.

Kim, S., M. J. Lee, and M. Bong (2009) "FMRI Study on the Effects of Task Interest and Perceived Competence during Negative Feedback Processing," paper presented at the Meetings of the American Educational Research Association, April, San Diego, CA.

Kintsch, W. (1980) "Learning from Text, Levels of Comprehension; or, Why Anyone Would Read a Story Anyway?" *Poetics*, 9: 87–98.

Kirschner, P. A., J. Sweller, and R. E. Clark (2006) "Why Minimal Guidance during Instruction Does Not Work: An Analysis of the Failure of Constructivist, Discovery, Problem-Based, Experiential, and Inquiry-Based Teaching," *Educational Psychologist*, 41 (1): 75–86.

Knogler, M., J. M. Harackiewicz, A. Gegenfurtner, and D. Lewalter (2015) "How Situational is Situational Interest? Investigating the Longitudinal Structure of Situational Interest," *Contemporary Educational* Psychology, 43: 39–50.

Knutson, B., and G. E. Wimmer (2007) "Reward: Neural Circuitry for Social Valuation," in E. Harmon-Jones and P. Winkielman (eds), *Social Neuroscience: Integrating Biological and Psychological Explanations of Social Behavior*, New York, NY: Guilford Press, pp. 157–175.

Köller, O., J. Baumert, and K. Schnabel (2001) "Does Interest Matter? The Relationship between Academic Interest and Achievement in Mathematics," *Journal for Research in Mathematics Education*, 32 (5): 448–470.

Konečni, V. J. (1978) "Daniel E. Berlyne: 1924–1976," *The American Journal of Psychology*, 91 (1): 133–137.

Krapp, A. (2002a) "An Educational-Psychological Theory of Interest and Its Relation to SDT," in E. L. Deci and R. M. Ryan (eds), *Handbook of Self-Determination Research*, Rochester, NY: University of Rochester Press.

Krapp, A. (2002b) "Structural and Dynamic Aspects of Interest Development: Theoretical Considerations from an Ontogenetic Perspective," *Learning and Instruction*, 12 (4): 383–409.

Krapp, A. (2005). "Basic Needs and the Development of Interest and Intrinsic Motivational Orientations," *Learning and Instruction*, 12: 383–409.

Krapp, A. (2007) "An Educational-Psychological Conceptualization of Interest," *International Journal of Educational and Vocational Guidance*, 7 (1): 5–21.

Krapp, A., and B. Fink (1992) "The Development and Function of Interests during the Critical Transition from Home to Preschool," in K. A. Renninger, S. Hidi, and A. Krapp (eds), *The Role of Interest in Learning and Development*, Hillsdale, NJ: Erlbaum, pp. 397–431.

Krapp, A., and D. Lewalter (2001) "Development of Interests and Interest-Based Motivational Orientations: A Longitudinal Study in Vocational School and Work Settings," in S. Volet and S. Järvela (eds), *Motivation in Learning Contexts: Theoretical Advances and Methodological Implications*, New York, NY: Elsevier, pp. 209–232.

Krapp, A., and M. Prenzel (2011) "Research on Interest in Science: Theories, Methods and Findings," *International Journal of Science Education*, 33 (1): 27–50.

Krapp, A., S. Hidi, and K. A. Renninger (1992) "Interest, Learning, and Development," in K. A. Renninger, S. Hidi, and A. Krapp (eds), *The Role of Interest in Learning and Development*, Hillsdale, NJ: Erlbaum, pp. 3–25.

Kunter, M., J. Baumert, and O. Köller (2007) "Effective Classroom Management and the Development of Subject-Related Interest," *Learning and Instruction*, 17 (5): 494–509.

Lammers, J. C. (2013) "Fangirls as Teachers: Examining Pedagogic Discourse in an Online Fan Site," *Learning, Media and Technology*, 38 (4): 368–386.

Lammers, J. C., J. S. Curwood, and A. M. Magnifico (2012) "Toward an Affinity Space Methodology: Considerations for Literacy Research," *English Teaching: Practice and Critique*, 11 (2): 44–58.

Lamont, A., D. J. Hargreaves, N. A. Marshall, and M. Tarrant (2003) "Young People's Music In and Out of School," *British Journal of Music Education*, 20 (3): 229–241.

Larson, R. W. (2000) "Toward a Psychology of Positive Youth Development," *American Psychologist*, 55 (1): 170–183.

Larson, R. W., K. C. Walker, N. Rusk, and L. B. Diaz (2015) "Understanding Youth Development From the Practitioner's Point of View: A Call for Research on Effective Practice," *Applied Developmental Science* 19 (2): 74–86.

Larson, S. C. (2014a) "Exploring the Roles of the Generative Vocabulary Matrix and Academic Literacy Engagement of Ninth Grade Biology Students," *Literacy Research and Instruction*, 53 (4): 287–325.

Larson, S. C. (2014b) "Using a Generative Vocabulary Matrix in the Learning Workshop," *The Reading Teacher*, 68 (2): 113–125.

Lee, M. (2007) "Spark Up the American Revolution with Math, Science, and More: An Example of an Integrative Curriculum Unit," *The Social Studies*, 98 (4): 159–164.

Lenhart, A., S. Arafeh, A. Smith, and A. Macgill (2008) "Writing, Technology, and Teens," *Pew Internet and the American Life Project*, available online at http://www.pewinternet.org/2008/04/24/writing-technology-and-teens/ (accessed October 20, 2015).

Lent, R. W., S. D. Brown, and G. Hackett (1994) "Toward a Unifying Social Cognitive Theory of Career and Academic Interest, Choice, and Performance," *Journal of Vocational Behavior*, 45 (1): 79–122.

Lent, R. W., M. J. Miller, P. E. Smith, B. A. Watford, R. H. Lim, K. Hui et al. (2013) "Social Cognitive Predictors of Adjustment to Engineering Majors across Gender and Race/Ethnicity," *Journal of Vocational Behavior*, 83 (1): 22–30.

Leotti, L. A., and M. R. Delgado (2011) "The Inherent Reward of Choice," *Psychological Science*, 22 (10): 1310–1318.

Lerner, R. M., J. V. Lerner, J. Almerigi, and C. Theokas (2005) "Positive Youth Development: A View of the Issues," *Journal of Early Adolescence*, 25 (1): 10–16.

Leslie, I. (2014) *Curious: The Desire to Know and Why Your Future Depends On It*, London: Anansi.

Levy, S. (1996) *Starting from Scratch: One Classroom Builds Its Own Curriculum*, Portsmouth, NH: Heinemann.

Lewalter, D., C. Geyer, and K. Neubauer (2014) "Comparing the Effectiveness of Two Communication Formats on Visitors' Understanding of Nanotechnology," *Visitor Studies*, 17 (2): 159–176.

Linnenbrink-Garcia, L., A. M. Durik, A. M. Conley, K. E. Barron, J. M. Tauer, S. A. Karabenick, and J. M. Harackiewicz (2010) "Measuring Situational Interest in Academic Domains," *Educational and Psychological Measurement*, 70 (4): 647–671.

Linnenbrink-Garcia, L., E. A. Patall, and E. E. Messersmith (2012) "Antecedents and Consequences of Situational Interest," *British Journal of Educational Psychology*, 83 (4): 591–614.

Linnenbrink-Garcia, L., K. J. Pugh, K. L. Koskey, and V. C. Stewart (2012) "Developing Conceptual Understanding of Natural Selection: The Role of Interest, Efficacy, and Basic Prior Knowledge," *The Journal of Experimental Education*, 80 (1): 45–68.

Lipstein, R., and K. A. Renninger (2007a) "Interest for Writing: How Teachers Can Make a Difference," *English Journal*, 96 (4): 79–85.

Lipstein, R., and K. A. Renninger (2007b) "'Putting Things into Words': 12–15-Year-Old Students' Interest for Writing," in P. Boscolo and S. Hidi (eds), *Motivation and Writing: Research and School Practice*, New York, NY: Kluwer Academic/Plenum Press, pp. 113–140.

Litman, J. A. (2005) "Curiosity and the Pleasures of Learning: Wanting and Liking New Information," *Cognition and Emotion*, 19 (6): 793–814.

Litman, J. A. (2008) "Interest and Deprivation Factors of Epistemic Curiosity," *Personality and Individual Differences*, 44 (7): 1585–1595.

Litman, J. A. (2010) "Relationships between Measures of I- and D-Type Curiosity, Ambiguity Tolerance, and Need for Closure: An Initial Test of the Wanting-Liking Model of Information-Seeking," *Personality and Individual Differences*, 48 (4): 397–402.

Litman, J. A., and T. L. Jimerson (2004) "The Measurement of Curiosity as a Feeling of Deprivation," *Journal of Personality Assessment*, 82: 147–157.

Litman, J. A., and P. Mussel (2013) "Validity of the Interest- and Deprivation-Type Epistemic Curiosity Model in Germany," *Journal of Individual Differences*, 34 (2): 59–68.

Litman, J. A., H. M. Crowson, and K. Kolinski (2010) "Validity of the Interest- and Deprivation-Type Epistemic Curiosity Distinction in Non-Students," *Personality and Individual Differences*, 49 (5): 531–536.

Logtenberg, A., C. A. M. Van Boxtel, G. L. J. Schellings, and B. H. A. M. Van Hout-Wolters (2011) "The Onset of Students' Questioning in History," paper presented at the European Association on Learning and Instruction, Exeter, UK.

Long, J. F., and P. K. Murphy (2005) "Connecting through Content: The Responsiveness of Teacher and Student Interest in a Core Course," paper presented at the Meeting of the American Educational Research Association, April, Montreal, Canada.

Low, K. D., M. Yoon, B. W. Roberts, and J. Rounds (2005) "The Stability of Vocational Interests from Early Adolescence to Middle Adulthood: A Quantitative Review of Longitudinal Studies," *Psychological Bulletin*, 131: 713–737.

Lowenstein, G. (1994) "The Psychology of Curiosity: A Review and Reinterpretation," *Psychology Bulletin*, 116 (1): 75–98.

Magner, U. I., R. Schwonke, V. Aleven, O. Popescu, and A. Renkl (2014) "Triggering Situational Interest by Decorative Illustrations Both Fosters and Hinders Learning in Computer-Based Learning Environments," *Learning and Instruction*, 29: 141–152.

Magnifico, A. M. (2012) "The Game of Nepean Writing," in E. R. Hayes and S. C. Duncan (eds), *Learning in Video Game Affinity Spaces*, New York, NY: Peter Lang, pp. 212–234.

Maltese, A. V., and J. A. Harsh (2015) "Student's Pathways of Entry into STEM," in K. A. Renninger, M. Nieswandt, and S. Hidi (eds), *Interest in Mathematics and Science Learning*, Washington, DC: American Educational Research Association, pp. 203–223.

Maltese, A. V., and R. H. Tai (2010) "Eyeballs in the Fridge: Sources of Early Interest in Science," *International Journal of Science Education*, 32 (5): 669–685.

Marjoribanks, K., and M. Mboya (2004) "Learning Environments, Goal Orientations, and Interest in Music," *Journal of Research in Music Education*, 52 (2): 155–166.

Markey, A., and G. Lowenstein (2014) "Curiosity," in R. Pekrun and L. Linnenbrink-Garcia (eds), *International Handbook of Emotions in Education*, London and New York, NY: Routledge, pp. 246–264.

Marsh, H., and S. Kleitman (2002) "Extracurricular School Activities: The Good, the Bad, and the Nonlinear," *Harvard Educational Review*, 72 (4): 464–515.

Marsh, H. W., U. Trautwein, O. Lüdtke, O. Köller, and J. Baumert (2005) "Academic Self-Concept, Interest, Grades, and Standardized Test Scores: Reciprocal Effects Models of Causal Ordering," *Child Development*, 76 (2): 397–416.

Mart, G. T. (2012) "Encouraging Young Learners to Learn English through Stories," *English Language Teaching*, 5 (5): 101–106.

Martin-Soelch, C., K. L. Leenders, A.-F. Chevalley, J. Missimer, G. Künig, S. Magyar, A. Mino, and W. Schultz (2001) "Reward Mechanisms in the Brain and Their Role in Dependence: Evidence from Neurophysiological and Neuroimaging Studies," *Brain Research Reviews*, 36 (2): 139–149.

Mayer, R. E., E. Griffith, I. T. N. Jurkowitz, and D. Rothman (2008) "Increased Interest-ingness of Extraneous Details in a Multimedia Science Presentation Leads to Decreased Learning," *Journal of Experimental Psychology: Applied*, 14 (4): 329–339.

McCarthey, S. J., A. M. López-Velásquez, G. E. García, S. Lin, and Y. H. Guo (2004) "Understanding Writing Contexts for English Language Learners," *Research in the Teaching of English*, 38 (4): 351–394.

McCrae, R. R., and P. T. Costa (1990) *Personality in Adulthood: A Five-Factor Theory Perspective*, London, UK: Guilford Press.

McDaniel, M. A., P. J. Waddill, K. Finstad, and T. Bourg (2000) "The Effects of Text-Based Interest on Attention and Recall," *Journal of Educational Psychology*, 92 (3): 492–502.

McDougall, W. (1932) *The Energies of Men*, London and New York, NY: Routledge.

McHale, S. M., J. Y. Kim, A. M. Dotterer, A. C. Crouter, and A. Booth (2009) "The Development of Gendered Interests and Personality Qualities from Middle Childhood through Adolescence: A Biosocial Analysis," *Child Development*, 80 (2): 482–495.

McKay, C., M. Sanders, and S. Wroblewski (2011) "Positive Youth Development and School Capacity Building," *School Social Work Journal*, 36 (1): 16–25.

McMullen, P. T., and M. J. Arnold (1976) "Preference and Interest as Functions of Distributional Redundancy in Rhythmic Sequences," *Journal of Research in Music Education*, 24 (1): 22–31.

Meredith, D. C., and E. F. Redish (2013) "Reinventing Physics for Life-Science Majors," *Physics Today*, 66 (7): 38–43.

Meyer, D. K. and J. C. Turner (2002) "Discovering Emotion in Classroom Motivation Research," *Educational Psychologist*, 37 (2): 107–114.

Michaelis, J. E. and M. J. Nathan (2015) "The Four-Phase Interest Development in Engineering Survey," paper presented at 2015 ASEE Annual Conference and Exposition, Seattle, Washington.

Mitchell, K., and S. Elwood (2012) "Engaging Students through Mapping Local History," *Journal of Geography*, 111 (4): 148–157.

Mitchell, M. (1993) "Situational Interest: Its Multifaceted Structure in the Secondary School Mathematics Classroom," *Journal of Educational Psychology*, 85 (3): 424–436.

Moore, H. T. (1921) "The Comparative Influence of Majority and Expert Opinion," *American Journal of Psychology*, 32: 16–20.

Mortillaro, M., M. Mehu, and K. R. Scherer (2011) "Subtly Different Positive Emotions Can Be Distinguished by Their Facial Expressions," *Social Psychological and Personality Science*, 2 (3): 262–271.

Murayama, K., M. Matsumoto, K. Izuma, A. Sugiura, R. M. Ryan, E. L. Deci, and K. Matsumoto (2015) "How Self-Determined Choice Facilitates Performance: A Key Role of the Ventromedial Prefrontal Cortex," *Cerebral Cortex*, 25: 1241–1251.

Murayama, K., R. Pekrun, S. Lichtenfeld, and R. Vom Hofe (2013) "Predicting Long Term Growth in Students' Mathematics Achievement: The Unique Contributions of Motivation and Cognitive Strategies," *Child Development*, 84 (4): 1475–1490.

Murphy, P. K., and P. A. Alexander (2000) "A Motivated Exploration of Motivation Terminology," *Contemporary Educational Psychology*, 25 (1): 3–53.

Myers, N. A., and M. Perlmutter (1978) "Memory in the Years from Two to Five," in P. A. Ornstein (ed.), *Memory Development in Children*, Hillsdale, NJ: Erlbaum, pp. 191–218.

Naizer, G., M. J. Hawthorne, and T. B. Henley (2014) "Narrowing the Gender Gap: Enduring Changes in Middle School Students' Attitude toward Math, Science and Technology," *Journal of STEM Education: Innovations and Research*, 15 (3): 29–34.

New London Group (1996) "A Pedagogy of Multiliteracies: Designing Social Futures," *Harvard Educational Review*, 66 (1): 60–92.

New York Hall of Science (2013) *Making Meaning (M2)*, Queens, NY: New York Hall of Science.

Niemivirta, M., and A. Tapola (2007) "Self-Efficacy, Interest, and Task Performance: Within-Task Changes, Mutual Relationships, and Predictive Effects," *Zeitschrift Für Pädagogische Psychologie*, 21 (3): 241–250.

Nieswandt, M. (2007) "Student Affect and Conceptual Understanding in Learning Chemistry," *Journal of Research in Science Teaching*, 44 (7): 908–937.

Nieswandt, M., and G. Horowitz (2015) "Undergraduate Students' Interest in Chemistry: The Roles of Task and Choice," in K. A. Renninger, M. Nieswandt, and S. Hidi (eds), *Interest in Mathematics and Science Learning*, Washington, DC: American Educational Research Association, pp. 225–242.

Nolen, S. B. (2001) "Constructing Literacy in the Kindergarten: Task Structure, Collaboration, and Motivation," *Cognition and Instruction*, 19 (1): 95–142.

Nolen, S. B. (2007a) "Young Children's Motivation to Read and Write: Development in Social Contexts," *Cognition and Instruction*, 25 (2): 219–270.

Nolen, S. B. (2007b) "The Role of Literate Communities in the Development of Children's Interest in Writing," in S. Hidi and P. Boscolo (eds), *Writing and Motivation*, Oxford, UK: Elsevier, pp. 241–255.

Nye, C. D., R. Su, J. Rounds, and F. Drasgow (2012) "Vocational Interests and Performance: A Quantitative Summary of over 60 Years of Research," *Perspectives on Psychological Science*, 7 (4): 384–403.

O'Keefe, P. A., and L. Linnenbrink-Garcia (2014) "The Role of Interest in Optimizing Performance and Self-Regulation," *Journal of Experimental Social Psychology*, 53: 70–78.

OECD (2006) *Assessing Scientific, Reading and Mathematical Literacy: A Framework for PISA 2006*, Paris, France: OECD.

OECD (2007) *PISA 2006: Science Competencies for Tomorrow's World*, vol. I: *Analysis*, Paris, France: OECD.

Ohland, M. W., C. E. Brawner, M. M. Camacho, R. A. Layton, R. A. Long, S. M. Lord, and M. H. Wasburn (2011) "Race, Gender, and Measures of Success in Engineering Education," *Journal of Engineering Education*, 100: 225–252.

Paige, D. D. (2011) "Engaging Struggling Adolescent Readers Through Situational Interest: A Model Proposing the Relationships Among Extrinsic Motivation, Oral Reading Proficiency, Comprehension, and Academic Achievement," *Reading Psychology*, 32: 395-425.

Pajares, F. (1996) "Self-Efficacy Beliefs in Academic Settings," *Review of Educational Research*, 66 (4): 543–578.

Palmer, D. H. (2004) "Situational Interest and the Attitudes towards Science of Primary Teacher Education Students," *International Journal of Science Education*, 26 (7): 895–908.

Palmer, D. H. (2009) "Student Interest Generated during an Inquiry Skills Lesson," *Journal of Research in Science Teaching*, 46 (2): 147–165.

Panksepp, J. (1998) *Affective Neuroscience: The Foundations of Human and Animal Emotion*, New York, NY: Oxford University Press.

Panksepp, J. (2000) "The Riddle of Laughter: Neural and Psychoevolutionary Underpinnings of Joy," *Current Directions in Psychological Science*, 9 (6): 183–186.

Papastergiou, M. (2008) "Online Computer Games as Collaborative Learning Environments: Prospects and Challenges for Tertiary Education," *Journal of Educational Technology Systems*, 37 (1): 19–38.

Patall, E. A. (2012) "The Motivational Complexity of Choosing: A Review of Theory and Research," in R. M. Ryan (ed.), *The Oxford Handbook of Human Motivation*. New York, NY: Oxford University Press, pp. 248–279.

Patall, E. A., H. Cooper, and C. J. Robinson (2008) "The Effects of Choice on Intrinsic Motivation and Related Outcomes: A Meta-Analysis of Research Findings," *Psychological Bulletin*, 134 (2): 270–300.

Paterson, D. G., R. M. Elliott, L. D. Anderson, H. A. Toops, and E. Heidbreder (1930) *Minnesota Mechanical Ability Tests*, Minneapolis, MN: University of Minnesota Press.

Pekrun, R., T. Goetz, L. M. Daniels, R. H. Stupnisky, and R. P. Perry (2010) "Boredom in Achievement Settings: Exploring Control-Value Antecedents and Performance Outcomes of a Neglected Emotion," *Journal of Educational Psychology*, 102 (3): 531–549.

Perlmutter, M., and G. Lange (1978) "A Developmental Analysis of Recall-Recognition Distinctions," in P. A. Ornstein (ed.), *Memory Development in Children*, Hillsdale, NJ: Erlbaum, pp. 243–258.

Perlmutter, M., and N. A. Myers (1974) "Recognition Memory Development in Two- to Four-Year-Olds," *Developmental Psychology*, 10 (3): 447–450.

Perlmutter, M., and N. A. Myers (1976) "Recognition Memory in Preschool Children," *Developmental Psychology*, 12 (3): 271–272.

Pestalozzi, J. H. (2004) *Letters on Education*, Syracuse, NY: C. W. Bardeen.

Philip, T. M., and A. D. Garcia (2013) "The Importance of Still Teaching the iGeneration: New Technologies and the Centrality of Pedagogy," *Harvard Educational Review*, 83 (2): 300–319.

Pinkard, N., and K. Austin (2014) "The Digital Youth Network Learning Model," in B. Barron, K. Gomez, N. Pinkard, and C. K. Martin (eds), *The Digital Youth Network: Cultivating Digital Media Citizenship in Urban Communities*, Cambridge, MA: MIT Press, pp. 17–40.

Pintrich, P. R. (2000) "Multiple Goals, Multiple Pathways: The Role of Goal Orientation in Learning and Achievement," *Journal of Educational Psychology*, 92 (3): 544–555.

Pintrich, P. R. (2003) "Motivation and Classroom Learning," in I. B. Weiner (ed.), *Handbook of Psychology*, vol. VII, New York, NY: Wiley.

Pintrich, P. R., and A. Zusho (2002) "The Development of Academic Self-Regulation: The Role of Cognitive and Motivational Factors," in A. Wigfield, and J. S. Eccles (eds), *Development of Achievement Motivation*, San Diego, CA: Academic Press, pp. 249–284.

Piotrowski, J. T., J. A. Litman, and P. Valkenburg (2014) "Measuring Epistemic Curiosity in Young Children," *Infant and Child Development*, 23 (5): 542–553.

Potvin, P., and A. Hasni (2014) "Interest, Motivation and Attitude towards Science and Technology at K–12 Levels: A Systematic Review of 12 Years of Educational Research," *Studies in Science Education*, 50 (1): 85–129.

Pressick-Kilborn, K. (2015) "Canalization and Connectedness in the Development of Science Interest," in K. A. Renninger, M. Nieswandt, and S. Hidi (eds), *Interest in Mathematics and Science Learning*, Washington, DC: American Educational Research Association, pp. 353–368.

Pressick-Kilborn, K., and R. Walker (2002) "The Social Construction of Interest in a Learning Community," in D. M. McInerney and S. Van Etten (eds), *Research on Sociocultural Influences on Learning and Motivation*, Greenwich, CT: Information Age Publishers, pp. 153–182.

Pugh, K. J., L. Linnenbrink-Garcia, K. L. Koskey, V. C. Stewart, and C. Manzey (2010) "Motivation, Learning, and Transformative Experience: A Study of Deep Engagement in Science," *Science Education*, 94 (1): 1–28.

Pugh, K., L. Linnenbrink-Garcia, M. Phillips, and T. Perez (2015) "Supporting the Development of Transformative Experience and Interest," in K. A. Renninger, M. Nieswandt, and S. Hidi (eds), *Interest in Mathematics and Science Learning*, Washington, DC: American Educational Research Association, pp. 369–383.

Randler, C., and F. X. Bogner (2007) "Pupils' Interest Before, During, and After a Curriculum Dealing with Ecological Topics and Its Relationship with Achievement," *Educational Research and Evaluation*, 13 (5): 463–478.

Rathunde, K. (1998) "Undivided and Abiding Interest: Comparisons across Studies of Talented Adolescents and Creative Adults," in L. Hoffmann, A. Krapp, K. A. Renninger, and J. Baumert (eds), *Interest and Learning*, Kiel, Germany: IPN, pp. 367–376.

Ray, M. (2013) *Powerful Problem-Solving: Activities for Making Sense with the Mathematical Practices*, Portsmith, NH: Heinemann.

Read, H. (1958) *Education through Art*, 3rd edn, New York, NY: Pantheon.

Reber, R., H. Hetland, W. Chen, E. Norman, and T. Kobbeltvedt (2009) "Effects of Example Choice on Interest, Control, and Learning," *Journal of the Learning Sciences*, 18 (4): 509–548.

Reeve, J. (1993) "The Face of Interest," *Motivation and Emotion*, 77 (4): 353–375.

Reeve, J. (1996) *Motivating Others: Nurturing Inner Motivational Resources*, Needham Heights, MA: Allyn & Bacon.

Reeve, J., and G. Nix (1997) "Expressing Intrinsic Motivation through Acts of Exploration and Facial Displays of Interest," *Motivation and Emotion*, 27 (3): 237–250.

Reeve, J., W. Lee, and S. Won (2015) "Interest as Emotion, Affect, and Schema," in K. A. Renninger, M. Nieswandt, and S. Hidi (eds), *Interest in Mathematics and Science Learning*, Washington, DC: American Educational Research Association, pp. 79–92.

Reid, J. (2011) "'We Don't Twitter, We Facebook': An Alternative Pedagogical Space that Enables Critical Practices in Relation to Writing," *English Teaching: Practice and Critique*, 10 (1): 58–80.

Reio, T. G., J. M. Petrosko, A. K. Wiswell, and J. Thongsukmag (2006) "The Measurement and Conceptualization of Curiosity," *The Journal of Genetic Psychology*, 167 (2): 117–135.

Renninger, K. A. (1989) "Individual Patterns in Children's Play Interests," in L. T. Winegar (ed.), *Social Interaction and the Development of Children's Understanding*, Norwood, NJ: Ablex, pp. 147–172.

Renninger, K. A. (1990) "Children's Play Interests, Representation, and Activity," in R. Fivush and J. Hudson (eds), *Knowing and Remembering in Young Children*, Cambridge, UK: Cambridge University Press, pp. 127–165.

Renninger, K. A. (1992) "Individual Interest and Development: Implications for Theory and Practice," in K. A. Renninger, S. Hidi, and A. Krapp (eds), *The Role of Interest in Learning and Development*, Hillsdale, NJ: Erlbaum, pp. 361–395.

Renninger, K. A. (2000) "Individual Interest and Its Implications for Understanding Intrinsic Motivation," in C. Sansone and J. M. Harackiewicz (eds), *Intrinsic Motivation: Controversies and New Directions*, San Diego, CA: Academic Press, pp. 373–404.

Renninger, K. A. (2003) "Effort and Interest," in J. Guthrie (ed.), *The Encyclopedia of Education*, 2nd edn, New York, NY: Macmillan, pp. 704–707.

Renninger, K. A. (2009) "Interest and Identity Development in Instruction: An Inductive Model," *Educational Psychologist*, 44 (2): 1–14.

Renninger, K. A. (2010) "Working with and Cultivating Interest, Self-Efficacy, and Self-Regulation," in D. Preiss and R. Sternberg (eds), *Innovations in Educational Psychology: Perspectives on Learning, Teaching and Human Development*, New York, NY: Springer, pp. 107–138.

Renninger, K. A., and J. E. Bachrach (2015) "Studying Triggers for Interest and Engagement Using Observational Methods," *Educational Psychologist*, 50 (1): 58–69.

Renninger, K. A. and A. L. Bishop (in press) "Interest, and Interest-Driven Learning," in K. Peppler (ed.), *The SAGE Encyclopedia of Out-of-School Learning*, New York, NY: Sage.

Renninger, K. A., and S. Hidi (2002) "Student Interest and Achievement: Developmental Issues Raised by a Case Study," in A. Wigfield and J. S. Eccles (eds), *Development of Achievement Motivation*, New York, NY: Academic Press, pp. 173–195.

Renninger, K. A., and S. Hidi (2011) "Revisiting the Conceptualization, Measurement, and Generation of Interest," *Educational Psychologist*, 46 (3): 168–184.

Renninger, K. A., and T. Leckrone (1991) "Continuity in Young Children's Actions: A Consideration of Interest and Temperament," in L. Oppenheimer and J. Valsiner (eds), *The Origins of Action: Interdisciplinary and International Perspectives*, New York, NY: Springer Verlag, pp. 205–238.

Renninger, K. A., and R. Lipstein (2006) "Come si sviluppa l'interesse per la scrittura; cosa volgliono gli studenti e di cosa hanno bisogno? [Developing Interest for Writing: What Do Students Want and What Do Students Need?]" *Età Evolutiva*, 84: 65–83.

Renninger, K. A., and M. W. Nam (2012) "Interest and Achievement among Those Who Continue in STEM," paper presented as part of the symposium, Interest Development and Its Relation to Academic Motivation, at the Meeting of the American Educational Research Association, April, Vancouver, BC, Canada.

Renninger, K. A., and R. K. Pozos-Brewer (2015) "Interest, Psychology of," in J. D. Wright (ed.), *The International Encyclopedia of Social and Behavioral Sciences: Motivation*, 2nd edn, Oxford: Elsevier, UK, vol. XII, pp. 378–385.

Renninger, K. A., and K. R. Riley (2013) "Interest, Cognition and Case of L- and Science," *Cognition and Motivation: Forging an Interdisciplinary Perspective*, Cambridge, UK: Cambridge University Press, pp. 352–382.

Renninger, K. A., and L. S. Schofield (2014) "Assessing STEM Interest as a Developmental Motivational Variable," poster presented at Current Approaches to Interest Measurement, American Educational Research Association, April, Philadelphia, PA.

Renninger, K. A., and S. Su (2012) "Interest and Its Development," in R. Ryan (ed.), *The Oxford Handbook of Human Motivation*, Oxford, UK: Oxford University Press, pp. 167–187.

Renninger, K. A., and M. E. Talian (in press) "Interest and School Subject Matter: What Do We Know? What Still Needs to Be Figured Out?" in A. M. O'Donnell (ed.), *Handbook of Educational Psychology*, Oxford, UK: Oxford University Press.

Renninger, K. A., and C. Y. Tibbetts (2010) "Triggers for Interest and Naturally Occurring Reconfiguration of Knowledge," paper presented at the Meeting of the Society for Research on Adolescence, March, Philadelphia, PA.

Renninger, K. A., and R. Wozniak (1985) "Effect of Interest on Attentional Shift, Recognition, and Recall in Young Children," *Developmental Psychology*, 21 (4): 624–632.

Renninger, K. A., L. Austin, J. E. Bachrach, A. Chau, M. S. Emmerson, R. B. King et al. (2014) "Going Beyond Whoa! That's Cool! Achieving Science Interest and Learning with the ICAN Intervention," in S. Karabenick and T. Urdan (eds), *Motivation-Based Learning Interventions*, Bingley, UK: Emerald, pp. 107–140.

Renninger, K. A., J. E. Bachrach, and S. K. Posey (2008) "Learner Interest and Achievement Motivation," *Social Psychological Perspectives*, 15: 461–491.

Renninger, K. A., M. Cai, M. Lewis, M. Adams, and K. Ernst (2011) "Motivation and Learning in an Online, Unmoderated, Mathematics Workshop for Teachers," *Special Issue: Motivation and New Media. Educational Technology, Research and Development*, 59 (2): 229–247.

Renninger, K. A., E. Ewen, and A. K. Lasher (2002) "Individual Interest as Context in Expository Text and Mathematical Word Problems," *Learning and Instruction*, 12 (4): 467–491.

Renninger, K. A., C. C. Kensey, S. J. Stevens, and D. L. Lehman (2015) "Perceptions of Science and Their Role in the Development of Interest," in K. A. Renninger, M. Nieswandt, and S. Hidi (eds), *Interest in Mathematics and Science Learning*, Washington, DC: American Educational Research Association, pp. 93–110.

Renninger, K. A., M. Nieswandt, and S. Hidi (2015a) "On the Power of Interest," in K. A. Renninger, M. Nieswandt, and S. Hidi (eds), *Interest in Mathematics and Science Learning*, Washington, DC: American Educational Research Association, pp. 1–14.

Renninger, K. A., M. Nieswandt, and S. Hidi (eds.) (2015b) *Interest in Mathematics and Science Learning*, Washington, DC: American Educational Research Association.

Renninger, K. A., C. Sansone, and J. L. Smith (2004) "Love of Learning," in C. Peterson and M. E. P. Seligman (eds), *Character Strengths and Virtues: A Handbook and Classification*, Oxford: Oxford University Press, pp. 161–179.

Reschly, A. L., and S. L. Christenson (2012) "Jingle, Jangle, and Conceptual Haziness: Evolution and Future Directions of the Engagement Construct," *Handbook of Research on Student Engagement*, New York, NY: Springer, pp. 3–19.

Rey, G. D. (2011) "Seductive Details in Multimedia Messages," *Journal of Educational Multimedia and Hypermedia*, 20 (3): 283–314.

Reynolds, R. E., and R. C. Anderson (1992) "Influence of Questions on the Allocations of Attention during Reading," *Journal of Educational Psychology*, 74 (5): 623–652.

Richards, J. B., J. A. Litman, and D. H. Roberts (2013) "Performance Characteristics of Measurement Instruments of Epistemic Curiosity in Third-Year Medical Students," *Medical Science Educator*, 23 (3): 355–363.

Risconscente, M. M. (2014) "Effects of Perceived Teacher Practices on Latino High School Students' Interest, Self-Efficacy, and Achievement in Mathematics," *The Journal of Experimental Education*, 82 (1): 51–73.

Rittmayer, M. A., and M. E. Beier (2008) "Overview: Self-efficacy in STEM," A Product of SWE-AWE (www.AWEonline.org) and NAE CASEE (www.nae.edu/casee-equity).

Rotgans, J. I., and H. G. Schmidt (2011) "Situational Interest and Academic Achievement in the Active-Learning Classroom," *Learning and Instruction*, 21 (1): 58–67.

Rotgans, J. I., and H. G. Schmidt (2014) "Situational Interest and Learning: Thirst for Knowledge," *Learning and Instruction*, 32: 37–50.

Rothwell, J. (2011) "Bodies and Language: Process Drama and Intercultural Language Learning in a Beginner Language Classroom," *Research in Drama Education: The Journal of Applied Theatre and Performance*, 16 (4): 575–594.

Rounds, J., and R. Su (2014) "The Nature and Power of Interests," *Current Directions in Psychological Science*, 23 (2): 98–103.

Rounds, J., R. Su, P. Lewis, and D. Rivkin (2010) *O*NET Interest Profiler Short Form Psychometric Characteristics: Summary*. Raleigh, NC: National Center for O*NET Development.

Ryan, R. M., and E. L. Deci (2000) "Self-Determination Theory and the Facilitation of Intrinsic Motivation, Social Development, and Well-Being," *American Psychologist*, 55 (1): 68–78.

Ryan, R. M. and E. L. Deci (2012) "Multiple Identities Within a Single Self: A Self-Determination Theory Perspective on Internalization within Contexts and Cultures," in M. R. Leary and J. P. Tangney (eds), *Handbook of Self and Identity*, New York, NY: The Guilford Press, pp. 224–246.

Sadoski, M. (2001) "Resolving the effects of concreteness on interest, comprehension, and learning important ideas from text," *Educational Psychology Review*, 13: 263–281.

Sahin, A. (2013) "STEM Clubs and Science Fair Competitions: Effects on Post-Secondary Matriculation," *Journal of STEM Education: Innovations and Research*, 14 (1): 5–11.

Sansone, C. (1986) "A Question of Competence: The Effects of Competence and Task Feedback on Intrinsic Interest," *Journal of Personality and Social Psychology*, 51 (5): 918–931.

Sansone, C. (2009) "What's Interest Got to Do with It? Potential Trade-Offs in the Self-Regulation of Motivation," in J. P. Forgas, R. Baumiester, and D. Tice (eds), *Psychology of Self-Regulation: Cognitive, Affective, and Motivational Processes*, New York, NY: Psychology Press, pp. 35–51.

Sansone, C., and J. M. Harackiewicz (1996) "I Don't Feel Like It: The Function of Interest in Self-Regulation," in L. Martin and A. Tesser (eds), *Striving and Feeling: The Interaction of Goals and Affect*, Hillsdale, NJ: Erlbaum, pp. 203–228.

Sansone, C., and J. L. Smith (2000) "Interest and Self-Regulation: The Relation between Having to and Wanting to," in C. Sansone and J. M. Harackiewicz (eds), *Intrinsic and Extrinsic Motivation: The Search for Optimal Motivation and Performance*, New York, NY: Academic, pp. 342–371.

Sansone, C., and D. B. Thoman (2005) "Interest as the Missing Motivator in Self-Regulation," *European Psychologist*, 10 (3): 175–186.

Sansone, C., T. Fraughton, J. Zachary, J. Butner, and C. Heiner (2011) "Self-Regulation of Motivation When Learning Online: The Importance of Who, Why and How," *Educational Technology Research and Development*, 59 (2): 199–212.

Sansone, C., J. L. Smith, D. B. Thoman, and A. Macnamara (2012) "Regulating Interest When Learning Online: Potential Motivation and Performance Trade-Offs," *The Internet and Higher Education*, 15 (3): 141–149.

Sansone, C., D. Thoman, and T. Fraughton (2015) "The Relation between Interest and Self-Regulation in Mathematics and Science," in K. A. Renninger, M. Nieswandt, and S. Hidi (eds), *Interest in Mathematics and Science Learning*, Washington, DC: American Educational Research Association, pp. 111–131.

Sansone, C., C. Weir, L. Harpster, and C. Morgan (1998) "Once a Boring Task Always a Boring Task? Interest as a Self-Regulatory Mechanism," *Journal of Personality and Social Psychology*, 63 (3): 379–390.

Savage, M. P., and L. B. Scott (1998) "Physical Activity and Rural Middle School Adolescents," *Journal of Youth and Adolescence* 27 (2): 245–253.

Schank, R. C. (1979) "Interestingness: Controlling Inferences," *Artificial Intelligence*, 12 (3): 273–297.

Scherer, K. P. (2009) "The Dynamic Architecture of Emotion: Evidence for Component Process Model," *Cognition and Emotion*, 23: 1307–1351.

Schiefele, H. (1978) *Lernmotivation Und Motivlernen* [*Learning Motivation and Learning of Motives*], 2nd edn, Munich: Ehrewirth.

Schiefele, U. (1991) "Interest, Learning, and Motivation," *Educational Psychologist*, 26 (3–4): 299–323.

Schiefele, U. (1996) "Topic Interest, Text Representation, and Quality of Experience," *Contemporary Educational Psychology*, 12 (1): 3–18.

Schiefele, U. (1999) "Interest and Learning from Text," *Scientific Studies of Reading*, 3 (3): 257–280.

Schiefele, U. (2001) "The Role of Interest in Motivation and Learning," in J. M. Collis and S. Messick (eds), *Intelligence and Personality: Bridging the Gap in Theory and Measurement*, Mahwah, NJ: Erlbaum, pp. 163–194.

Schiefele, U. (2009) "Situational and Individual Interest," in K. Wentzel and A. Wigfield (eds), *Handbook of Motivation at School*, London and New York, NY: Routledge, pp. 197–222.

Schiefele, U., and M. Csikszentmihalyi (1994) "Interest and the Quality of Experience in Classrooms," *European Journal of Psychology of Education*, 9 (3): 251–270.

Schiefele, U., and A. Krapp (1996) "Topic Interest and Free Recall of Expository Text," *Learning and Individual Differences*, 8 (2): 141–160.

Schiefele, U., A. Krapp, K.-P. Wild, and A. Winteler (1993) "Eine Neue Version des Fragebogens zum Studieninteresse (FSI) Untersuchungen zur Reliabilität und Validität [A New Version of the Study Interest Questionnaire (SIQ)]," *Diagnostica*, 3 (4): 335–351.

Schinka, J. A., D. A. Dye, and G. Curtiss (1997) "Correspondence between Five-Factor and RIASEC Models of Personality," *Journal of Personality Assessment*, 68 (2): 355–368.

Schlechty, P. C. (2011) *Engaging Students: The Next Level of Working on the Work*, San Francisco, CA: Wiley.

Schraw, G., and R. S. Dennison (1994) "The Effect of Reader Purpose on Interest and Recall," *Journal of Reading Behavior*, 26 (1): 1–18.

Schukajlow, S., and A. Krug (2014) "Do Multiple Solutions Matter? Prompting Multiple Solutions, Interest, Competence, and Autonomy," *Journal for Research in Mathematics Education*, 45 (4): 497–533.

Schultz, W. (1998) "Predictive Reward Signal of Dopamine Neurons," *Journal of Neurophysiology*, 80 (1): 1–27.

Schultz, W. (2007) "Reward," *Scholarpedia*, 2 (3): 1652.

Schunk, D. H., and E. L. Usher (2012) "Social Cognitive Theory and Motivation," in R. M. Ryan (ed.), *The Oxford Handbook of Human Motivation*, Oxford, UK: Oxford University Press, pp. 13–27.

Schunk, D. H., and B. J. Zimmerman (1994) "Self-Regulation of Learning and Performance: Issues and Educational Applications," in S. Hidi and P. Boscolo (eds), *Writing and Motivation*, Oxford, UK: Elsevier, pp. 241–255.

Schunk, D. H., and B. J. Zimmerman (2007) "Influencing Children's Self-Efficacy and Self-Regulation of Reading and Writing through Modeling," *Reading and Writing Quarterly*, 23 (1): 7–25.

Schwan, S., A. Grajal, and D. Lewalter (2014) "Understanding and Engagement in Places of Science Experience: Science Museums, Science Centers, Zoos, and Aquariums," *Educational Psychologist*, 49 (2): 70–85.

Senko, C., and J. M. Harackiewicz (2002) "Performance Goals: The Moderating Role of Context, Achievement Orientation, and Feedback," *Journal of Experimental Social Psychology*, 38 (6): 603–610.

Senko, C., C. S. Hulleman, and J. M. Harackiewicz (2011) "Achievement Goal Theory at the Crossroads: Old Controversies, Current Challenges, and New Directions," *Educational Psychologist*, 46 (1): 26–47.

Shao, J. (2012) "A Study of Multimedia Application-Based Vocabulary Acquisition," *English Language Teaching*, 5 (10): 202–207.

Shernoff, D. J. (2010) "Engagement in After-School Programs as a Predictor of Social Competence and Academic Performance," *American Journal of Community Psychology*, 45 (3–4): 325–327.

Shernoff, D. J. (2013) *Optimal Learning Environments to Promote Student Engagement*, New York, NY: Springer.

Shernoff, D. J., and L. Hoogstra (2001) "Continuing Motivation beyond the High School Classroom," *New Directions for Child and Adolescent Development*, 93: 73–87.

Shernoff, D. J., and J. A. Schmidt (2008) "Further Evidence of an Engagement-Achievement Paradox among US High School Students," *Journal of Youth and Adolescence*, 36 (5): 891–903.

Shernoff, D. J., M. Csikszentmihalyi, B. Schneider, and E. Steele Shernoff (2003) "Student Engagement in High School Classrooms from the Perspective of Flow Theory," *School Psychology Quarterly*, 18 (2): 158–176.

Shirey, L. L., and R. E. Reynolds (1988) "Effect of Interest on Attention and Learning," *Journal of Educational Psychology*, 80 (2): 159–166.

Silvia, P. J. (2001) "Interest and Interests: The Psychology of Constructive Capriciousness," *Review of General Psychology*, 5 (3): 270–290.

Silvia, P. J. (2006) *Exploring the Psychology of Interest*, Oxford, UK: Oxford University Press.

Simon, H. A. (1967) "Motivational and Emotional Controls of Cognition," *Psychological Review*, 74 (1): 29–39.

Simpkins, S. D., J. Fredricks, and J. S. Eccles (2015) "Parent Beliefs to Youth Choices: Mapping the Sequence of Predictors from Childhood to Adolescence," *Monographs of the Society for Research in Child Development*, 80 (2): 1–169.

Sinatra, G. M., and P. R. Pintrich (eds) (2003) *Intentional Conceptual Change*, London and New York, NY: Routledge.

Skinner, B. F. (1935) "The Generic Nature of the Concepts of Stimulus and Response," *The Journal of General Psychology*, 12 (1): 40–65.

Skinner, B. F. (1976) *About Behaviorism*, New York, NY: Vintage Books.

Slavin, R. E. (1983) *Cooperative Learning*, New York, NY: Longman.

Slavin, R. E. (1991) *Student Team Learning: A Practical Guide to Cooperative Learning*, Washington, DC: National Education Association Professional Library.

Sloboda, J. (1990) "Musical Excellence: How Does It Develop?" in M. J. A. Howe (ed.), *Encouraging the Development of Exceptional Skills and Talents*, London, UK: Wiley, pp. 165–178.

Sloboda, J. (1996) "The Acquisition of Musical Performance Expertise: Deconstructing the 'Talent' Account of Individual Differences in Musical Expressivity," in K. Ericsson (ed.),

The Road to Excellence: The Acquisition of Expert Performance in the Arts and Sciences, Sports, and Games, Mahwah, NJ: Erlbaum, pp. 107–126.

Sloboda, J. (2004) "The Acquisition of Musical Performance Expertise: Deconstructing the 'Talent' Account of Individual Differences in Musical Expressivity," in K. Ericsson (ed.), *The Road to Excellence: The Acquisition of Expert Performance in the Arts and Sciences, Sports, and Games*, Mahwah, NJ: Erlbaum, pp. 107–126.

Sloboda, J. A., and J. W. Davidson (1995) "The Young Performing Musician," in I. Delidge and J. A. Sloboda (eds), *The Origins and Development of Musical Competence*, Oxford, UK: Oxford University Press, pp. 171–190.

Small, S., and M. Memmo (2004) "Contemporary Models of Youth Development and Problem Prevention: Toward an Integration of Terms, Concepts, and Models," *Family Relations*, 53 (1): 3–11.

Sosniak, L. A. (1985) "Learning to Be a Concert Pianist," in B. Bloom (ed.), *Developing Talent in Young People*, New York, NY: Ballantine, pp. 19–67.

Sosniak, L. A. (1990) "The Tortoise, the Hare, and the Development of Talent," in M. Howe (ed.), *Encouraging the Development of Exceptional Skills and Talents*, Leicester, UK: British Psychological Society, pp. 149–164.

Springer, M. (1994) *Watershed: A Successful Voyage into Integrative Learning*, Westerville, OH: National Middle School Association.

Springer, M. (2006) *Soundings: A Democratic, Student-Centered Education*, Westerville, OH: National Middle School Association.

Steinkuehler, C., E. King, E. Alagoz, G. Anton, S. Chu, J. Elmergreen et al. (2011) "Let Me Know When She Stops Talking: Using Games for Learning Without Colonizing Play," in *Proceedings of the 7th International Conference on Games+ Learning+ Society Conference*, Pittsburgh, PA: ETC Press, pp. 210–220.

Strong, E. K., Jr. (1925) *The Psychology of Selling and Advertising*, New York, NY: McGraw-Hill.

Strong, E. K., Jr. (1943) *Vocational Interests of Men and Women*, Palo Alto, CA: Stanford University Press.

Sun, H., A. Chen, C. D. Ennis, R. Martin, and B. Shen (2008) "An Examination of the Multidimensionality of Situational Interest in Elementary School Physical Education," *Research Quarterly for Exercise and Sport*, 79 (1): 62–70.

Swarat, S., A. Ortony, and W. Revelle (2012) "Activity Matters: Understanding Student Interest in School Science," *Journal of Research in Science Teaching*, 49 (4): 515–537.

Tanaka, A., and K. Murayama (2014) "Within-Person Analyses of Situational Interest and Boredom: Interactions between Task-Specific Perceptions and Achievement Goals," *Journal of Educational Psychology*, 106 (4): 1–13.

Thoman, D.B., Sansone, C., and Pasupathi, M. (2007) "Talking about Interest: Exploring the Role of Social Interaction for Regulating Motivation and the Interest Experience," *Journal of Happiness Studies*, 8 (3): 335–370.

Thomas, A. (2007) *Youth Online: Identity and Literacy in the Digital Age*. New York, NY: Peter Lang.

Thorndike, E. L. (1905) "Measurement of Twins," *The Journal of Philosophy, Psychology, and Scientific Methods*, 2 (20): 399–406.

Thorndike, E. L. (1912) "Measurement of Educational Products," *The School Review*, 20 (5): 399–406.

Thorndike, E. L. (1935) "The Interests of Adults: I. The Permanence of Interests," *Journal of Educational Psychology*, 26 (6): 401–410.

Tobias, S. (1994) "Interest, Prior Knowledge, and Learning," *Review of Educational Research*, 64 (1): 37–54.

Todt, E., and S. Schreiber (1998) "Development of Interests," in L. Hoffmann, A. Krapp, K. A. Renninger, and J. Baumert (eds), *Interest and Learning*, Kiel, Germany: IPN, pp. 3–11.

Toku, M. (2001) "What Is Manga? The Influence of Pop Culture in Adolescent Art," *Art Education*, 54 (2): 1–17.

Tolman, E. C. (1932) *Purposive Behavior in Animals and Men*, New York, NY: Century.

Tomkins, S. (1962) *Affect, Imagery Consciousness*, vol. I: *The Positive Affects*, London: Tavistock.

Travers, R. M. W. (1978) *Children's Interests*, Kalamazoo, MI: Western Michigan University, College of Education.

Tsai, Y. M., M. Kunter, O. Lüdtke, U. Trautwein, and R. M. Ryan (2008) "What Makes Lessons Interesting? The Role of Situational and Individual Factors in Three School Subjects," *Journal of Educational Psychology*, 100 (2): 460–472.

Tulis, M., and S. M. Fulmer (2013) "Students' Motivational and Emotional Experiences during Academic Challenge in Mathematics and Reading," *Learning and Individual Differences*, 27: 35–46.

Turner, J. C., A. Christensen, H. Z. Kackar-Cam, M. Trucano, and S. M. Fulmer (2014) "Enhancing Students' Engagement Report of a 3-Year Intervention with Middle School Teachers," *American Educational Research Journal*, 51 (6): 1–32.

Turner, J. C., H. Z. Kackar, and M. Trucano (2015) "Teachers Learning How to Support Student Interest in Mathematics and Science," in K. A. Renninger, M. Nieswandt, and S. Hidi (eds), *Interest in Mathematics and Science Learning*, Washington, DC: American Educational Research Association, pp 243–257.

Unsworth, N., and B. D. McMillan (2013) "Mind Wandering and Reading Comprehension: Examining the Roles of Working Memory Capacity, Interest, Motivation, and Topic Experience," *Journal of Experimental Psychology: Learning, Memory, and Cognition*, 39 (3): 832–842.

Upadyaya, K., and J. S. Eccles (2014) "How Do Teachers' Beliefs Predict Children's Interest in Math from Kindergarten to Sixth Grade?" *Merrill-Palmer Quarterly*, 60 (4): 403–430.

Urdan, T., and E. Schoenfelder (2006) "Classroom Effects on Student Motivation: Goal Structures, Social Relationships, and Competence Beliefs," *Journal of School Psychology*, 44 (5): 331–349.

Vollmeyer, R., and F. Rheinberg (2000) "Does Motivation Affect Performance Via Persistence?" *Learning and Instruction*, 10 (4): 293–309.

Wade, S. E. (1992) "How Interest Affects Learning from Text," in K. A. Renninger, S. Hidi, and A. Krapp (eds), *The Role of Interest in Learning and Development*, Hillsdale, NJ: Erlbaum, pp. 255–277.

Wade, S. E., and R. B. Adams (1990) "Effects of Importance and Interest on Recall of Biographical Text," *Journal of Reading Behavior: A Journal of Literacy*, 22 (4): 330–353.

Wade, S. E., W. Buxton, and M. Kelly (1999) "Using Think-Alouds to Examine Reader-Text Interest," *Reading Research Quarterly*, 34 (2): 194–216.

Walkington, C. A. (2013) "Using Adaptive Learning Technologies to Personalize Instruction to Student Interests: The Impact of Relevant Contexts on Performance and Learning Outcomes," *Journal of Educational Psychology*, 105 (4): 932–945.

Walkington, C. A., and M. L. Bernacki (2014) "Motivating Students by 'Personalizing' Learning around Individual Interests: A Consideration of Theory, Design, and Implementation Issues," in S. A. Karabenick and T. C. Urdan (eds), *Advances in Motivation and Achievement*, vol. XVIII: *Motivational Interventions*, Bingley, UK: Emerald, pp. 139–177.

Walkington, C. A., A. Petrosino, and M. Sherman (2013) "Supporting Algebraic Reasoning through Personalized Story Scenarios: How Situational Understanding Mediates Performance," *Mathematical Thinking and Learning*, 15 (2): 89–120.

Walsh, W. B., and S. H. Osipow (eds) (1986) *Advances in Vocational Psychology*, vol. I: *The Assessment of Interests*, London and New York, NY: Routledge.

Watson, J. B. (1913) "Psychology as the Behaviorist Views It," *Psychological Review*, 20 (2): 158–177.

Whitley, M. T. (1929) "Children's Interest in Collecting," *Journal of Educational Psychology*, 2 (3): 249–261.

Wigfield, A., and J. Cambria (2010) "Students' Achievement Values, Goal Orientations, and Interest: Definitions, Development, and Relations to Achievement Outcomes," *Developmental Review*, 30 (1): 1–35.

Wigfield, A. and J. S. Eccles (2000) "Expectancy-Value Theory of Achievement Motivation," *Contemporary Educational Psychology*, 25 (1): 68–81.

Wigfield, A. and J. S. Eccles (2002) "The Development of Competence Beliefs, Expectancies for Success, and Achievement Values from Childhood through Adolescence," in A. Wigfield and J. S. Eccles (eds), *Development of Achievement Motivation*, San Diego, CA: Academic Press, pp. 249–284.

Wigfield, A., J. Cambria, and J. S. Eccles (2012) "Motivation in Education," in R. C. Ryan (ed.), *Oxford Handbook of Motivation*, Oxford, UK: Oxford University Press, pp. 463–478.

Wigfield, A., J. Eccles, U. Schiefele, R. Roeser, and P. Davis-Kean (2006) "Development of Achievement Motivation," in R. Lerner and W. Damon (eds), *Handbook of Child Psychology*, 6th edn, vol. III: *Social, Emotional, and Personality Development*, New York, NY: Wiley, pp. 933–1002.

Wigfield, A., J. S. Eccles, K. S. Yoon, R. D. Harold, A. J. Arbreton, C. Freedman-Doan, and P. C. Blumenfeld (1997) "Change in Children's Competence Beliefs and Subjective Task Values across the Elementary School Years: A 3-Year Study," *Journal of Educational Psychology*, 89 (3): 451–469.

Xu, J., L. T. Coats, and M. L. Davidson (2012) "Promoting Student Interest in Science: The Perspectives of Exemplary African American Teachers," *American Educational Research Journal*, 49 (1): 124–154.

Zahorik, J. A. (1996) "Elementary and Secondary Teachers' Reports of How They Make Learning Interesting," *The Elementary School Journal*, 96 (5): 551–564.

Zhang, W., and C. Han (2012) "A Case Study of the Application of a Blended learning Approach to Web-based College English Teaching Platform in a Medical University in Eastern China," *Theory and Practice in Language Studies*, 2 (9): 1961–1970.

Zhu, X., A. Chen, C. D. Ennis, H. Sun, C. Hopple, M. Bonello, M. Bae, and S. Kim, (2009) "Situational Interest, Cognitive Engagement, and Learning Achievement in Physical Education," *Contemporary Educational Psychology*, 34 (3): 221–229.

Zilversmit, A. (1993) *Changing Schools: Progressive Education Theory and Practice, 1930–1960*, Chicago, IL: University of Chicago Press.

Zimmerman, B. J. (2000) "Self-Efficacy: An Essential Motive to Learn," *Contemporary Educational Psychology*, 25 (1): 82–91.

Zimmerman, B. J. (2002) "Becoming a Self-Regulated Learner: An Overview," *Theory into Practice*, 41 (2): 64–70.

Zimmerman, B. J., and A. Bandura (1994) "Impact of Self-Regulatory Influences on Writing Course Attainment," *American Educational Research Journal*, 31 (4): 845–862.

Zimmerman, B. J., and T. J. Cleary (2009) "Motives to Self-Regulate Learning," in K. Wentzel, A. Wigfield, and D. Miele (eds), *Handbook of Motivation at School*, London and New York, NY: Routledge, pp. 247–264.

Zimmerman, B. J., and A. Kitsantas (1996) "Self-Regulated Learning of a Motoric Skill: The Role of Goal Setting and Self-Monitoring," *Journal of Applied Sport Psychology*, 8 (1): 60–75.

Zimmerman, B.J., and A. Kitsantas (1997) "Developmental Phases in Self-Regulation: Shifting from Process Goals to Outcome Goals," *Journal of Educational Psychology*, 89 (1): 29–36.

Zimmerman, B. J., and A. Kitsantas (1999) "Acquiring Writing Revision Skill: Shifting from Process to Outcome Self-Regulatory Goals," *Journal of Educational Psychology*, 91 (2): 241–250.

Zimmerman, B. J., and A. Kitsantas (2002) "Acquiring Writing Revision and Self-Regulatory Skill through Observation and Emulation," *Journal of Educational Psychology*, 94 (4): 660–668.

Zimmerman, B. J., and D. H. Schunk (2004) "Self-Regulating Intellectual Processes and Outcomes: A Social Cognitive Perspective," in D. Dai and R. Sternberg (eds), *Motivation, Emotion, and Cognition: Integrative Perspectives on Intellectual Functioning and Development*, Mahwah, NJ: Erlbaum, pp. 323–349.

Zimmerman, T. G., D. Johnson, C. Wambsgans, and A. Fuentes (2011) "Why Latino High School Students Select Computer Science as a Major," *TOCE*, 11 (2): 1–17.

Zink, C. F., G. Pagnoni, M. E. Martin-Skurski, J. C. Chappelow, and G. S. Berns (2004) "Human Striatal Responses to Monetary Reward Depend on Saliency," *Neuron*, 42 (3): 509–517.

Zink, C. F., G. Pagnoni, M. E. Martin-Skurski, M. Dhamala, and G. S. Berns (2003) "Human Striatal Response to Salient Nonrewarding Stimuli," *Journal of Neuroscience*, 23 (22): 8092–8097.

AUTHOR INDEX

SUBJECT INDEX